STUDY GUIDE

FOR

Cole & Cole's

The
Development
of Children

Third Edition

STEPHANIE STOLARZ-FANTINO
San Diego State University

W. H. Freeman and Company
New York

ISBN: 0-7167-2807-9

Printed in the United States of America

First printing 1997, RRD

Contents

To The Student

This Study Guide was written to help you understand and remember the ideas and facts presented in the second edition of The Development of Children. The guide has 16 chapters corresponding to the 16 chapters of the textbook; each chapter has the following sections, intended to enhance your studying in a different way:

- The introduction will orient you to the ideas presented. You may want to read it before reading the text chapter.
- The detailed Chapter Outline can be read before the textbook chapter, as preparation, or afterward, as a review; it will also be useful when studying for quizzes and exams. Reading the outline cannot, however, substitute for reading the text; while it contains the basic ideas, it leaves out many important examples and illustrations that will help you understand and remember these ideas.
- The Key Terms listed at the end of each textbook chapter are reproduced. There is space for you to define the terms and a matching exercise that will give you the opportunity to test your understanding by identifying examples that illustrate key terms.
- The Fill-in Questions recapitulate important points made in the chapter. Uncover the answers in the margin as you complete each statement.
- Multiple-Choice Questions cover material that is especially likely to appear on exams.
- Short-Answer Questions are intended to make you think about important topics introduced in the chapter. Sometimes you will need to utilize ideas presented in different sections of the chapter to answer these questions.
- Putting It All Together appears in some, but not all, chapters of the guide. It contains exercises that require you to combine material from the chapter you are currently studying with information from previous chapters to help you gain a better overall view of development.
- Sources of More Information supplement the additional readings listed at the end of each text chapter.
- An Answer Key in each chapter lists the correct answers for the key terms matching exercise, the multiple-choice questions, and, where appropriate, for the putting it all together section.

The Study Guide also includes suggestions for observing children. It is hoped that you will find your study of child development to be interesting and enjoyable.

Ideas For Observing Children

As you learn about children's development, you may become interested in observing their behavior. Perhaps you will want to conduct some formal observations or you may be assigned this task by your instructor. These suggestions will help you get started.

There are many opportunities for casual observation of children's behavior in everyday settings. A children's shoe store is a good place to hear the ways preschoolers use language as they argue for one pair of shoes or another. Restaurants provide opportunities to view children's social interactions and observe their fine motor skills. Children can be observed using the equipment at playgrounds, playing in parks, visiting zoos and amusement parks with their parents, and just "hanging around" with their friends at public libraries, in shopping centers, and at beaches or swimming pools. Babies can be observed—sitting in strollers, carried by their parents, and taking their first, unsteady steps—in many of the same settings as they accompany their parents and older siblings. It is also possible to view children in more formal settings—at day-care centers, schools, or in such activities as scouting or Little League. In fact, a good way to get firsthand experience with children is to work as a volunteer in one of these settings. Baby-sitting also provides excellent opportunities to observe children's behavior in detail.

Observations may focus on particular behaviors—noting instances of aggression among a group of preschoolers—or may consist of records of all the behavior a child performs within a specified period of time. In the first example, you might prepare a chart with the children's names on one axis and the aggressive behaviors under study—hitting, biting, pushing, and so on—on the other. Specific instances of aggression could then be recorded by checking appropriate boxes corresponding to the particular children and behaviors. Other types of behavior would not, of course, be recorded. In the second type of observation, you would target a particular child, a 4-year-old named Jill, for example. First, you would set the scene—"Jill is seated on the floor, cross-legged, in the block area of the classroom. Mark is nearby but is not facing Jill."—then make a detailed description of everything that occurs, keeping track of the time in the left margin (2- or 5-minutes intervals). Motor movements should be described in detail, especially when observing babies, and conversations should be recorded whenever possible. Naturally, when performing such a detailed observation, it is necessary to take frequent breaks.

When you conduct observations, keep in mind the criteria of scientific description discussed in Chapter 1. Your observations should, first of all, be objective. This will be easier to accomplish if you separate your own comments and interpretations ("Jill is angry with Mark") from the facts of the observation ("Jill does not respond to Mark's request") either by placing them in a separate, parallel column or by putting them in parentheses. Observations also need to be reliable. For example, when studying aggression, two observers should be able to agree on whether a particular act was, in fact, an instance of hitting. Validity is important as well; for example, crying when their mothers leave the room may be a valid measure of attachment in 1-year-olds, but is a less appropriate measure of 6-year-olds' attachment.

Observers also need to remember the ethical guidelines for research with children, also discussed in Chapter 1. In particular, always obtain permission from parents or teachers before conducting a formal observation of a particular child, and be sure not to follow or approach children in any way that might alarm or frighten them. If you use common sense in obtaining subjects, your observations will be enjoyable to carry out and will add greatly to your understanding of children's development.

Entire books have been written about techniques for observing children. Those listed below will give you additional ideas about how to conduct this kind of psychological research.

Cohen, Dorothy H. and **Virginia Stern** with **Nancy Balaban.** *Observing and Recording the Behavior of Young Children*, 3rd ed. New York: Teachers College Press, 1983.

Irwin, D. Michelle and **M. M. Bushnell**. *Observational Strategies for Child Study*. New York: Holt, 1980.

Isaksen, Judith G. *Watching and Wondering: Observing and Recording Child Development*. Palo Alto, CA.: Mayfield, 1986.

The Study of Human Development

For centuries, philosophers have asked, "What is human nature?" Within this question are others, about how individual humans become what they are, and about how the events of their lives help or hinder their development.

Today developmental psychologists bring the techniques of scientific research to bear on these questions. Using interviews, observations, and experiments, they gather information on human behavior and interpret it within the framework of theory.

This research is not of interest solely to philosophers. It helps all of us to make informed decisions in diverse areas; for example: public policy, by asking such questions as "What kinds of day-care arrangements are best for children?"; education, by asking under what conditions children learn best; and child rearing, by asking about what techniques are most likely to help children grow up happy and well-adjusted.

Psychologists do not yet have answers to all our questions. But each year psychological research adds something to our understanding of human nature and to our appreciation of the development of individual children.

Chapter Outline

I.   A Child of Nature?

Victor, the "Wild Boy of Aveyron," remains something of a mystery nearly two centuries after his discovery. Was he, as believed by many authorities of his time, abandoned by his parents because of innate mental deficiency? Or, as his benefactor Jean-Marc Itard believed, was his development stunted by years of isolation in the forest? These questions, though unanswered, are relevant to the modern-day study of human development, the sequence of changes that begins at conception and continues throughout life.

II.   The Legacy of Itard

In his work with Victor, Itard showed that science could be applied to problems of human behavior, and that practical applications can come from such work. The case of the Wild Boy also demonstrated that scientific work has implications for philosophical and political issues. The combination of scientific, philosophical, and public policy goals remains important to today's developmental psychologists.

A.   Scientific concern about children grew out of social concerns as the industrial revolution in Europe and America resulted in large numbers of children working long hours in unhealthy factory conditions. Charles Darwin's theory of evolution also focused interest on children, as their development provided evidence that humans are related to other species. By the late nineteenth century, G. Stanley Hall had formed the Child-Study Association and the first child development journal had begun publication. The U.S. government and various organizations dedicated to social reform became interested in educating parents about child rearing. Child welfare reform was under way.

B.   Developmental psychologists are dedicated to accumulating knowledge about *development*—the sequence of physical and psychological changes that human beings undergo as they grow older—and to applying their knowledge in helpful ways. Their general goal—increasing our understanding of human nature and its development—should be kept in mind while using the textbook.

III.   The Central Questions of Developmental Psychology

Developmental psychologists seek answers to three major questions:
   • To what extent is development a process of continuous change and to what extent is it characterized by more sudden transformations?

> • What are the contributions of the body's genetic program and forces in the environment in directing development?
> • How do individual differences develop, making each human being unique?
> • Psychologists' assumptions about these issues influence the theoretical viewpoints they adopt to explain developmental changes.

A. Within the question about continuity are several issues:
    • Are human beings distinctive? This is a question about *phylogeny*, the evolutionary history of a species. There is disagreement among evolutionary theorists as to whether the process of evolutionary change is continuous or discontinuous. Certainly, humans have much in common with other animals; however, we have unique attributes as well, especially our highly developed systems of language and *culture*—the accumulation of knowledge, beliefs, and values.
    • Is individual development continuous? This is a question about *ontogeny*—the course of development during an individual person's lifetime—and concerns the notion that children pass through a set of qualitatively different *stages* on their way to maturity. Some psychologists emphasize these discontinuities, while others stress underlying processes, such as learning, that remain the same throughout life.
    • Are there *critical periods* in development? Critical periods are times during which particular events must occur in order for development to proceed normally. Critical periods occur in human physiological development and may occur in behavioral development as well.

B. The question about the roles of genes and environment in development is often thought of as a debate about the relative importance of *nature* (a person's inborn capacities and limitations) and *nurture* (the social environment's influences on the person). This debate, which has its roots in philosophical theories about the nature of mankind, has striking implications for politics and education. The ideas of the English philosopher John Locke, who saw the infant's mind as a blank slate (*tabula rasa*), and the French philosopher Jean-Jacques Rousseau, who conceived of the child as "natural man," continue to influence our ideas about the nature of children and society's responsibility toward them. These ideas are discussed in Box 1.1

C. The question about individual differences asks what makes people different from one another and whether their characteristics remain stable over their lifetimes—for example, can you predict their behavior as adults from their traits in infancy? Apparently, the stability of characteristics over time depends, to some degree, on how they are measured; it is also influenced by the stability of a person's environment.

IV. THE DISCIPLINE OF DEVELOPMENTAL PSYCHOLOGY

Developmental psychologists want to be able to understand the behavior of individuals and relate it to information about human beings as a group. In order to do this, they collect information using various types of research designs.

A.   Psychologists judge their findings according to four general criteria:
      • Observations should have *objectivity*—that is, they should not be biased by the investigator's preconceived ideas.
      • Observations should have *reliablility*—they should be consistent when observed on more than one occasion, and particular observations should be agreed on by independent observers.
      • The measures used should have *validity*—the data being collected should actually reflect the underlying process the researcher is using it to measure.
      • When other investigators perform a *replication*—that is, when they perform the same study using the same procedures—they should obtain the same results.

It is also important that the subjects being studied are a *representative sample* of the group about which the investigator is drawing conclusions.

B.   There are several ways in which psychologists obtain information:
      • *Self-reports* include interviews and responses to questionnaires. Self-reports can provide information not obtainable by other methods. However, people's accuracy in reporting their own behavior is often questionable.
      • *Naturalistic observation* is a method in which behavior is studied in real-world settings. Observations may be made in a single setting or in many different settings. Some developmental psychologists carry out work in this tradition, studying behavior in the context in which it has adaptive significance. *Baby biographies*—diaries recording observations of children—are also examples of naturalistic observation. Naturalistic observation is important in the discipline of *ethology*, the study of the biological bases of behavior. It is also used to discover children's *ecology*, the range of situations they encounter, and the roles they play. A child's place in the community can be thought of as a *developmental niche*.

A problem with collecting data through naturalistic observation is that, while there may be a *correlation* between factors being observed, it is not possible to determine which factors are causal. The issue of correlation and causation is discussed in Box 1.2.

      • *Experiments* are often used to get around the problem of determining causation. In these studies, investigators introduce a change into a child's experience while, if possible, holding all other factors constant; then they measure the effect of this change on the child's behavior. The group of children whose experience is changed are called the *experimental group*. Their behavior is compared with that of the *control group*, who are treated as much as possible like the experimental group except for not undergoing the change. Because some research is potentially harmful to children, researchers must carry out their investigations accordingto strict standards of ethics, as described in Box 1.3. If carried out effectively, an experiment supports or disproves a *hypothesis*, an assumption that is precise enough to be tested scientifically. A possible problem with experiments is that they often involve artificial situations that may elicit different behavior from that seen in natural settings.

• The *clinical method* involves tailoring interview techniques to the individual subject; the answers to questions determine the direction the questioning will take. The clinical method can reveal a great deal about individual behavior; however, it may be difficult to arrive at general conclusions using this technique. This method also relies a great deal on verbal expression and therefore may underestimate children's abilities.

C. In order to determine how the factors influencing development work over time, psychologists use several types of research designs:
• In a *longitudinal design*, the same individuals are studied at more than one age. Unfortunately, subjects may drop out during the course of a study, changing the sample from its original composition. To get around this problem, researchers can use *microgenetic methods*, which provoke change in the course of a relatively short time interval, allowing them to observe developmental mechanisms in action. Longitudinal designs also may confound age changes in behavior with changes due to other influences relating to the subject's *cohort*—the group of people born at about the same time who share particular experiences unique to those growing up during that era. Using a *cohort-sequential design*, in which the longitudinal study is carried out on several cohorts, helps researchers to separate cohort-related factors from changes due to age.
• In a *cross-sectional design*, groups of people of different ages are each studied at a single time. This type of design is less expensive and requires less commitment from participants; however, it does not allow researchers to see how behavior actually changes over time.

D. Each of these research designs, like each technique for collecting data, has advantages and disadvantages; keeping these in mind, investigators must choose the most practical methods for conducting their particular studies.

E. The information psychologists obtain about children's behavior is only meaningful in the context of a *theory*—a broad conceptual framework within which facts can be interpreted. Today, psychologists' attempts to understand development reflect four broad theoretical frameworks described below. The textbook organizes information from the point of view of these perspectives; information relating to an additional perspective—the *psychodynamic approach*—is incorporated within these frameworks.
• According to the biological-maturation framework, the basic changes characterizing development are *endogenous* (coming from "inside"), and *maturation* is therefore the major cause of development; from this perspective, the environment plays a secondary role. Sigmund Freud and Arnold Gesell are important biological-maturation theorists.
• According to the environmental-learning framework, biological factors provide a foundation, but *learning* is the major cause of developmental change. This perspective emphasizes *exogenous* factors (those coming from "outside"). B. F. Skinner is an important environmental-learning theorist.
• According to the constructivist framework, nature and nurture both play important roles, the specifics of which vary with the type of development being examined. Thus, development is "co-constructed" by children and their caretakers. Developmental

psychologist Jean Piaget emphasized children's roles as active constructors of their own development.

• The cultural-context framework is similar to the constructivist perspective; however, it emphasizes the role of children's cultural groups in organizing their experiences, since the same biological or environmental factors may have different consequences for development when they appear in different cultural contexts. The work of psychodynamic theorist Erik Erikson fits well within this framework.

V.   THIS BOOK AND THE FIELD OF DEVELOPMENTAL PSYCHOLOGY

Psychologists have not yet developed one unifying theory to integrate and interpret the facts of children's development. The major theoretical orientations regard development as encompassing seven major periods: the prenatal period, infancy, early childhood, middle childhood, adolescence, adulthood, and old age. However, there is little agreement about whether these divisions are simply convenient verbal classifications or whether each is an actual developmental stage. The textbook organizes its discussion of developmental change from conception through adulthood around a series of bio-social-behavioral shifts, outlined in Table 1.4. These shifts are points at which converging changes in children's biology and behavior—which, in turn, cause them to be treated differently by other people—lead to the emergence of distinctively new forms of behavior.

It will be useful, in reading the text, to keep in mind the questions introduced in this chapter about the nature of development and what it means to be human. The information gathered by numerous researchers and presented in the following chapters ultimately bears on these recurring themes.

Key Terms I

Following are important terms introduced in Chapter 1. In the space to the right, write the definition of each term. In the space to the left, write the letter of the example that best illustrates the term.

_____ baby biography _____

_____ clinical method _____

_____ coefficient of correlation _____

_____ cohort _____

_____ cohort-sequential design _____

_____ control group _____

_____ cross-sectional design _____

_____ experiment _____

_____ experimental group _____

_____ longitudinal design _____

_____ microgenetic method _____

_____ naturalistic observation _____

_____ objectivity _____

_____ reliability _____

_____ replication _____

_____ representative sample _____

_____ self-report _____

_____ validity _____

a.   This type of diary of infants' behavior is still used in studying language development.
b.   This expresses the relationship that exists when changes in one factor are associated with changes in another, for example, the association between age and height in children.
c.   A person filling out a questionnaire about his or her behavior would be participating in this method of observation.
d.   This occurs when other researchers redo a study and get the same results.
e.   Watching children interact on the playground at recess is a form of this.
f.   This describes research designs that are not biased by preconceived ideas.
g.   A measure has this characteristic when it reflects what it is purported to. (For example, in order to have it, a written memory test would need to be given to subjects who could read.)
h.   A group of subjects in an experiment who undergo a manipulation of their environment.
i.   A psychologist who is comparing a group of 8-year-olds, a group of 10-year-olds, and a group of 12-year-olds on a problem-solving task is conducting this type of study.
j.   Psychologists try to obtain this in selecting subjects so that they can generalize their results to a larger population.

k.   Subjects in an experiment who do not receive the experimental manipulation, but are otherwise treated the same as those who do.

l.   A measure has this if, when subjects are tested on more than one occasion, they earn nearly the same scores.

m.   An example is "American children beginning kindergarten in 1992."

n.   In this way of studying development, questions are tailored to the person being interviewed.

o.   A psychologist who is studying one group of children's social relationships from kindergarten through sixth grade is conducting this type of study.

p.   When researchers test the effectiveness of a new way to teach spelling by teaching one group with the new method and comparing results with those of a group taught by the previous method , they are conducting this type of study.

q.   A researcher studying adolescence follows several groups of children from 10 through 15 years of age, adding a new group of 10-year-olds to the study every five years.

r.   This helps avoid some of the problems that can be encountered in longitudinal studies.

Key Terms II

Following are important terms introduced in Chapter 1. In the space to the right, write the definition of each term. In the space to the left, write the letter of the example that best illustrates the term.

_____ bio-social-behavioral shift _____

_____ critical period _____

_____ culture _____

_____ development _____

_____ developmental niche _____

_____ ecology _____

_____ endogenous _____

_____ ethology _____

_____ exogenous _____

_____ hypothesis _____

_____ learning _____

_____ maturation _____

_____ nature _____

_____ nurture _____

_____ ontogeny _____

_____ phylogeny _____

_____ psychodynamic approach _____

_____ stage _____

_____ theory _____

a. An individual's developmental history.
b. A broad conceptual framework within which facts can be interpreted.
c. The process by which new behaviors arise when the organism is modified by experience.
d. The knowledge and beliefs of a group of people are an example of this.
e. The sequence of physical and behavioral changes that occur from conception to maturity.
f. Influences on development that come from "inside"—from the child's biological heritage.
g. A species' evolutionary history.
h. Genetically determined patterns of change that occur during development.
i. Influences on development that come from "outside"—from the child's interaction with the environment.
j. This term, derived from the Greek word for "home," refers, in psychology, to the range of situations in which people's behavior occurs.
k. A distinctive period of development marked by discontinuity from the periods occurring before and after.
l. This represents the influence of the environment on the individual.
m. A reorganization of behavior, such as the one that occurs at the end of infancy, which comes about as a result of changes in several different areas of development.
n. A time in a person's life when certain experiences are necessary if normal development is to occur.
o. This refers to the individual's inborn, biologically based capacities.
p. A term used by ecologists to refer to the child's place within the community.
q. This involves observing the behavior of animals or people in natural settings, rather than in the laboratory.

r. An idea that can be tested, for example, the idea that locomotion plays an important role in the development of fear of heights.

s. This involves developing clinical techniques designed to treat mental illness.

Fill-In Questions

Cover the list of answers next to the statements below and fill in each blank with the word or phrase that correctly completes the sentence.

development
1. The study of human _____ involves the changes beginning at conception and continuing throughout life.

evolution
2. Scientific interest in children grew both out of social concern and interest in Darwin's theory of _____.

apply
3. Modern developmental psychologists accumulate knowledge about human behavior and _____ their knowledge to enhance development.

qualitative
genetic
differences
4. Several major questions guide developmental psychologists: whether development is best understood as quantitative or _____ in nature; whether development is guided mainly by the body's _____ program or by environmental influences; and what are the sources of the individual _____ that make each individual unique?

phylogeny

culture
5. When we ask about ways in which human beings are distinctive, we are asking questions about _____—the evolutionary history of our species. One important difference between human beings and other creatures is _____, the accumulation of knowledge, beliefs, and artifacts of a society.

ontogeny
6. Questions about continuity from birth through adulthood relate to _____—an individual person's development.

stages
7. One question about ontogeny concerns whether, on the way to maturity, individuals pass through qualitatively different _____ of development.

critical
8. There is some evidence that _____ periods—times during which particular events must happen for normal development to take place—occur in human psychological development.

9. Questions about the relative importance of genes and environment are often phrased as a debate about the relative influence of nature and _____.

    nurture

10. In conducting research, psychologists strive for observations with _____, or freedom from bias.

    objectivity

11. When observations are agreed upon by more than one observer, they have _____.

    reliability

12. Observations have _____ when they actually reflect the process they are used to measure.

    validity

13. _____—obtaining the same result when a study is repeated—helps an investigator's findings to be accepted by the scientific community.

    Replication

14. Sometimes investigators obtain _____ from subjects by asking them about their own behavior.

    self-reports

15. Sometimes researchers document behavior through naturalistic _____—studying people in one or more settings as they go about their daily lives.

    observation

16. When performing _____, investigators introduce changes into an environment and study the effects on behavior.

    experiments

17. When groups of people are studied, the group whose members experience a change is called the _____ group; their behavior is compared with that of the _____ group.

    experimental
    control

18. When conducting research with children, investigators must follow strict _____ standards in order to avoid harm to the participants.

    ethical

19. Research using the _____ method involves interview techniques that are tailored to the individual subject.

    clinical

20. In _____ studies, researchers examine the effect of time on development by studying the same group of people at more than one age.

    longitudinal

21. In _____ studies, investigators compare single observations of people from different age groups.

    cross-sectional

theory   22. A _____ provides a conceptual framework within which
                           researchers can interpret the facts they uncover.

                      23. According to the biological-maturation framework, the major
maturation   cause of development is _____.

environmental-learning 24. The _____ framework emphasizes
                           learning as the main source of developmental change.

contructivist   25. The _____ framework acknowledges the importance of both
                           nature and nurture in development.

                      26. The cultural-context framework emphasizes the importance of
cultural   the _____ group in organizing children's experience.

                      27. This textbook organizes its discussion of development around
                           points in children's lives at which changes in biology, behavior,
                           and social expectations converge. New forms of behavior emerge
shifts   from these biosocial-behavioral _____.

Multiple-Choice Questions

Circle the letter of the word or phrase that correctly completes each statement.

1. It was hoped that the case of Victor, the Wild Boy of Aveyron, could help answer
    questions about
    a. why parents abandon their children.
    b. what people would be like if they grew up completely apart from others.
    c. how wild animals raised their young.
    d. the causes of mental retardation.

2. John Locke, the seventeenth-century English philosopher, believed that most
    differences between people were
    a. caused by genetic differences.
    b. unimportant.
    c. due to the way they were brought up.
    d. due more to influences in later life than to influences during childhood.

3. Jean-Jacques Rousseau's ideas about _____ remain influential today.
    a. the child's mind as a "blank slate"
    b. original sin
    c. the importance of beginning formal education at an early age
    d. the stagelike character of development

4. The history of a species over thousands or millions of years is called
   a. ontogeny.
   b. continuity.
   c. phylogeny.
   d. development.

5. Knowledge about how to live is passed from one generation of humans to another through
   a. culture.
   b. the genetic code.
   c. mutations.
   d. unknown means.

6. Using the concept of stage to explain development (for example, saying that John has tantrums because he's in the "terrible twos")
   a. helps to understand children's behavior.
   b. is widely accepted by developmental psychologists.
   c. confirms the usefulness of stage theories.
   d. does not help us understand children's behavior.

7. A possible example of a critical period in human development is the following: In order to develop normally with respect to this behavior, children need to
   a. form a primary attachment during the first year of life.
   b. acquire some form of language before 7 years of age.
   c. learn to walk before 18 months of age.
   d. learn to play an instrument before 10 years of age.

8. How can we tell when a child reaches a new stage of development?
   a. quantitative change (for example, the ability to remember more words)
   b. slow, steady improvement (for example, being able to walk more quickly)
   c. simultaneous change in several areas of behavior
   d. the appearance of new behaviors with no obvious input from the environment

9. Which statement best represents psychologists' current attitudes toward replication of studies?
   a. The findings of a study are more likely to be accepted when, by following the same procedures, other investigators obtain the same results.
   b. To be accepted as true, a study should yield the same results more than once, even when different procedures are used.
   c. A study with conclusive findings is generally accepted as accurate even if other investigators are unable to obtain the same results.
   d. It is a waste of time and money to replicate research that has already been carried out.

10. A person who fills out a consumer questionnaire about what household products he or she uses is participating in which form of data collection?
a. naturalistic observation
b. self-report
c. experiment
d. clinical interview

11. In order to be able to generalize their results to other groups, researchers need to conduct their work using
a. both children and adults as subjects.
b. as representative a sample as possible.
c. identical questions for all age groups.
d. naturalistic observation.

12. When conducting an experiment, researchers usually compare the performance of the experimental group with that of a control group that
a. is assigned to a different experimental treatment.
b. undergoes no experience at all.
c. consists of people who did not volunteer to be in the experimental group.
d. is treated like the experimental group except for not receiving the experimental treatment.

13. When psychologists compare the performance of 3-year-olds, 5-year-olds, and 7-year-olds on a vocabulary test, they are conducting
a. a kinship study.
b. a clinical study.
c. a cross-sectional study.
d. a longitudinal study.

14. The _____ framework views development as being due mainly to factors "inside" the child.
a. environmental-learning
b. cultural-context
c. constructivist
d. biological-maturation

15. The cultural-context framework is similar to the _____ perspective, but also emphasizes the effect on development of the prior experience of the society into which a child is born.
a. biological-maturational
b. environmental-learning
c. constructivist
d. sociobiological

Short-Answer Questions

Write a brief answer in the space below each question.

1. What might be some reasons why Victor, the Wild Boy of Aveyron, never developed completely normal behavior, despite Itard's educational efforts?

2. What did seventeenth-century English philosopher John Locke consider to be the role of early experience?

3. What is "culture" as psychologists use the term? Why is it important to consider the role of culture in development?

4. Compare the advantages and disadvantages of naturalistic observation and experiments for studying children's behavior.

5. Describe how researchers might use a longitudinal design or a cross-sectional design to gather information on the same aspect of development. What are the advantages and disadvantages of each?

Sources of More Information

Barker, Roger G, and Herbert F. Wright. *One Boy's Day: A Specimen Record of Behavior.* New York: Harper & Row, 1951.
This book, which records in detail a day in the life of a 7-year-old boy, illustrates one method of naturalistic observation.

Elkind, David. *Children and Adolescents: Interpretive Essays on Jean Piaget*, 3rd Edition. New York: Oxford University Press, 1981.
Although most of the material has been inspired by Piaget, this book also contains sections comparing the Piagetian and psychometric approaches to development and comparing the work and goals of Piaget and Maria Montessori.

Fraiberg, Selma H. *The Magic Years. Understanding and Handling the Problems of Early Childhood*. New York: Charles Scribner's Sons, 1959.
This book entertainingly describes development during the first five years of life from a psychodynamic point of view.

Gesell, Arnold, Frances L. IIg, Louise Bates Ames, and Janet Learned Rodell. *Infant and Child in the Culture of Today: The Guidance of Development in Home and Nursery School*, Rev. Ed. New York: Harper & Row, 1974.
This book presents Gesell's maturational approach to infancy and early childhood, with an emphasis on the child's increasing abilities of self-regulation.

Irwin, D. Michelle, and M. Margaret Bushnell. *Observational Strategies for Child Study*. New York: Holt, Rinehart and Winston, 1990.
This book serves as an introduction to observing children, and contains both general guidelines and specific suggestions for using checklists, event sampling, rating scales and other techniques, and instruction on writing up observation reports. Information on theoretical perspectives and history is also included.

Jones, N. Blurton, ed. *Ethological Studies of Child Behavior*. New York: Cambridge University Press, 1972.
This book contains many different ethological studies, including examples of child-child and mother-child interaction.

Patterson, Gerald. *Living With Children: New Methods for Parents and Teachers*. Champaign, Ill.: Research Press, 1976.
In this book, parents and teachers are shown how to change children's behavior for the better by arranging environmental contingencies to encourage desired behaviors and eliminate undesired ones. This book illustrates the environmental-learning approach to development.

Answer Key

Answers to Key Terms I: a, n, b, m, q, k, i, p, h, o, r, e, f, l, d, j, c, g

Answers to Key Terms II: m, n, d, e, p, j, f, q, i, r, c, h, o, l, a, g, s, k, b

Answers to Multiple-Choice Questions: 1. b, 2. c, 3. d, 4. c, 5. a, 6. d, 7. b, 8. c, 9. a, 10. b, 11. b, 12. d, 13. c, 14. d, 15. c.

The Human Heritage: Genes and Environment

In many ways, all human beings seem very much alike. Yet within that basic similarity, the details of appearance and behavior vary a great deal. In fact, people exhibit an amazing diversity of both talents and troubles.

How do genes and the environment combine to create our unique characteristics as human beings? If we were all raised in identical environments, would we behave completely alike? Nearly all psychologists would say "No." Human development is an interaction between biologically based tendencies and the environmental circumstances in which people live. Nearly all of us are genetically unique, so a hypothetical universal environment would affect each person in a different way. On the other hand, under ordinary circumstances, even genetically identical individuals—monozygotic twins—develop individual interests, abilities, and characters.

Some of the differences among people are shaped systematically by the cultures in which they live. Human beings can adapt to changing conditions through cultural evolution, building upon the expertise of countless generations.

Because biological and cultural evolution have occurred together for so long, it is not easy to distinguish their separate influences on development. But by studying the effects on development of mutations—mistakes in gene replication—and inherited genetic disorders, psychologists can learn more about how genes and environment interact to produce each unique person.

Chapter Outline

I.   SEXUAL REPRODUCTION AND GENETIC TRANSMISSION

The similarities and differences among people result from the interaction of the environments in which they develop and the *genes* they inherit from their parents.

Each person's genes are found on the 46 *chromosomes*—23 inherited from each parent—present in the *zygote*, the single cell from which all the individual's body cells will derive.

A.   The zygote creates these new cells through *mitosis*, a process of duplication and division. This is also the way new *somatic* cells are created and replaced throughout a person's lifetime.

B.   *Meiosis* is the process by which *germ cells* (sperm and ova) are derived. It results in cells with 23 chromosomes—half the usual number. When a sperm cell fertilizes an ovum, the resulting zygote will have 46 chromosomes.
• The mixing of genes during sexual reproduction and the process of *crossing over* (an exchange of genetic material between two chromosomes) during meiosis make each human being—with the exception of *monozygotic twins*— generically unique.
• Occasionally (1 of every 250 births) the daughter cells separate during one of the early mitotic divisions to form two generically alike individuals: monozygotic, or identical, twins. *Dizygotic*, or fraternal, *twins* result from the fertilization of two eggs by two sperm; these twins are no more alike genetically than any brothers or sisters.

C.   The twenty-third pair of chromosomes in normal females are both X chromosomes; normal males have one X chromosome and one Y chromosome. While an ovum always contains an X chromosome, a sperm may contain an X or a Y; thus, the sperm cell determines the genetic sex of the resulting child. More boy babies than girl babies are conceived. This may reflect boy babies' greater vulnerability: by 18 years of age there are equal numbers of males and females, and females outnumber males thereafter.

II.   THE LAWS OF GENETIC INHERITANCE

Some characteristics are inherited through a simple type of genetic transmission in which one pair of genes determines a trait. The genes controlling the trait (for example, blood type) may have alternative forms, or *alleles* (for example, A, B, and O). People who have inherited the same allele from both parents are *homozygous* for the trait; those who have inherited different alleles are *heterozygous*. How an allelic form of a trait is expressed in a heterozygous person depends on whether the allele is *dominant* (in which case it will be expressed), *recessive* (in which case it will not be expressed), or whether the two alleles have *codominance* (in which case a distinctively different outcome will result). In those instances in which neither allele is dominant, an intermediate outcome will occur (as it may in the case of skin color).

A.   An individual's *genotype* represents that person's genetic endowment; the *phenotype*, or the individual's observable characteristics, results from an interaction between that person's inherited traits and the environment. Most phenotypic characteristics (height is an example) are *polygenic traits* resulting from the combined action of many genes as well as a great deal of influence from the environment.

Genes interact with each other in several ways:
• *Modifier genes* influence the expression of other genes; without the action of modifier genes on the allelic forms of the gene for eye color, all people would have either blue or brown eyes.
• Some genes are *complementary* to one another; both must be present for a characteristic to be expressed
• *Masking genes* prevent or lessen the expression of other genes.

B.   *Sex-linked characteristics* are determined by genes found only on the X or Y chromosomes; because the X chromosome carries more genes, the phenotypic expression of these traits is seen more often in males, who have only one X chromosome, than in females, whose second X chromosome may contain an allele that will prevent expression. Because of this, certain recessive genetic defects, ranging from red-green color blindness to a form of muscular dystrophy, are far more common among males. Sex-linked abnormalities also vary in frequency among ethnic groups, reflecting differences in the frequencies with which the corresponding alleles occur in different *gene pools*—the total genetic information possessed by a sexually reproducing population.

III.   GENES, THE ORGANISM, AND THE ENVIRONMENT

Because genes do not exist in isolation, development occurs only within the context of an organism's *environment*, the totality of things, conditions, and circumstances that surround the organism.

A. Environmental variations may have large effects on an individual's phenotypic characteristics. By varying genotypes within the same environment, or by varying the environment of individuals with the same genotype, researchers are able to learn how genes and environment interact to produce particular characteristics. *Range of reaction* is the term used for the changes in phenotype caused by varying the environment of a particular genotype. *Behavioral geneticists* study the way genetic and environmental factors combine to produce individual differences. When a trait is said to be "genetically influenced," this influence may be the work of a single gene or, more commonly, by multiple genes in interaction with the environment.

B. Some genetically determined traits are not easily influenced by the environment. Developmental geneticist Conrad Waddington called this *canalization*. The tendency for children to learn language is a highly canalized process; only severe and prolonged deprivation would prevent it from occurring.

C. It would be unethical to study the range of reaction for human genotypes in the way we can for plants, insects, and animals, (see Box 2.2 for additional information on ethical issues) but *family studies*—comparisons among members of the same biological family—help in estimating which traits have a substantial genetic contribution. If two closely related people are increasingly similar with respect to a trait, this is evidence for an inherited factor. Of course, people who are biologically related also share similar environments; this limits our ability to test for genetic influences using kinship studies. *Adoption studies* are another strategy for estimating the contribution of genes and environment to particular traits. Some researchers studying individual differences have pointed out that family members are often quite different from one another, despite their close genetic relationship (see Box 2.3). Besides having different combinations of genes, individuals in a family experience unique environments, having their own particular teachers, friends, and sibling relationships.

D. Genotypes, phenotypes, and environment do not interact as unrelated factors in development; complex feedback mechanisms exist. As pointed out by Sandra Scarr and Kathleen McCartney, babies inherit both their genes and their early environment from their parents, and babies' own characteristics influence the types of environments their parents provide. Different babies might experience the same environment in different ways. Many different characteristics and incidents combine to make each person's experience unique.

IV. MUTATIONS AND GENETIC ABNORMALITIES

A *mutation* is an error in gene replication that results in a change in the molecular structure of genetic material. The majority of mutations are lethal, resulting in spontaneous abortions early in pregnancy. But about 3.5 percent of babies born have some kind of genetic aberration; because most of these are recessive, they are not often phenotypically expressed.

Table 2-2 describes some common genetic diseases and conditions. By studying mutations and generic abnormalities, researchers can better understand the interaction of genes and environment, and may find ways of preventing defects or lessening their impact.

A.   Sickle-cell anemia, a serious blood disorder, is caused by a recessive gene, carried by 8 to 9% of Americans of African descent. People who are heterozygous for the gene have the sickle-cell trait but usually do not suffer from symptoms of the disease; in fact, they have been found to be more resistant to malaria than people without the sickle cell trait. This explains why another wise unadaptive trait might remain at a relatively high level in the population. Twenty percent of the people in West Africa, where malaria is common, carry the sickle-cell gene, while the incidence is falling among African-Americans, who are rarely exposed to malaria.

B.   Down's syndrome is caused by an extra chromosome on the twenty-first pair (Trisomy 21) and results in mental retardation as well as a number of distinctive physical characteristics and a susceptibility to leukemia and respiratory problems. The older a woman is when she conceives, the greater her chance of producing a child with this disorder, suggesting that environmental agents may damage the genetic material. Children with Down's syndrome have a wide range of levels of functioning, depending on the severity of the disorder and the environmental interventions they receive. Down's syndrome affects about 1 of every 1000 children born in the United States.

C.   The most common abnormalities of the chromosomes that determine sex are: Klinefelter's syndrome, in which a boy has an extra X chromosome (XXY); Fragile X syndrome, a cause of mental retardation; and Turner's syndrome, in which a girl has only one X chromosome (XO).

D.   Phenylketonuria (PKU) is an inherited metabolic disorder that results in brain damage leading to mental retardation. However, by altering the environment of children with this disorder-specifically, by removing from their diets foods high in the amino acid phenylalanine—the children's brains can develop normally. A blood test given to newborn babies can detect most cases of PKU, so that dietary intervention can begin immediately.

It is now possible to detect some abnormalities before birth. Following *amniocentesis*, a technique in which a needle is inserted into the mother's uterus in order to sample the fluid in the sac surrounding the fetus, amniotic fluid is analyzed for chemical imbalances and fetal cells floating in the fluid are examined for certain genetic disorders. In *chorionic villus sampling*, the fetal cells are harvested from the hairlike projections (villi) on the chorion— the tissue that forms the placenta. The *alpha-fetoprotein test* is a blood test that is used to detect defects in the neural tube.

Parents who have had a child with a genetic defect or who think they may be carriers of a particular disorder can often be helped by genetic counseling (see Box 2.4). Through test results and family histories, the genetic counselor will try to determine the probability that a couple's future children will be affected. Using this information, the couple can make an informed decision about whether to risk a future pregnancy.

V.   BIOLOGY AND CULTURE

At the time Darwin wrote *The Origin of Species*, people tended to confuse the processes that produce biological change with those that produce historical change.

A.   For example, as explained by the French biologist Jean Baptiste Lamarck, characteristics acquired by parents during their lifetimes could be passed on biologically, it was thought, to their children. Today we know that this process does not account for biological evolutionary change; however, it does illustrate the occurrence of human cultural evolution, in which the skills and knowledge of each generation build on those of the generations before.

B.   Evidence from archeology and paleontology tells us that *coevolution* of human biological and cultural characteristics has been occurring from the time of the early ancestors of modern humans. The fact of coevolution makes it extremely difficult, when comparing people from different parts of the world, to determine whether the differences between them are due to genetically transmitted characteristics or to differences in the cultures in which they have been raised. Nearly every instance of human development is the result of complex interactions between genes and environment.

Key Terms I

Following are important terms introduced in Chapter 2. In the space to the right, write the definition of each term. In the space to the left, write the letter of the example that best illustrates the term.

_____ allele _____

_____ canalization _____

_____ chromosome _____

_____ codominance _____

_____ complementary genes _____

_____ crossing over _____

_____ dominant allele _____

_____ environment _____

_____ gene pool _____

_____ genes _____

_____ heterozygous _____

_____ homozygous _____

_____ masking gene _____

_____ modifier gene _____

_____ phenotype _____

_____ recessive allele _____

_____ X chromosome _____

_____ Y chromosome _____

a. There are 46 of these threadlike structures in the nucleus of each cell.
b. This sex-determining chromosome can be inherited only from the father.
c. These molecules, found on chromosomes, contain "blueprints" for development.
d. The cells of normal females contain two of these.
e. This exchange of material between chromosomes helps to increase genetic diversity.
f. This term expresses the tendency for some characteristics, such as children's ability to learn language, to follow the same developmental path for everyone, despite most environmental variations.
g. An alternative form of a gene; for example, the O form of the gene for blood type.
h. A gene that prevents another gene from completely expressing itself.
i. This kind of gene influences the action of other genes, producing, in one example, hazel eye color.
j. A person's observable characteristics, developing through interaction between genes and environment.
k. Genes that can only produce their effect if other genes are also present.
l. The generic information available in a whole reproducing population.
m. When a child inherits an allele for type A blood from his mother and an allele for type 0 blood from his father, we use this term to describe his genotype for blood type.
n. A child inherits an allele for type O blood from each parent; this term describes her genotype for blood type.

o. A less powerful allele—for example, the allele for type O blood—that is not expressed when a more powerful allele is present.

p. A trait is contributed to by two different alleles; for example, type AB blood.

q. An allele whose effects show up phenotypically—in type A blood, for example—even in the presence of another allele (such as the O allele).

r. Children's development results from the interaction of this with their genetic inheritance.

Key Terms II

Following are important terms introduced in Chapter 2. In the space to the right, write the definition of each term. In the space to the left, write the letter of the example that best illustrates the term.

_____ adoption study _____

_____ behavioral geneticist _____

_____ coevolution _____

_____ dizygotic twins _____

_____ family studies _____

_____ genotype _____

_____ germ cells _____

_____ heritability _____

_____ meiosis _____

_____ mitosis _____

_____ monozygotic twins _____

_____ mutation _____

_____ polygenic traits _____

_____ range of reaction _____

_____ sex-linked characteristics _____

_____ somatic cells _____

_____ zygote _____

a.   These come in two varieties: sperm and ova.
b.   This expresses the degree to which genetic factors influence the amount of variability in a trait.
c.   Nearly all the body's cells are produced by this process of duplication and division.
d.   All the cells in the body with the exception of the sperm and ova.
e.   These result from the fertilization of two ova by two sperm.
f.   Exposure to radiation can cause this change in the structure of the genetic material.
g.   This term refers to a person's genetic endowment.
h.   The process through which sperm and ova contain 23 chromosomes, rather than 46.
i.   Members of the same family are compared to assess their similarity for a particular trait.
j.   Characteristics influenced by the interaction of several genes, as in the case of height and many other human characteristics.
k.   This single cell results from the joining of sperm and ovum at conception.
l.   Red-green color blindness is one of these.
m.   The fact that this occurs makes it difficult to pinpoint the source of differences between people who have grown up in very different parts of the world.
n.   The full range of gene-environment interactions that are compatible with life for a particular genotype.
o.   A researcher who studies the effects of genes and environment on individual differences.
p.   Two individuals with exactly the same genotype.
q.   This involves studying genetically related individuals who are raised in different environments.

Fill-In Questions

Cover the list of answers next to the statements below and fill in each blank with the word or phrase that correctly completes the sentence.

1.   People's similarities and differences come from an interaction between _____ and environment.   **genes**

2.   The body's cells contain _____ chromosomes, 23 inherited from each parent.   **46**

3.   New cells are created by the process of _____.   **mitosis**

Y

males

alleles

heterozygous

dominant
recessive

phenotype

Sex-linked

males

reaction

Family

genetic

environments

interact

canalized

Mutations

spontaneous

4. The cells of females contain two X chromosomes; those of males contain one X chromosome and one _____ chromosome.

5. Although a greater number of _____ are conceived and born, by 18 years of age there are equal numbers of males and females.

6. The genes determining a trait can have alternative forms called _____. People who inherit the same allele from both parents are called homozygous for the trait; those who inherit a different allele from each parent are _____.

7. When two alleles are present but only one is expressed, we say that the one whose characteristic are expressed is a _____ allele. The one that is not expressed is a _____ allele.

8. A person's genetic endowment is represented by his or her genotype; _____ represents the individual's observed characteristics.

9. _____ characteristics are determined by genes found on the X chromosome. They are phenotypically expressed more often in _____ than in females.

10. By varying the environments of organisms with the same genotype and observing the phenotypic results, researchers can determine the range of _____ for a particular genotype.

11. _____ studies compare people who are related to one another to assess their similarities. They help to determine what traits might have a substantial _____ contribution.

12. One problem with family studies is that closely related people usually have similar _____.

13. Genotype and environment _____ in complex ways to produce phenotypic characteristics.

14. A characteristic that is relatively unaffected by environmental influences during development is one which is highly _____.

15. _____ are changes in genetic material caused by errors in gene replication.

16. The majority of mutations result in _____ abortions early in pregnancy.

17. People who have the sickle-cell _____ do not develop sickle-cell anemia; in addition, they have increased resistance to _____.

trait

malaria

18. _____ syndrome is a chromosomal disorder that results in mental retardation and characteristic physical abnormalities.

Down's

19. Klinefelter's and Turner's syndromes are caused by abnormalities of the _____ chromosomes.

sex

20. Today the inherited metabolic defect PKU need not lead to mental retardation if the _____ of an affected child is controlled.

diet

21. Passing on acquired characteristics from one generation to the next is accomplished through _____, not biological, evolution.

cultural

22. We give the name _____ to the process in which biological and cultural evolution have interacted with one another over the last several million years.

coevolution

Multiple-Choice Questions

Circle the letter of the word or phrase that correctly completes each statement.

1. The somatic cells of the body each contain
   a.   23 chromosomes.
   b.   23 pairs of chromosomes.
   c.   46 pairs of chromosomes.
   d.   50 pairs of chromosomes.

2. A person who is genetically male receives, at conception,
   a.   an X chromosome from his mother and a Y chromosome from his father.
   b.   a Y chromosome from his mother and an X chromosome from his father.
   c.   an X chromosome from each parent.
   d.   a Y chromosome from each parent.

3. Sex-linked characteristics are
   a. passed from one generation to the next on the Y chromosome.
   b. phenotypically expressed more often in females than in males.
   c. limited to characteristics that determine a person's physical and psychological sex.
   d. phenotypically expressed more often in males than in females.

4. When two alleles for a trait are present but only one is expressed, we call the one that is not expressed
   a. dominant.
   b. codominant.
   c. complementary.
   d. recessive.

5. The development of _____ traits is resistant to environmental influence.
   a. learned
   b. canalized
   c. physical
   d. psychological

6. Which is an example of a polygenic trait?
   a. height
   b. blood type
   c. hemophilia
   d. sickle-cell anemia

7. Errors in gene replication, called _____, often have lethal results.
   a. meioses
   b. canalizations
   c. mutations
   d. recessive traits

8. _____ is a genetic disorder caused by an extra chromosome.
   a. Down's syndrome
   b. Sickle-cell anemia
   c. Phenylketonuria
   d. Turner's syndrome

9. A _____ gene prevents another gene from expressing itself completely.
   a. complementary
   b. masking
   c. modified
   d. recessive

10. Which of the following is *not* a test used to detect birth defects prenatally?
    a.   amniocentesis
    b.   range of reaction
    c.   chorionic villus sampling
    d.   alpha-fetoprotein test

11. The total genetic material in a reproducing population is called the
    a.   genotype.
    b.   phenotype.
    c.   range of reaction.
    d.   gene pool.

12. If a child receives an allele for type A blood from her mother and an allele for type B blood from her father, she is _____ with respect to blood type.
    a.   heterozygous
    b.   recessive
    c.   homozygous
    d.   complementary

13. Meiosis is
    a.   the process by which the body's cells reproduce.
    b.   the process by which the germ cells come to contain fewer chromosomes than the somatic cells.
    c.   an error in gene replication.
    d.   a polygenic trait.

14. Behaviors such as reading, writing, and numeric calculation are passed from one generation of people to the next through
    a.   evolution.
    b.   culture.
    c   genetic transmission.
    d.   mutation.

15. _____ make(s) it difficult to tell whether differences between people are genetically transmitted or environmentally caused.
    a.   Coevolution of physical and cultural characteristics
    b.   Family studies
    c.   Mutations
    d.   Recessive traits

Short-Answer Questions

1.   What is a sex-linked genetic effect and how is it transmitted from one generation to another? Describe two examples of such an effect.

2.   Describe how family studies are used to separate genetic and environmental contributions to behavior. What are some problems with such studies?

3.   How does feedback complicate the study of gene-environment interactions? Give an example.

4.   How does coevolution affect attempts to separate the contributions of nature and nurture to human differences? Describe an example of a human characteristic shaped by coevolution.

Sources of More Information

Asimov, Isaac. *The Genetic Code*. New York: New American Library of World Literature, 1962.
This book traces the research that led to the discovery of DNA.

Darwin, Charles. *The Origin of Species*. New York: New American Library of World Literature, 1958.
Charles Darwin's classic account of the origin of man.

Genes: Our Individual Programming System. Bostonia, Sept./Oct. 1984: 26-33.
This article reviews findings about how genes, hormones, and environment affect biological sex characteristics and gender identity.

Jensen, Arthur R. *The Heritability of Intelligence.* Saturday Evening Post, Summer, 1972.
The author marshals evidence for genetic influences on intelligence and explains how heritability is determined.

Kimura, Doreen. *Male Brain, Female Brain: The Hidden Difference.* Psychology Today, Nov. 1985: 50-52.
This article examines the relationship between genetic sex, physiological functioning, and some forms of behavior.

Kitcher, Philip. *The Lives to Come: The Genetic Revolution and Human Possibilities.* New York: Simon & Schuster, 1996.
This book addresses some of the ethical dilemmas that accompany new discoveries in the field of genetics.

Stockton, William. *Altered Destinies: Lives Changed by Genetic Flaws.* New York: Doubleday, 1979.
A medical reporter follows the lives and experiences of families affected by genetically based disorders.

Vishup, Amy. *Perfect People?* New York Magazine, July 27, 1987: 26-34.
This article discusses genetic testing techniques and the moral dilemmas that accompany their increasingly widespread use.

Whimbey, Arthur. *Something Better than Binet?* Saturday Review, June 1, 1974.
The author argues that, while genetic factors affect the development of intelligence, the extent of their influence depends upon the environment in which children are raised.

Answer Key

Answers to Key Terms I: g, f, a, p, k, e, q, r, l, c, s, m, n, h, i, j, o, d, b

Answers to Key Terms II: q, o, m, e, i, g, a, b, h, c, p, f, j, n, l, d, k.

Answers to Multiple-Choice Questions: 1. b, 2. a, 3. d, 4. d, 5. b, 6. a, 7. c, 8. a, 9. b, 10. b, 11. d, 12. a, 13. b, 14. b, 15. a.

Prenatal Development and Birth

During the 9 months between conception and birth, rapid development transforms the human organism from a single cell to a baby capable of life outside the mother's body. Development proceeds through the processes of differentiation and integration: differentiation of one type of cell into many, and integration of bodily systems into a smoothly functioning whole.

At no time during the course of prenatal development is the developing organism completely buffered from the outside world. On the one hand, while still in the womb, the fetus registers signals from its sense organs, particularly those of balance and hearing. It may even learn to recognize familiar experiences. On the other hand, outside influences such as malnutrition, chemicals, and disease organisms may set obstacles to normal development.

Birth is a dramatic transition, both physically and behaviorally. It also marks the beginning of children's first social relationships, starting with their first face-to-face encounters with their parents. And finally, at birth, the beliefs and customs of the cultural group into which children are born begin to shape their development in more direct ways. The influence of culture can be seen in how preparations for childbirth are carried out—whether in a hut or a hospital—in the rituals surrounding the process, and in the expectations with which the infant is greeted by parents and other members of the community.

Chapter Outline

Many developmental theorists consider an understanding of development during the 9 months from conception to birth to be essential for explaining the processes of development that occur throughout postnatal life.

I.   THE PERIODS OF PRENATAL DEVELOPMENT

As a zygote develops from one-celled organism to newborn baby, it passes through three periods of development: the *germinal period*, the *period of the embryo*, and *the period of the fetus*. Each period is characterized by distinctive patterns of growth and interaction with the environment.

A.   The germinal period begins at conception and lasts until, 8 to 10 days later, the organism is implanted in the uterine wall. During its journey through the fallopian tube, the zygote—contained within the *zona pellucida*, an envelope only a few molecules thick—divides, through the process of mitosis. These initial mitotic divisions are called *cleavage*. In this process, cells divide at different times, rather than all together (*heterochrony*), which results in different parts of the organism developing at different rates (*heterogeneity*). After the first few cleavages occur, a cluster of identical cells—the *morula*—takes shape. By the time it reaches the uterus, the organism is a *blastocyst* consisting of about 100 cells. Interaction with the environment results in differentiation of the blastocyst into the *inner cell mass*, that will become the organism itself, and the *trophoblast*, which will become the membranes that will supply it with nourishment. *Implantation* occurs when the trophoblast puts out branches which burrow into the uterine wall and contact maternal blood vessels.

A major question in embryology is: How do new forms arise from a single type of cell? According to one explanation, *preformationism*, new forms do not arise; they are already present in the first cells. An alternative viewpoint that is favored today explains the development of new forms through *epigenesis*, interactions between previous forms and their environment.

B.   The period of the embryo begins at implantation and continues until, at about the end of the eighth week of gestation, the bones begin to ossify. During this period, the basic organs take shape and the embryo begins to respond to stimulation.
       • From the trophoblast come the membranes that will protect and nourish the developing embryo: the *amnion*, holder of the fluid surrounding the embryo; and the

chorion, which becomes the fetal portion of the *placenta*, which is made from both maternal and embryonic tissue. The placenta is linked to the embryo by the *umbilical cord*. It delivers nutrients and oxygen to the embryo and carries away waste products.

• The inner cell mass differentiates into three cell layers: the outermost, or *ectoderm*, from which the skin and nervous system, among other things, develop; the *mesoderm*, which becomes the bones, muscles, and circulatory system; and the innermost, or *endoderm*, which develops into the digestive system and lungs.

• Beginning during the prenatal period and continuing through adolescence, development occurs in *cephalocaudal* (from the head down) and *proximodistal* (from the midline outward) patterns. The pattern of development for all but the sexual organs is the same for all human embryos. As discussed in Box 3. 1, sexual differentiation for genetically male (XY) embryos begins in the seventh week of gestation with the formation of the testes, while the formation of ovaries in genetically female (XX) embryos will not begin until several weeks later. The rest of the process of sexual differentiation is controlled by hormones: in the presence of the male hormone testosterone, the external genitalia will be male; in the absence of testosterone, female genitalia will develop.

• By about 4 weeks after conception, the embryo's heart begins to beat; by 8 weeks, it can open its mouth, turn its head, and flex its body in response to a stimulus.

C. During the period of the fetus, which lasts from the eighth or ninth week of gestation until birth, the organ systems integrate their activities and the central nervous system undergoes a great deal of development. The fetus greatly increases in length and in strength.

• The fetus also becomes more active, engaging in more varied and smoother movements that, by the end of the fourth month, can be felt by the mother. Some fetal activity is *endogenous*, arising directly for the maturation of tissues, while other instances are responses to environmental stimulation (*exogenous*). The fetus's activity decreases temporarily at 17 or 18 weeks, inhibited by the maturing of higher brain regions. From the sixth month on, activity once again increases. Experiments with fetuses of other species suggest that fetal movement may be necessary for normal development to take place; for example, chick embryos paralyzed with drugs fail to demonstrate the elimination of excess *neurons*—nerve cells—that ordinarily accompanies neuromuscular development, and their joints become fused as a result. The exact role of fetal movement in human prenatal development is, however, not known.

II. THE DEVELOPING ORGANISM IN THE PRENATAL ENVIRONMENT

Even though it is protected and nourished by the mother's body, the fetus interacts with both the uterine environment and the outside world. Some influences are beneficial, while others are potentially harmful.

A.   An understanding of the fetus's sensory capacities helps to determine how its development is affected by the environment.
• About 5 months after conception, the fetus begins to develop a sense of balance and can sense changes in its mother's posture. The fluid-filled amniotic sac provides it with support and protection.
• Toward the end of pregnancy, fetuses are able to respond to light and may actually see light through the stretched wall of the mother's abdomen.
• Fetuses hear, and respond to, loud noises in the outside environment, though these sounds are muffled by background noise in the uterus.

B.   While there is no evidence that fetuses' prenatal experiences have significant effects on their later behavior, it does appear that, after birth, they recognize some familiar sounds, such as their mothers' heartbeats, to which they were repeatedly exposed prenatally. Some studies have shown that newborns appear to "recognize" stories read to them repeatedly before birth.

C.   Fetuses are indirectly affected, biochemically, by events affecting their mothers.
• Psychological stress during pregnancy puts women at risk for miscarriage and premature or difficult labor. Their babies may be irritable and have eating and sleeping difficulties. Having a supportive mate can reduce a woman's stress during pregnancy. As discussed in Box 3.2, fathers-to-be also must adjust to the changes that a pregnancy brings. Their involvement sometimes even includes sharing their wives' physical discomforts.
• Adequate maternal nutrition during pregnancy is necessary for normal fetal development. Extreme malnutrition early in pregnancy can lead to spontaneous abortions, malformations, or stillbirths; for those born alive, it can result in *low birth weight*. Less extreme nutritional deprivation is also harmful, in particular because it usually accompanies low income, poor health care, and lack of educational opportunity; together, these factors may interfere with babies' cognitive development. Studies suggest that food supplementation for low-income pregnant women helps reduce the health costs of undernutrition. And special educational help added to health care and nutritional supplementation can improve the cognitive and social development of children who have been undernourished prenatally.

D.   *Teratogens* are environmental agents—for example, drugs, radiation, infections, and chemical pollutants—that can kill the developing embryo or fetus or cause serious abnormalities.
• Drugs, both prescription and nonprescription, can cross the placenta to affect the developing child. Some, like thalidomide, cause major deformities; no drug should be taken during pregnancy without medical advice.
• Smoking increases the rate of stillbirths and is associated with low birth weight and sudden infant death syndrome.
• Heavy alcohol consumption during pregnancy, particularly during the first 3 months, can lead to the set of abnormalities known as *fetal alcohol syndrome*. Even moderate drinking is thought to put the fetus at some risk.

• Cocaine use during pregnancy puts the fetus at risk for spontaneous abortion, stroke, birth defects, postnatal irritability, lack of motor coordination and learning problems.

• Narcotics addiction (for example, to heroin or methadone) on the part of mothers results in the birth of addicted infants who are also at risk for prematurity, low birth weight, respiratory illness, and impaired motor control.

• Infections can be passed to an embryo or fetus across the placental barrier or during the birth process. Rubella (German measles) and AIDS (Acquired Immune Deficiency Syndrome) are two examples. Rubella causes major developmental defects; transmission of the AIDS virus causes the baby to be infected with the disease.

• Rh incompatibility can result in a mother forming antibodies that destroy the red blood cells of the fetus. Rh disease can be treated by blood transfusions; however, most cases are now prevented by an anti-Rh serum that prevents an Rh-negative mother from forming antibodies to their Rh-positive child's blood.

• Radiation exposure can lead to spontaneous abortions, malformations, and mental retardation, and can also cause genetic damage to future generations.

• Pollution by chemicals in air, food and water which become concentrated in the body can cause birth defects in unborn children. Additional research is needed to determine the effects of many of the chemicals to which we are routinely exposed.

Principles of teratogenic effects:

• The impact of teratogens on the developing organism depends on when exposure occurs. Exposure during the first 2 weeks may destroy the organism; after that time, exposure will affect whatever system is in the process of developing.

• Each teratogen causes a particular pattern of abnormal development.

• Not every developing organism will be equally affected by the same exposure to a teratogen.

• Factors such as the mother's age and health can intensify or decrease the risk from exposure to a teratogen.

• The greater the concentration of a teratogen to which the organism is exposed, the greater the risk.

• Levels of a teratogen that can harm the developing organism may produce little or no effect on the mother.

III. PRENATAL DEVELOPMENT RECONSIDERED

In examining prenatal development, some general principles become clear: sequence and timing of development are important; development consists of both differentiation and integration; development occurs unevenly and appears stagelike; and regressions in development occur during periods of reorganization. In many respects, prenatal development remains a mystery; however, these principles, according to many psychologists, can help us to gain some understanding of the processes involved.

IV. BIRTH: THE FIRST BIO-SOCIAL-BEHAVIORAL SHIFT

At birth, important changes take place in the newborn's body and environment, and the social relationship between parents and child also begins.

A. Labor, the process that forces the fetus out of the mother's body, occurs approximately 266 days after conception, and is customarily divided into three stages:
   • During the first stage of labor, contractions of the uterus dilate, or open, the cervix—the opening of the uterus into the vagina.
   • The second stage of labor begins when the baby's head enters the vagina and continues until the baby's head, then body, emerge from the mother's body.
   • During the third stage of labor, the placenta and membranes are expelled.

B. The experience of giving birth depends, in part, on the traditions surrounding it in the culture in which the mother lives. These customs vary widely from culture to culture, but all give the mother and community a set of procedures to follow and a set of expectations about what will occur.

C. In the United States today, most women give birth in hospitals. The change to hospital-based birth has helped to lower infant mortality to less than 9 of 1000 births and maternal mortality to less than 8.4 of every 100,000 births. However, medical intervention in childbirth is not without controversy.
   • Drugs used to relieve the pain of childbirth may affect babies' breathing and sucking responses and other postnatal behavior. In large doses, they may have long-term effects. For some women, prepared childbirth techniques are an alternative to the use of medication during labor and delivery.
   • Medical interventions—for example induction of labor or caesarean section—are thought to occur more frequently than is necessary. As discussed in Box 3.3, the stresses of labor and delivery may actually help babies adapt to postnatal life; caesarean-born infants are more likely to have breathing difficulties than those born vaginally.

V. THE NEWBORN'S CONDITION

A. Newborn babies weigh, on average, 7 to 7 1/2 pounds (5 1/2 to 10 pounds is the normal range) and are, on average, 20 inches in length.

   The neonate's physical and behavioral condition can be assessed using rating scales:
   • The *Apgar Scale* measures babies' heart rate, respiratory effort, muscle tone, reflex responsivity, and color at 1 and 5 minutes after birth.
   • The *Brazelton Neonatal Assessment Scale* tests reflexes, muscle tone, motor capacities, responsiveness to objects and people, and infants' ability to control their own behavior

and attention. Scales like Brazelton's do well in pointing out babies who need medical intervention, but are less useful in predicting later development from neonatal behavior.

B.   Some babies are at risk for developmental problems, often because they are born prematurely and/or underweight.
    • *Premature*, or preterm, babies are born before 37 weeks of gestation. Prematurity affects 10% of births in the United States. While expert medical care now allows more premature babies to survive, they may have immature digestive and respiratory systems. The causes of prematurity are not well understood; however, mothers who are poor, very young, in poor health, who smoke, or who are carrying more than one fetus are more likely to give birth prematurely than those without these risk factors.
    • *Low birth weight* means birth weight of 2500 grams or less, whether or not they are born prematurely. A newborn who has a particularly low weight for gestational age is said to suffer from *fetal growth retardation.* This is associated with multiple births, maternal malnutrition, smoking or drug use, infections, and abnormalities of the placenta or umbilical cord.
    • The smaller a baby is at birth, whether preterm or not, the more likely that he or she will suffer some permanent impairment. Low-birth-weight babies frequently have some decrease in intellectual capacity. Premature babies of normal weight for their gestational age are most likely to catch up with their full-term peers. Those with low birth weights and medical complications are at risk for developmental problems. Premature and low-birth-weight babies who grow up under supportive environmental conditions are less likely to suffer negative effects.

VI. BEGINNING THE PARENT-CHILD RELATIONSHIP

Human infants are helpless creatures; their relationship with their parents is crucial for their well-being. The attachment between parents and child forms over a long period of time. However, the events immediately after birth set the stage for their future interactions.

A.   In trying to understand the source of love between parents and infants, some psychologists have borrowed from *ethology*—the study of animal behavior and its evolutionary bases—the idea that newborn infants' appearance of *babyness* influences the responses of parents to their offspring. There is evidence that adults find the large heads, protruding cheeks, and large, low-set eyes of infants to be appealing. Research shows that, beginning at about the age of puberty, children switch from preferring to look at pictures of adults to preferring pictures of babies. There is also evidence that adults interact more frequently with attractive babies than with those who are less attractive in appearance.

B.   Animal mothers will often reject babies who are removed from them immediately after birth, unless they have first had the opportunity to interact with them. According to Marshall Klaus, John Kennell, and their colleagues, human mothers given extra contact with their infants after birth are later more responsive to them. These findings have not been consistently replicated, however. In any case, we know that strong parent-infant attachments can be formed in the absence of extended contact immediately after birth.

C.   When a baby is born, parents must begin to adapt to their actual child, not the child they may have imagined, as illustrated in Box 3.4. From the time of birth, parents' reactions to their infants reflect their, and their societies', beliefs and expectations. Boys may be described as "big," girls are "cute," regardless of their actual appearance. From the beginning, parents treat their infants in ways consistent with the community's ideas and knowledge about people and their future roles. The parent-infant relationship will serve as the foundation for children's future development.

Key Terms I

Following are important terms introduced in Chapter 3. In the space to the right, write the definition of the term. In the space to the left, write the letter of the example that best illustrates the term.

_____ amnion _____

_____ blastocyst _____

_____ chorion _____

_____ cleavage _____

_____ ectoderm _____

_____ endoderm _____

_____ epigenesis _____

_____ heterochrony _____

_____ heterogeneity _____

_____ inner cell mass _____

_____ mesoderm _____

_____ morula _____

_____ preformationism _____

_____ trophoblast _____

_____ zona pellucida _____

a. A membrane that develops into the fetal component of the placenta.
b. The layer of cells from which the lungs and digestive system develop.
c. The unevenness seen between the levels of development of different parts of an embryo is an example of this.
d. The layer of cells from which the bones and muscles are formed.
e. A thin but tough membrane that contains the fluid surrounding the embryo.
f. This extremely thin "envelope" forms the boundary that separates the zygote from the outside world.
g. The skin and the central nervous system develop from this layer of cells.
h. A cluster of identical cells that forms during the first few days after conception.
i. The name for the organism very early in development when, for the first time, two different types of cells can be distinguished.
j. A layer of cells within the blastocyst that develops into the protective membranes which will surround the developing organism.
k. The idea that new forms arise during development through interaction of existing forms with the environment.
l. A knot of cells within the blastocyst that develops into the organism itself.
m. About 24 hours after conception, the zygote divides into two daughter cells that, in turn, each divide into two daughter cells.
n. The idea that the adult forms of the body are each already present in some way within the fertilized ovum.
o. This refers to the fact that not all cells divide at the same rate during embryonic development.

Key Terms II

Following are important terms introduced in Chapter 3. In the space to the right, write the definition of the term. In the space to the left, write the letter of the example that best illustrates the term.

_____ Apgar Scale _____

_____ Brazelton Neonatal Assessment Scale _____

_____ cephalocaudal pattern _____

_____ fetal alcohol syndrome _____

_____ fetal growth retardation _____

_____ germinal period _____

_____ implantation _____

_____ low birth weight _____

_____ period of the embryo _____

_____ period of the fetus _____

_____ placenta _____

_____ premature _____

_____ proximodistal pattern _____

_____ teratogens _____

_____ umbilical cord _____

a. The period of prenatal development, lasting about 6 weeks, during which the body's basic organs take shape.
b. This structure links the embryo to the placenta.
c. The blastocyst attaches itself to the wall of the uterus.
d. The period of prenatal development that begins at conception and ends when implantation occurs.
e. This is illustrated by the fact that the embryo's arms begin to form earlier than its legs.
f. These come from the environment and harm the developing fetus by causing deviations in development.
g. This organ, made from tissues of both the mother and the embryo, helps the embryo obtain nourishment and dispose of wastes.
h. The period of prenatal development during which the organ systems develop sufficiently to allow the fetus to survive outside the mother's body.
i. Examples are that the upper arm develops before the forearm and the forearm before the hand.
j. Birth that occurs before the 37th week of gestation.
k. An assessment of the baby's physical condition at 1 and 5 minutes after birth.
l. An underdeveloped brain, heart disease, and malformations of the face are some of the indicators of this.
m. When this occurs, babies are particularly small for their gestational ages.
n. Babies have this if they weigh 2500 grams or less.
o. This evaluates newborns' neurological condition by testing their behavior.

Fill-In Questions

Cover the list of answers next to the statements below. Then uncover each answer after you complete each statement.

1. The germinal period begins at the time of conception and lasts until _____, 8 to 10 days later.   **implantation**

2. The single-celled zygote divides again and again; eventually, the organism becomes a _____ with two distinctly different kinds of cells: some cells form the inner cell mass; others form the _____, which nourishes and protects the developing organism.

    blastocyst

    trophoblast

3. Preformationism assumes that all the different types of cells and physical features that characterize adults are already present at the time of _____; according to an alternative view— _____— these forms emerge later, through interaction with the environment.

    conception

    epigenesis

4. After implantation, the period of the _____ begins, and continues for about 6 weeks.   **embryo**

5. The embryo is surrounded by fluid that is contained by the _____, a thin but tough membrane; another membrane, the chorion, becomes a component of the _____, which contains both maternal and embryonic tissue.

    amnion

    placenta

6. Different layers of the inner cell mass form the various organ systems of the body: the digestive system and lungs are formed from the inner layer, or _____; the middle layer, or _____, becomes the bones, muscles, and circulatory system; and the outer layer, or _____, gives rise to, among other things, the skin, nails, and central nervous system.

    endoderm, mesoderm

    ectoderm

7. Embryonic development occurs in patterns that are cephalocaudal—from the _____ down—and _____—from the inside out.

    top, proximodistal

8. Sexual differentiation begins at 7 weeks gestation for male embryos, several weeks _____ than for females; most of sexual differentiation depends on the presence or absence of male _____, especially testosterone.

    earlier

    hormones

male, XX

9. An XY pattern of sex chromosomes results in a person who is genetically _____ ; an _____ pattern results in a person who is genetically female.

fetus

10. The period of the _____ begins once the basic organ systems have been formed.

11. Although it has been capable of activity for sometime, it is not until about the end of the fourth month that the mother can feel

move, decrease

the fetus _____; fetal activity may temporarily _____ at 17 or 18 weeks, due to inhibition by higher brain centers.

respond

12. Fetuses are able to _____ to light, sound, and changes in their mothers' posture; there is some evidence that newborns may recognize certain sounds, such as the mother's heartbeat, that

prenatally

became familiar to them _____.

13. The changes associated with pregnancy can cause a mother-to-be

stress
undernourished

to experience psychological _____, which can adversely affect the fetus; the fetus may also suffer if the mother is _____, either because of economic deprivation or poor eating habits.

teratogens

14. Drugs, radiation, or pollutants—which are all _____—can kill the embryo or fetus or cause it to develop abnormalities.

when

15. The effects of teratogen exposure depend on _____ during gestation exposure occurs; in general, whatever system is in the

developing

process of _____ is the one that will be affected.

Labor

16. _____, the process that forces the fetus out of the mother's body, begins at about 266 days after conception.

17. During the first stage of labor, contractions of the uterus cause

cervix, second

the _____ to dilate; during the _____ stage, the mother feels the urge to bear down and push the baby out.

head

18. Under ordinary circumstances, the baby's _____ is the first part to emerge from the mother's body.

placenta

19. The _____ and membranes are delivered during the third stage of labor.

drugs

20. It is now known that _____ administered during childbirth can cross the placenta and affect the fetus.

21. The stresses of the birth process stimulates fetuses to produce adrenaline and other _____, which help their breathing and circulation adjust to postnatal conditions.

hormones

22. Average American babies weigh 7 to 7 1/2 pounds at birth, but _____ several ounces during the first few days of postnatal life; their length, 20 inches on average, is mainly determined by the size of the _____.

lose

uterus

23. The _____ Scale assesses a baby's condition at 1 and 5 minutes after birth; the Brazelton Scale evaluates a baby's _____ condition after delivery.

Apgar
neurological

24. Infants born at fewer than 37 weeks are considered _____; they may have difficulty sucking, swallowing, and _____.

preterm
breathing

25. Infants are classified as having a _____ birth weight if they weigh less than 2500 grams at birth.

low

26. Preterm infants reach early developmental milestones, such as sitting up and crawling, somewhat _____ than those born at normal gestational age; whether they "catch up" with their full-term peers depends in part on what _____ conditions they are exposed to after birth.

later

environmental

27. Infant humans and many infant animals have physical characteristics, such as large eyes and round cheeks, that signify _____ and evoke caregiving behaviors in adults of their species.

babyness

28. Parents' _____ about their infants, shaped by culturally organized beliefs, are an important source of continuity in development.

expectations

Multiple-Choice Questions

Circle the letter of the word or phrase that correctly completes each statement.

1. During the prenatal period, the one-celled _____ develops into a fully formed baby.
   a. ovum
   b. blastocyst
   c. zygote
   d. embryo

2. The germinal period of development begins at conception and ends when
    a. the organism divides into two cells.
    b. the organism is implanted in the uterine wall.
    c. the major organ systems are formed.
    d. the heart begins to beat.

3. According to the _____ explanation for development, new forms occur through differing interactions of existing forms with the environment.
    a. epigenetic
    b. embryonic
    c. preformationist
    d. constructivist

4. The fluid-filled _____ protects and supports the developing embryo.
    a. chorion
    b. placenta
    c. amnion
    d. zona pellucida

5. The bones and muscles of the developing organism are formed from which layer of the inner cell mass?
    a. endoderm
    b. mesoderm
    c. ectoderm
    d. trophoblast

6. During prenatal development, the embryo's arms
    a.   are formed earlier than the legs.
    b. are formed at the same time as the legs.
    c. are formed later than the legs.
    d. are formed later than the hands.

7. In the absence of testosterone during prenatal development, the external genitalia will be _____ in appearance.
    a. male
    b. undifferentiated
    c. both male and female
    d. female

8.   Studies of fetal hearing indicate that
   a.   fetuses are capable of hearing, but the uterine environment is very quiet, so there is little to hear.
   b.   fetuses "hear" only by feeling vibrations on their body surfaces, not with their ears.
   c.   fetuses hear most sounds in the immediate vicinity of their mothers, including most conversations.
   d.   fetuses hear only very distinct sounds from the world outside, as the background noise level in the uterus is fairly high.

9.   Women who are under stress during pregnancy
   a.   secrete hormones that affect their fetuses' behavior.
   b.   give birth to larger babies than women who experience peaceful pregnancies.
   c.   give birth to babies who are placid and regular in their bodily functions.
   d.   experience no special problems or advantages in their pregnancies.

10.   Which of the following causes birth defects?
   a.   alcohol
   b.   radiation
   c.   environmental pollutants
   d.   All of these

11.   Exposure to a teratogen during prenatal development
   a.   invariably leads to fetal death.
   b.   affects whatever system is developing at the time of exposure.
   c.   affects all fetuses with comparable exposure in the same way.
   d.   does not affect the fetus at exposure levels that are safe for the mother.

12.   The baby actually emerges from the mother's body during
   a.   the first stage of labor.
   b.   the second stage of labor.
   c.   the third stage of labor.
   d.   the fourth stage of labor.

13.   The main problem with obstetric medications is that
   a.   they are not effective in relieving the pain of labor.
   b.   while they do not affect the fetus, they may adversely affect the mother.
   c.   they enter the bloodstream of the fetus and may cause adverse effects.
   d.   in order to use them, it is necessary to give birth in a hospital.

14.   The "stress" hormones that babies produce during labor are now thought to
   a.   help their circulation and respiration adjust to life outside the womb.
   b.   be the basis for psychological birth trauma.
   c.   prevent them from making a smooth adjustment to postnatal life.
   d.   have no effect on them.

15. The _____ evaluates the baby's condition at 1 and 5 minutes after birth.
    a.   Apgar Scale
    b.   PKU test
    c.   Brazelton Neonatal Assessment Scale
    d.   Bayley Mental and Motor Scale

16. Women who _____ are more likely than others to give birth prematurely.
    a.   are of middle-class socioeconomic status
    b.   are carrying more than one fetus
    c.   are in their twenties
    d.   have no known risk factors

17 Which is *not* a sign of babyness, as Konrad Lorenz described it?
    a.   small head in proportion to body
    b.   round cheeks
    c.   large eyes
    d.   high forehead

18. Parents tend to describe their newborns as
    a.   "easy" if they are girls, and "difficult" if boys
    b.   "big" if they are boys, and "cute" if girls.
    c.   "big" and "beautiful," regardless of sex.
    d.   "resembling their mothers," regardless of sex.

Short-Answer Questions

1. What are the major features of the three periods of prenatal development? How would exposure to a teratogen affect development during each of these periods?

2. In the context of the epigenetic hypothesis, what is the environment? Give an example.

3.   Why is it difficult to determine the effect on development of nutritional deprivation alone?

4.   Why is it difficult to predict which premature babies will have long-term developmental problems? What are some predictors of their developmental outlook?

5   What are some positive and negative aspects of parents' expectations about their newborns on the basis of the infant's sex or other characteristics?

Putting It All Together

As discussed in Chapter 1, developmental psychologists interpret the facts they collect in terms of three major questions about development:
 • Is development continuous or do stagelike changes take place?
 • What are the roles of development genetic factors and environmental forces in development?
 • What are the sources of individual differences?

Using what you know about prenatal development, find an example of each of the following as it occurs during the prenatal period:

 • stages of development

 • continuous change

- critical periods

- genetic influence

- effects of the environment

- cultural influences

Sources of More Information

Kitzinger, Sheila. *The Complete Book of Pregnancy and Childbirth*. New York: Knopf, 1994.
This is a comprehensive discussion of pregnancy and the process of childbirth, aimed at helping the pregnant woman to understand what is happening and what to expect.

Klaus, Marshall and John H. Kennell. *Maternal-Infant Bonding*. St. Louis: The C.V. Mosby Co., 1976.
The physician-authors hypothesize a sensitive period for the formation of parent-infant attachment. This idea is controversial but has had great impact on hospital policies.

Lamaze, Fernand. *Painless Childbirth: The Lamaze Method*. Chicago: Contemporary Books, 1984.
A popular method of prepared childbirth is explained by the physician who brought it from the Soviet Union to France.

Nilsson, Lennart. *A Child Is Born: The Completely New Edition*. New York: Delacorte, 1990.
A photographic record of prenatal development.

Poole, William. The First Nine Months of School. *Hippocrates* July/Aug. 1987: 68-73.
This article gives the reader a lighthearted, though scientifically accurate, look at learning.

Profet, Margie. *Protecting Your Baby-to-Be: Preventing Birth Defects in the First Trimester.* Reading, Mass.: Addison-Wesley, 1995.
This book takes the view that pregnancy sickness serves the purpose of protecting the embryo during its most vulnerable period. Suggestions are included for managing pregnancy sickness and avoiding teratogens.

Vaughn, Christopher. *How Life Begins: The Science of Life in the Womb.* New York: Random House, 1996.
This is a readable discussion of prenatal development in a scientific context, written by a science journalist.

Answer Key

Answers to Key Terms I: e, i, a, m, g, b, k, o, c, l, d, h, n, j, f.

Answers to Key Terms II: k, o, e, l, m, d, c, n, a, h, g, j, i, f, b.

Answers to Multiple-Choice Questions: 1. c, 2. b, 3. a, 4. c, 5. b, 6. a, 7. d , 8. d, 9. a, 10. d, 11. b, 12. b, 13. c, 14. a, 15. a, 16. b, 17. a, 18. b.

Early Infancy: Initial Capacities and the Process of Change

During the first few postnatal months, infants are mainly adjusting to life outside their mothers' bodies, and parents are adjusting their lives to accommodate their new offspring. Some changes seem to be the result of maturation of infants' nervous systems. For example, several reflexes present at birth—stepping and involuntary grasping, for example—disappear during the first weeks or months. But learning also plays a role, and other reflexes are modified by use, becoming part of more complex behaviors, as when rooting, sucking, swallowing, and breathing become integrated with one another (and with maternal behaviors as well) in nursing.

Cultural variations in the ways parents organize their infants' experiences exert some influence on development. For example, infants from cultures—such as that of the U.S.—in which they are expected to sleep all night without waking to feed will, in fact, learn to sleep through the night sooner than infants from cultures in which this is not an important expectation.

The various broad approaches to the study of development—biological-maturation, environmental-learning, constructivist, and cultural-context—each emphasize different factors in explaining the changes of the first months of infancy. But at the end of about 2 1/2 months, it is possible to see how changes at all levels—biological, behavioral, and social—move infants to a new level of development, in a bio-social-behavioral shift.

Chapter Outline

I. EARLIEST CAPACITIES

Psychologists now know that infants are born able to perceive and react to the world in ways that help them to survive.

A. Newborns' sensory systems are all functioning, but some capacities are more mature than others. Psychologists study infants' sensory capacities by observing their reactions to stimuli—for example, does a child turn his or her head in the direction of a sound? Another common method relies on infants' tendency to pay less and less attention to a repeatedly presented stimulus (*habituation*); if the stimulus is changed in a way that makes it seem new to the infant, he or she will once again pay attention (*dishabituation*).

Newborns turn their heads toward the sources of sounds, startle when they hear loud noises, and can even distinguish—and prefer—the human voice compared to other sounds. Newborns are also able to perceive distinctions between the basic speech sounds called *phonemes*—even ones not present in the language they hear around them.

Infants' vision is not fully developed at birth. There is some disagreement about what colors newborns perceive; however, by about 2 months of age their color vision is equal to that of adults. Newborns are quite nearsighted, with an acuity that has been estimated as between 20/300 and 20/800. However, they can see fairly clearly objects about as far away as their mothers' faces when they are nursing. By the time infants are crawling, at about 7 or 8 months of age, their acuity is close to that of adults.
• Newborns demonstrate endogenous looking, which originates in the neural activity of the brain and occurs even in the dark. They also demonstrate exogenous looking, which is stimulated by the external environment, for example, by changes in illumination.
• While newborn babies prefer to look at patterned figures rather than unpatterned ones, they do not scan them in the same way adults do. Instead, they focus on areas of high contrast. By 3 months of age, they are able to scan figures more thoroughly.
• Studies by Robert Fantz in the early 1960's indicated that babies could distinguish a schematic face from a facelike figure in which the features were scrambled. But when

other investigators controlled for factors such as brightness, contrast, and complexity—all factors other than "faceness"—it was found that a definite preference for schematic faces is shown by 12-week-olds but not by 6-week-olds. Evidently, movement is an important factor in babies' perception. Even newborns prefer a moving schematic face to one with scrambled features.

• Newborns are sensitive to a variety of odors and can distinguish them from one another. Their sense of taste is acute, and they prefer sweet substances.

• Newborns are sensitive to touch, to changes in temperature, and to changes in position.

B. Infants are born with a number of ways to respond to or act on the world.

• They are equipped with an array of *reflexes*—involuntary and specific responses to specific types of stimulation.

• They appear to express *emotions*, the feeling tone with which individuals respond to their circumstances. Infants display facial expressions that, to adults, look like indications of surprise, interest, joy, and sadness. Some psychologists see this as evidence of an inborn set of emotions, although it is difficult to know whether infants' emotional expressions have the same meanings as those of adults. Other psychologists believe that only two emotional states—one positive, one negative—are present at birth and these *differentiate* into different emotions as the baby develops.

• Many psychologists believe that the elements of *temperament*—reflecting dominant mood and the tendency to react to the world in characteristic ways—are present at birth.

Alexander Thomas, Stella Chess, and their colleagues found that babies could be classified as *easy* (playful, adaptable, and regular in biological functions), *difficult* (irritable, negative toward new experiences), and *slow to warm up* (low in activity level and needing some time to adapt to new situations). There appear to be genetic influences on infant temperament; for example, identical twins are more similar to one another in temperament than are fraternal twins, and differences in temperament have been found among babies of different ethnic groups. However, as with other psychological phenomena, stability of temperament over time depends, in part, upon the measures used and upon the environment in which the child develops.

II. Becoming Coordinated

Coordination of babies' inborn abilities with their parents' caretaking skills allows babies' basic needs to be met. In addition, when babies and parents coordinate their schedules—for example, for eating and sleeping—babies fit smoothly into their families' lives.

A. An important area for coordination is sleep. Peter Wolff, studying newborns' activity patterns, found that they display seven different states of alertness, in four of which they are asleep or nearly asleep. Electroencephalographic research indicates that different brainwave patterns accompany these levels of arousal.

• For the first 2 to 3 months of life, babies begin their sleep periods with active or REM (rapid eye movement) sleep, and later enter quiet or NREM sleep. After a few months, this pattern is reversed.

• Newborns sleep about two-thirds of the time, but their sleep comes in many short periods. As they grow older, sleep periods become longer and begin to coincide with adult day/night schedules.

• Both cultural expectations and brain maturation affect how quickly babies adopt adultlike sleep cycles. American expectations for babies to sleep through the night may be at the limit of what they can adjust to. Coordination of sleeping arrangements is discussed in Box 4.1.

B.   Adults and babies must also coordinate feeding schedules. If fed on demand, newborns prefer to eat about every 3 hours, but adjust, by 7 to 8 months, to eating about four times per day.

C.   Crying alerts parents to babies' discomfort. At first, it is coordinated by structures in the brain stem; it is several months before the cortex is involved, at which point "voluntary" crying becomes possible. At birth, pain and hunger cries can be distinguished both by sound patterns and by adult listeners, as can those of "at risk" and normal babies. Still, parents may not always be able to interpret their babies' cries. Adults react to infant cries with increased heart rate and blood pressure, and even, among nursing mothers, with milk flow.

• Hunger and gastrointestinal pain are two major causes of crying, but all infants have periods in the first few months during which they cry for no identifiable reason.

• Changing their diapers often quiets babies, but it may be the handling involved in diapering that has this effect. As discussed in Box 4.2, holding babies to the shoulder, rocking, patting, cuddling, swaddling, and giving them pacifiers to suck—all effective techniques—provide babies with rhythmic stimulation while reducing the sensations from their own movements. Crying gradually decreases during the first few months of life.

III. Mechanisms of Developmental Change

A.   During early infancy, existing behaviors become more efficient and new behaviors develop. Nursing provides a good example. At birth, rooting, sucking, swallowing, and breathing are not yet smoothly coordinated. By 6 weeks, however, the components of nursing occur in an efficient, integrated sequence. Since each of the four broad developmental frameworks introduced in Chapter 1 emphasizes different factors in explaining its development, nursing is a behavior that can be used to compare these approaches.

B.   The biological-maturation perspective emphasizes the way changes in physical structure and physiological processes bring about development, and assigns only a small role to the environment. According to this approach, postnatal development is a continuation of embryological processes, and changes in behavior, such as the development of nursing, are accounted for by changes in infants' nervous systems. Infants' reflexes illustrate some of these changes.

• Infants' simplest behaviors are spinal reflexes, involving sensory receptors (*neurons* that receive information from the environment), motor neurons, and *synapses* (the gaps between neurons) in the spinal cord. The hand withdrawal reflex (in response to pain) is an example.

• More complex reflexes such as sucking involve additional neurons both in the spinal cord and in the *brain stem*. The brain stem also controls newborns' vital functions, such as sleeping and breathing, and is involved in their emotional responses.

• When sensory inputs are directed to the *cerebral cortex*, memories of past events are integrated with current information, and information from several sources can be combined, and also compared with memories of past experience.

The central nervous system undergoes many changes after birth. For example, the hippocampus, a structure that is important in memory, progresses from being 40% mature at birth to being fully mature at 1 1/2 years of age. Another developmental change involves *myelination*, a process in which neurons are covered by *myelin*, a fatty sheath that allows nerve impulses to be transmitted more quickly. As myelination better connects the cortex to underlying parts of the nervous system, infants' abilities expand. Structural developments in the *primary motor area*, the first area of the cortex to undergo important development, allow infants first to raise their heads voluntarily, to control their arms, trunks, and legs, and, finally, to walk.

Changes in the *primary sensory areas* (including those responsible for touch, vision, and hearing) take place mainly during the first 3 months after birth.

• According to the biological-maturation perspective, development of the brain allows babies to interact with the environment in more complex ways. Supporting evidence comes from the observation that babies born with intact brain stems but without cerebral cortexes can suck, yawn, stretch, cry, and track visual stimuli, but do not develop the well-coordinated behaviors, such as nursing, seen in normal babies the same age.

• More evidence that brain maturation influences development comes from studies of reflexes. After birth, the cerebral cortex becomes increasingly active and certain reflexes disappear. The *Moro reflex* occurs in response to a sudden noise or to the sensation of being dropped. It resembles the clinging of infant apes and disappears for good by about the fifth month; the *stepping reflex* disappears by 2 months. Some researchers feel that the stepping reflex, inhibited by cortical activity, reappears later as voluntary walking (at about 1 year of age) under cortical control; others believe that the stepping reflex is not directly related to voluntary walking. As the visual and motor systems develop, visually initiated reaching (or *prereaching*), based on independent and reflexive reaching and grasping movements, is replaced at about 3 months after birth by the more coordinated movements of visually guided reaching.

The prefrontal cortex, which helps in inhibition of movement, develops during the first 2 years; the frontal cortex, essential for planned, voluntary behavior, continues to mature throughout childhood.

As discussed in Box 4.3, interaction with the environment affects development of the nervous system. Austin Riesen demonstrated that chimpanzees needed visual stimulation for normal development of their retinas and visual cortexes, and Hirsch and Spinelli demonstrated the effect of visual simulation in kittens. Mark Rosenzweig and his colleagues found that rats allowed to actively explore enriched environments developed larger brains and learned faster than those housed in standard laboratory conditions. Thus, not only does the brain affect behavior, but behavior affects development of the brain.

C.   The environmental-learning perspective emphasizes the role of learning in the coordination of innate reflexes with environmental events. One type of learning, habituation, was described earlier in the chapter. Another type, imitation, is discussed in Box 4.4. Other types of learning are *classical conditioning* and *operant conditioning*.
   • Through classical conditioning, infants learn what events in the environment tend to occur together. They are then able to anticipate events rather than simply react to them. Classical conditioning was first described by physiologist Ivan Pavlov during his experiments on digestion in dogs. In his studies, a tone served as a *conditional stimulus* (CS), which was paired with food in the dog's mouth—an *unconditional stimulus* (UCS). This UCS invariably caused salivation—*an unconditional response* (UCR). After many pairings, presentation of the CS alone caused the dog to salivate—a *conditional response* (CR) had been learned.

It appears that babies can learn expectancies through classical conditioning within hours of birth. For example, Elliot Blass and his colleagues demonstrated that newborns could learn to pucker their mouths (CR) in response to being stroked on the forehead (CS), when the stroking had been paired with a sugar-water solution (UCS).
   • While classical conditioning explains how behaviors come to be elicited by new circumstances, instrumental or operant conditioning provides a means for adding new forms of behavior to infants' repertoires. Actions that produce rewarding consequences are repeated; such a consequence is called *reinforcement*. Actions that are not followed by reinforcing consequences, or are punished, will not be likely to be repeated. Einar Siqueland demonstrated that newborns could learn to either turn their heads (experimental group) or keep their heads still (control group) in order to obtain the opportunity to suck on a pacifier (a reinforcing stimulus).

The environmental-learning perspective has proved important as a counterweight to biological-maturation theories; however, it tends to view developmental change as an accumulation of learned modifications of behavior, discounting the genetic effects much as the biological-maturation approach discounts environmental effects on development.

D. The constructivist perspective originated in the work of Jean Piaget, who criticized as incomplete both the biological-maturation and the environmental-learning theories of his day. In Piaget's view, development begins with reflexes, which are early examples of *schemas*—mental structures that serve as models for action in similar situations. Schemas are strengthened and transformed through two processes of *adaptation*: *assimilation* and *accommodation*. Piagetian theory sees infants as active organisms whose actions shape the ways in which the environment acts on them.

Experience is assimilated to infants' schemas much the same as food is assimilated by their digestive systems. Infants may assimilate breast, bottle, pacifier, and fingers to their inborn sucking schemas.

At the same time, it is necessary for infants to modify their schemas to fit the variety of objects to which they are applied. This process is called accommodation. Somewhat different sucking techniques are necessary to suck on a nipple, on a pacifier, a blanket, or a toy truck. An infant may have to accommodate the sucking schema to each.. *Equilibration* is a balancing of assimilation and accommodation, bringing children to a new level of development. Soon, however, biological changes or environmental demands will create new imbalances that will in turn push children's development even further.
• Piaget identified six substages within infancy, which he referred to as the *sensorimotor stage*. Substages 1 and 2 are described in this chapter.

In substage 1 (birth to about 1or 1 1/2 months), infants mainly learn to coordinate and control their first schemas, the initial reflexes. The most important aspect of this practice is that the reflexes themselves produce further stimulation, which then stimulates further reflex activity.

Substage 2 (from about 1 to about 4 months) is characterized by *primary circular reactions*: infants now repeat, for their own sake, actions that are centered on their own bodies, such as sucking their fingers, waving their hands, or kicking their feet. These actions are also called circular because they lead back to themselves, serving only to prolong interesting events.
• Although Piaget did not actually study the social context of early development, it is clear that changes in the mother's behavior are essential to an infant's development. In nursing, for example, the mother's behavior (holding the infant properly or jiggling the infant during pauses in sucking) combines with the baby's efforts to maximize the amount of milk received.

E. The cultural-context perspective emphasizes cultural variations in the way that adults arrange their interactions with their children. For example, children may be breastfed by their mothers, fed by a wet nurse, or given infant formula in a bottle. More important for development than these variations in feeding practices, though, are the larger cultural patterns of which they are a part. The ways in which infants are treated in a particular culture depend on what that culture views babies to be. For example,

American mothers, who have a high opinion of newborns' capacities, react to them as though each of their behaviors were highly meaningful. The Kaluli of Papua New Guinea (as studied by Eleanor Ochs and Bambi Schieffelin), view infants as quite helpless and speak for their infants to other members of the social group, rather than speaking to their infants.

IV. Integrating the Separate Threads of Development

Children's behaviors do not develop in isolation, but as part of a complex system. Because it is not possible to study all aspects of this system at once, Robert Emde and his colleagues developed a strategy for tracing development in biological, behavioral, and social domains as they relate to one another. Periodically, changes in these domains converge, resulting in a qualitative reorganization that represents a new level of development, a bio-social-behavioral shift.

A.   The first bio-social-behavioral shift occurs in full-term babies at about 2 1/2 months after birth. Changes in smiling illustrate the importance of this shift for infants' interactions with the world.

Robert Emde, T.J. Gaensbauer, and R.J. Harmon observed that infants' earliest smiles were controlled by events occurring in the brain stem. These have been called REM smiles because they are associated with drowsiness and REM sleep. In the first few months, these endogenous smiles are replaced by exogenous smiles, which are reactions to environmental stimuli. Between 1 month and 2 1/2 months of age, infants may smile in response to nearly any outside stimulus.

At 2 1/2 to 3 months of age, as part of the first bio-social-behavioral shift, infants' smiles become truly social—they smile in response to others' smiles and, in turn, elicit others' smiles. At this point, parents report a new quality of emotional contact with their infants.

B.   Feedback from the social world—in the form of others smiling back—is important in the development of social smiling. Blind infants, unable to make these visual connections, may not shift to social smiling at 2 1/2 months. According to Selma Fraiberg, parents of blind infants often use touch to stimulate their babies' smiles; in this way, they establish the kind of social interaction seen in sighted babies and their parents.

VI. SUMMING UP THE FIRST TWO AND A HALF MONTHS

During the first 2 1/2 months of postnatal life, infants grow larger and stronger, their nervous systems develop, and they perform reflexive behaviors more efficiently. These developments take place in close coordination with their caregivers' behavior. As signaled by the development of social smiling, at about 2 1/2 months after birth, converging developments in the biological, behavioral, and social domains result in a new level of development and a new kind of social relationship between infants and their caregivers.

Key Terms I

Following are important terms introduced in Chapter 4. In the space to the right, write the definition of the term. In the space to the left, write with the letter of the example that best illustrates the term.

_____ accommodation _____

_____ adaptation _____

_____ assimilation _____

_____ emotion _____

_____ Equilibration _____

_____ Myelination _____

_____ Neuron _____

_____ prereaching _____

_____ primary circular reaction _____

_____ primary motor area _____

_____ primary sensory areas _____

_____ schema _____

_____ sensorimotor stage _____

_____ stepping reflex _____

_____ temperament _____

a.   The time of life during which developments in behavior primarily involve coordination between motor behaviors and sensory circumstances.
b.   A baby learns to suck differently to get milk from a bottle than to nurse from its mother's breast.
c.   A process through which schemas are strengthened and transformed.
d.   A baby sees its hand pass across its field of vision, finds this interesting, then repeats the movement over and over again.
e.   This balance between assimilation and accommodation brings the child into a new stage of development.
f.   The area responsible for the sense of touch is the first of these to become active.
g.   Development in this part of the cortex allows changes such as that from prereaching to voluntary reaching.
h.   A baby uses its sucking schema to explore a pacifier.
i.   When held upright on her parents' bed, a week-old girl repeatedly touches the surface with first one foot, then the other.
j.   As this process occurs, the cerebral cortex becomes more directly connected to the lower-lying areas of the nervous system.
k.   According to Piaget, the infant's early reflexes (for example, sucking) are primitive examples of this unit of psychological functioning.
l.   A newborn girl stretches out her hand toward her mother's bright necklace.
m.   Some examples of this—including anger, pleasure, and surprise—appear to be present at birth.
n.   This is another word for "nerve cell."
o.   One example of this is "slow to warm up."

Key Terms II

Following are important terms introduced in Chapter 4. In the space to the right, write the of the term. In the space to the left, write the letter of the example that best illustrates the term.

_____ brain stem _____

_____ cerebral cortex _____

_____ classical conditioning _____

_____ conditional response _____

_____ conditional stimulus _____

_____ cishabituation _____

_____ habituation _____

_____ myelin _____

_____ operant conditioning _____

_____ phonemes _____

_____ reflex _____

_____ reinforcement _____

_____ synapse _____

_____ unconditional response _____

_____ unconditional stimulus _____

a. An infant learns to suck a pacifier in order to activate a mobile above its crib.
b. A baby makes sucking movements with its mouth when it sees a nursing bottle approaching.
c. The part of the nervous system that controls vital functions such as breathing and inborn reflexes.
d. This substance coats nerve fibers, allowing nerve impulses to travel more efficiently.
e. Through this process, infants learn to anticipate events rather than simply react to them.
f. A stimulus that automatically elicits some response (as a puff of air in the eye elicits blinking).
g. This type of well-integrated but involuntary response comprises much of the newborn's behavior.
h. In simple reflexes, the small gaps between sensory and motor neurons.
i. In Pavlov's study, a tone, which signaled that food was about to be presented.
j. An infant smiles at his father and receives a smile in return, making him more likely to direct smiles at his father in the future.
k. This part of the nervous system allows infants to integrate new sensory information with memories of previous experiences.
l. A response that automatically occurs in response to a particular stimulus (as when a baby turns its head in the direction of a touch on the cheek).
m. These are responsible for the difference in sound between "pear" and "bear."
n. A newborn who stops paying attention to the washing machine has this response pattern.
o. A baby who has stopped paying attention to the radio and perks up when the station is changed has this response pattern.

Fill-in Questions

Cover the list of answers next to the statements below and fill in each blank with the word or phrase that correctly completes the sentence.

habituation

voice

language

nearsighted
crawl

faces
moving

sweet

reflexes

emotions

short

maturation

three

hunger

Nursing

1. Researchers sometimes study newborns' sensory capacities using _____—the tendency for infants to stop paying attention to a repeated stimulus.

2. Newborn infants prefer the sound of the human _____ to other sounds, and, by several days after birth, may prefer the sounds of the _____ spoken around them.

3. Infants are quite _____ at birth, but their visual acuity is close to that of adults by the time they are old enough to _____ on their own.

4. Although it is not clear what aspects they are responding to, newborns like to look at human _____, especially if they are _____.

5. Newborns have a well-developed sense of taste, and prefer _____ tastes to sour ones.

6. Infants are born with many _____—for example, blinking and grasping—which represent specific responses to specific kinds of stimulation.

7. Even very young infants appear to feel _____ such as interest, anger, and surprise.

8. Newborns sleep for a large number of fairly _____ periods.

9. Both brain _____ and cultural expectations affect the age at which babies adopt an adult-like sleep cycle.

10. If fed on demand, newborns prefer being fed about every _____ hours.

11. Both adult listeners and electronic analysis can distinguish between newborns' cries evoked by pain and their cries evoked by _____.

12. _____ is not a reflex, but involves coordination of the sucking, swallowing, and breathing reflexes.

13. The _____ perspective explains developmental change in infancy as a continuation of embryological processes.

biological-maturation

14. An infant's simplest _____ involve a sensory neuron, a motor neuron, and a synapse in the spinal cord.

reflexes

15. The _____ controls newborns' sleeping and breathing, and is involved in their emotional responses.

brain stem

16. The _____ is involved in psychological processes such as language and memory.

cerebral cortex

17. In the months after birth, _____ of neurons more closely connects the cortex to the brain stem and spinal cord.

myelination

18. While the primary motor area is not fully developed until sometime in the second year, the primary _____ area is relatively mature by 3 months after birth.

sensory

19. Some reflexes present at birth—for example, the Moro and stepping reflexes—disappear in the next few months, possibly due to maturation of higher _____ centers.

brain

20. The _____ perspective emphasizes the importance of learning in explaining developmental change.

environmental-learning

21. There is controversy about whether the form of learning called _____ occurs in newborn infants.

imitation

22. In classical conditioning, a _____ stimulus (for example, a bell), when paired with an unconditional stimulus (for example, food), comes to elicit a conditional _____ (for example, salivation).

conditional

response

23. In _____ conditioning, behavior increases in frequency when followed by _____ (rewards or escape from unrewarding circumstances).

operant
reinforcement

24. The _____ framework, exemplified by Piaget's theory, emphasizes the role of children's own activity in developmental change.

constructivist

25. In Piaget's theory, the basic psychological units are _____—for example, sucking, grasping, and looking.

schemas

assimilation
accommodation

26. In the process of _____, schemas are applied to new experiences; through _____ the schemas are modified to fit the demands of the environment.

Equilibration

27. _____—the balancing of assimilation and accommodation—brings children to new levels of development.

sensorimotor
six

28. Piaget referred to the first 2 years as the _____ stage of development. He divided this period into _____ substages.

reflexes present at birth

29. In substage 1 (birth to about 1 1/2 months), infants learn to control and coordinate their first schemas, the _____.

circular

30. During substage 2 (1 to 4 months), infants engage in primary _____ reactions, such as sucking their fingers and kicking their feet.

cultural-context

31. The _____ perspective emphasizes the ways in which development is affected by cultural differences in adults' interactions with their children.

bio-social-behavioral
2 1/2

32. When developments in the biological, behavioral, and social domains converge, the result is the qualitative reorganization of development known as a _____ shift. The first such shift takes place at about _____ months of age.

Social

33. _____ smiling (smiling in response to others' smiles and eliciting the smiles of others) occurs as part of the first bio-social-behavioral shift.

Multiple-Choice Questions

Circle the letter of the word or phrase that correctly completes each statement.

1. On which would a newborn best be able to focus?
   a. his mother's face while he nurses
   b. a mobile hanging over the far end of his crib
   c. a person standing across the room
   d. All of the above equally well

2. When 1-month-olds are shown simple geometric figures,
    a.   they look away.
    b.   they focus on areas of high contrast.
    c.   they systematically scan the outline of the figure.
    d.   they look first at the outline, then scan the interior.

3. Infants who are regular in biological functions, playful, and adaptable have been labeled "easy" with respect to
    a.   motor development.
    b.   personality.
    c.   temperament.
    d.   emotion.

4. Babies' cries usually cause adults to
    a.   react with increased heart rate and blood pressure.
    b.   avoid contact with the babies.
    c.   react with decreases in heartrate.
    d.   react with signs of depression.

5. Nursing
    a.   is present at birth in the same form as seen in older infants.
    b.   develops greater efficiency and coordination during the first weeks of life.
    c.   is composed of several reflexes that are and remain separate from one another.
    d.   takes longer in older infants than in newborns.

6. Theorists with the _____ perspective view development during infancy as a continuation of embryological processes.
    a.   environmental-learning
    b.   cultural-context
    c.   constructivist
    d.   biological-maturation

7. The _____ controls vital functions such as breathing and sleeping.
    a.   cerebral cortex
    b.   cerebellum
    c.   brain stem
    d.   midbrain

8. Myelination is
    a.   a process of brain growth through the formation of new neurons.
    b.   the formation of a fatty sheath around nerve fibers.
    c.   a structural part of brain development that is nearly complete at birth.
    d.   the formation of reflex arcs in the spinal cord.

9. The _____ reflex involves flinging out the arms, then hugging them back to the center of the body.
    a. grasping
    b. reaching
    c. swimming
    d. Moro

10. Through _____, babies learn to anticipate events that often occur together.
    a. operant conditioning
    b. imitation
    c. classical conditioning
    d. habituation

11. When an infant turns her head, she is given a taste of sugarwater. After a series of trials, she turns her head consistently. This is an example of
    a. habituation.
    b. classical conditioning
    c. imitation.
    d. operant conditioning.

12. Piaget's theory of intellectual development views infants as
    a. active, problem-solving organisms.
    b. helpless and unable to initiate behavior.
    c. completely dependent on the environment for stimulation.
    d. having intellectual potential that unfolds automatically as they mature.

13. Which might be a primary circular reaction?
    a. An infant opens his mouth for milk when he sees his mother approach.
    b. An infant repeatedly brings her hand to her mouth and briefly sucks her fingers.
    c. A baby learns to ignore the sound of the highway outside its window.
    d. A newborn copies its mother when she opens her eyes wide in a surprised expression.

14. American mothers generally behave as though everything their infants do is
    a. random.
    b. evidence of helplessness.
    c. meaningful.
    d. evidence of superior intelligence.

15. Which is associated with the first postnatal bio-social-behavioral shift?
    a. social smiling
    b. complete development of the cerebral cortex
    c. walking
    d. the first meaningful spoken words

Short-Answer Questions

1. What types of visual stimuli do newborns prefer to look at? What changes take place in their looking behavior over the first few months of life?

2. In what ways do researchers determine that infants are experiencing emotions? Can we know for certain that infant and adult emotions are similar? Why or why not?

3. What do psychologists mean by "temperament"? What evidence is there that it has a heritable component?

4. How do both mother and infant contribute to the development of efficient nursing?

5. How do infants form expectancies through classical conditioning? Describe a situation in which this might actually occur.

6. Show how biological, behavioral, and social factors interact in infants' development of social smiling.

Putting It All Together

Find examples from prenatal development and early infancy to show what happens when higher centers in the nervous system begin to take charge of particular motor functions.

Additional Resources

Bower, T. G. R. *Development in Infancy*. San Francisco: W.H. Freeman and Co., 1982.
This discussion of perceptual and cognitive development during infancy gives readers a look at how a clever researcher tries to determine what babies really know.

Brazelton, T. Berry. *What Every Baby Knows*. New York: Ballantine Books, 1987.
This account of early development follows five families during the first two years of their children's lives, showing how they solve problems and adapt to the changes brought about by their children's births.

Ginsburg, Herbert P. and Sylvia Opper. *Piaget's Theory of Intellectual Development*, Third Edition. Englewood Cliffs, N.J.: Prentice-Hall, 1988.
This is a readable, up-to-date presentation of Piaget's work and theory, aimed at undergraduate-level students.

Haith, Marshall. *Rules That Babies Look By*. Hillsdale, NJ: Erlbaum, 1980.
The characteristics of early visual behavior in early infancy are described by an expert in the field.

Metzger, Mary and Cynthia Whittaker. *The Childproofing Checklist. A Parent's Guide to Accident Prevention From Birth to Age Five*. New York: Doubleday, 1988.
This book deals with one of the major adjustments that must be made by families with new babies—making the home safe for infants and young children.

Montagu, Ashley. *Touching. The Human Significance of the Skin*, Third Edition. New York: Harper & Row, 1986.
The author describes the importance of tactile interaction for human development.

Pryor, Karen. *Nursing Your Baby*. New York: Pocket Books, 1991.
In this book, nursing is discussed from the point of view of the prospective mother; it should, nevertheless, be interesting to students of infant development.

Schaffer, Rudolph. *Mothering*. Cambridge: Harvard University Press, 1977.
The author describes the organization of infants' behavior in the context of their mothers' stimulation of and reaction to them.

Towle, Alexandra (Ed.). *Mother*. New York: Simon & Schuster, 1988.
This book contains many views of motherhood, expressed through the words and images of famous writers and poets.

Answer Key

Answers to Key Terms I: b, c, h, m, e, j, h, l, d, g, f, k, a, i, o

Answers to Key Terms II: c, k, e, b, i, o,n, d, a, m,g, j, h, l, f

Answers to Multiple-Choice Questions: 1. a, 2. b, 3. c, 4. a, 5. b, 6. d, 7. c, 8. b, 9. d, 10. c, 11. d, 12. a, 13. b, 14. c, 15. a.

The Achievements of the First Year

At no time after birth does development occur so quickly as in the first year. During their first 12 months, infants move from relative helplessness to independent locomotion. Gradually, they gain control over their bodies. By 1 year of age, they can reach for and grasp objects smoothly and accurately and let them go voluntarily; they can even, using thumb and fingers, pick up objects the size of a bead or a raisin.

Infants' growing cognitive abilities parallel the development of their motor skills. Toward the end of the first year, they demonstrate newly developed powers of memory and are able to coordinate actions to reach a goal. Linguistically, they are also making progress; their strings of babbling begin to resemble adult speech.

Changes are occurring in infants' social lives as well. By 7 or 8 months of age, they begin to be wary of strangers and to resist being separated from their caretakers. In fact, they depend on their caretakers' reactions to show them how to react in unfamiliar situations.

These many changes in different domains result in a bio-social-behavioral shift between about 7 and 9 months of age. At this time, infants are prepared for more active exploration of their physical and social worlds.

Chapter Outline

I.   BIOLOGICAL CHANGES

Changes in babies' motor and cognitive abilities between 2 1/2 months and 1 year depend on changes in the physical structures of their bodies and brains.

A.   Most babies grow about 10 inches and triple their weight during the first year—their fastest growth spurt until adolescence. Their bodies grow differentially; by 12 months, their heads account for a smaller proportion and their legs a greater proportion of overall length than they did at birth. This lowers their center of gravity and makes walking easier.

B.   Infants' bones start to ossify, or harden, beginning with those of the hands and wrists. Their muscles become longer and thicker, another development that prepares them for walking. Girls mature faster than boys. By the time of birth, their skeletons are 4 to 6 weeks more mature than those of male newborns. By puberty, girls will lead boys in physical maturity by 2 years.

C.   Babies' nervous systems—especially the cortexes of their brains—grow and become more complex. Growth and myelination lead, between 7 and 9 months, to increased functioning of the frontal and prefrontal areas and to the appearance of new patterns in electrical activity. Behavior comes more under voluntary control and babies are, for the first time, able to inhibit their impulses.

II.   PERCEPTUAL AND MOTOR DEVELOPMENT

Dramatic improvements occur during the first year in babies' ability to explore the environment through *perception, locomotion*—the ability to move about on their own—, and by manipulating objects.

A.   Babies begin to visually guide their reaching toward objects at the time of the first postnatal bio-social-behavioral shift. During the next months, their movements become more refined and accurate. By 12 months, they can pick up objects using thumb and fingers and are well enough coordinated to eat with a spoon and drink from a cup.

B.   Babies can hold up their heads at about 2 months of age and coordinate their arm movements at about 4 months, but are usually not skilled at crawling until, at 8 or 9 months of age, the actions of arms and legs are coordinated with one another. Walking generally follows several months later; however, there is wide variation in the ages at which children reach various milestones in motor development.

C.   Giving babies practice in specific motor skills—walking, for example—causes them to learn these skills at earlier ages. However, for skills involved in basic motor development, untrained children quickly catch up. There may be some lasting advantage for early training of culture-specific activities such as sports skills, dance, and playing musical instruments.

III. COGNITIVE CHANGES

Psychologists' beliefs about infants' *cognitive processes* depends to some extent on the methods they use to assess them. However, there is no doubt that, during this time, babies are improving in their ability to remember their experiences and to think about them in more systematic ways.

A.   As discussed in Chapter 4, Piaget viewed development as arising from children's own actions on the world. In substages 1 and 2 of the sensorimotor stage, infants first practiced their initial reflexes (substage 1), then developed ways of making enjoyable activities continue (substage 2). Between 4 and 12 months, they will complete substages 3 and 4.
   • In substage 3 (4 to 8 months), babies perform *secondary circular reactions*, in which they repeat actions that cause interesting results in the outside environment; for example, kicking at a mobile in order to see the dangling objects move.
   • In substage 4 (8 to 12 months), they become able to combine secondary circular reactions in order to reach a goal. For example, a baby may sweep a cushion out of the way (one schema) in order to reach for and grasp a stuffed toy (a second schema).

B.   Piaget believed that newborns had no sense of *object permanence* but gradually develop it during the sensorimotor period. Until babies actively began to search for hidden objects, he thought, it was not possible to know that they believed in the objects' continued existence when out of sight. This notion has generated a considerable amount of scientific work.

C.   Piaget traced six levels of understanding of object permanence, which parallel the six substages of the sensorimotor period.
   • In stages 1 and 2 (birth to 4 months), when an object disappears, babies stare at the place where they last saw it, then turn their attention elsewhere.
   • During stage 3 (4 to 8 months), they will reach for a covered object if it is only partially hidden. However, they are not bothered by the appearance of the "same" object in two or more places at once.
   • During stage 4 (8 to 12 months), babies search for an object that has been completely hidden under a cover, showing that they believe in the object's continued existence. However, if an object that was first hidden in one location is then hidden in a second location—in full view of the babies—they continue to search for it in the first location, where they had previously found it. This is called the *A-not-B error*.

D. It is possible, by using clever experimental techniques, to show that infants of less than 8 months of age actually know more about hidden objects than they appeared to in Piaget's observations. For example, Renee Baillargeon and her colleagues demonstrated that 3 1/2-month-olds continued to believe in the existence of a hidden object by showing that the infants were surprised when a screen appeared to pass through the space where the object was supposed to be. Why, then, do they fail to actively search? Adele Diamond varied the time before babies could search for an object and found that memory limitations were a factor in their performance. However, neither memory limitations nor lack of motor coordination can provide a complete explanation for babies' errors on object permanence tests. Looking at all the results together, it seems likely that infants have some understanding of object permanence by 4 months of age but cannot act on it until their motor skills become smoothly enough coordinated so that reaching for covered objects can be done without forgetting about the object altogether.

Piaget's views on the importance of children's own activity in cognitive development have led to many studies. As discussed in Box 5.1, Richard Held and Alan Hein, working with kittens, discovered that experience with locomotion is necessary for developing an understanding of spatial relations. Joseph Campos and his colleagues demonstrated that babies who had experience with moving around in baby walkers developed fear of heights (as measured on a visual cliff) at an earlier age and also were better at locating hidden objects than children of the same age without walker experience. They also found that babies whose locomotion was delayed were correspondingly delayed on a hidden object task.

E. For many years, it was assumed that, at birth, babies respond to the sight, sound, and other sense impressions of objects as though these impressions were completely separate. *Cross-modal perception* was thought to be acquired through a long learning process. Recent studies, however, indicate that babies are either born with the ability to integrate their sense impressions or learn this ability quite early in infancy. For example, Elizabeth Spelke found that when 4-month-old infants were shown two different films but heard only one soundtrack, they spent more time looking at the film that matched the sounds they heard. Other research has provided additional support for infants' ability to integrate sense impressions.
    • There is some evidence that infants can perceive the number of items in a display, so long as there are four or fewer items, and that they are even sensitive to numerical relations such as subtraction.
    • Infants' ability to *categorize*—to respond to different objects in a similar way—increases substantially during the first year. Studies by Carolyn Rovee-Collier and her colleagues and by Peter Eimas and Paul Quinn have shown that 3-month-old infants can form *perceptual categories*. Later in the first year they will begin to form *conceptual categories* in which objects are grouped according to function or behavior rather than by perceptual similarity.

F.   Infants also improve in their ability to remember what they learn. Carolyn Rovee-Collier and her colleagues found that, when they were taught to move a mobile by kicking it, 3-month-olds remembered their training for about a week; however, if "reminded" by being shown the mobile the day before testing, they remembered how to move the mobile even after a month. Older infants could remember for longer periods of time.

G.   Studies of infant memory that involve learning reveal a picture of continuous improvement involving the same processes present early on. Somewhat different results are obtained by studying babies' recall of events that they have merely observed. For example, studies have demonstrated that 9- to 11-month-olds can imitate actions they have seen someone else perform the day before. Some researchers believe this to be a new form of memory that emerges around the middle of the first year.

Once infants can recognize what is familiar, they also recognize other situations as unfamiliar. Rudolph Schaffer found that, while 4-month-olds immediately reached for an unfamiliar object, 6-month-olds hesitated a short time, and 9-month-olds hesitated longer or turned away from the object. Nathan Fox, Jerome Kagan, and Sally Weiskopf suggest that infants become wary when confronted with objects and events which do not fit into any familiar category. Andrew Meltzoff and Keith Moore argue, on the basis of infants' imitation of facial expressions, that recall memory appears as early as 6 weeks of age. Other researchers such as Jean Mandler feel that this type of imitation is a reflexive behavior that does not involve true recall.

These changes in cognitive abilities are linked to changes in babies' emotional relationship with their caretakers and in their ability to communicate.

IV.   A NEW RELATIONSHIP WITH THE SOCIAL WORLD

A.   Babies are fairly limited in the ways in which they can function in the world; therefore, they depend on adults to help them perform many actions that they will later be able to perform by themselves. Cultural-context theorist Lev Vygotsky called this a *zone of proximal development*. The adults perform only those parts of the action that the child cannot yet perform; thus, their actions are finely tuned to those of the child. In a study with 6- to 13-month-olds, Christine Mosier and Barbara Rogoff found that older babies were more likely to solicit their mothers' help to perform a task. In doing this, they were dependent on their mothers' ability to understand what they wanted. Because only familiar adults can be counted on to perform according to babies' expectation, babies may feel uncertain about how to interact with unfamiliar adults, and are therefore wary of them.

B.   At about the same time that infants begin to crawl and to react with wariness to unfamiliar people, their emotional relationships with their caretakers take on a new quality, which psychologists call *attachment*. According to Eleanor Maccoby, the signs of attachment are:
   • Seeking to be near the caretaker
   • Showing distress if separated
   • Being happy when reunited
   • Orienting (for example, watching, or listening for) toward the other caretaker.

   Attachment appears between 7 and 9 months of age and undergoes changes in later infancy.

C.   As babies become more independent physically, they show different forms of communication with their caretakers. In early infancy, their face-to-face interactions display a kind of coordinated turn-taking called *primary intersubjectivity*. But at around 7 months of age, a further development—*secondary intersubjectivity*—appears, allowing infants and caretakers to share understanding of events beyond themselves. For example, now infants can follow their mothers gaze to look at something she is looking at. Another example is *social referencing*, a form of communication in which babies' reactions to unusual situations are affected by their mothers' facial expressions—the expressions tell them "how to feel." Baby girls are somewhat more likely than baby boys to be wary of objects that make their mothers appear worried. Once babies move around on their own, new forms of vocal communication allow mothers and babies to remain coordinated even when out of sight of one another.
   • From the first 10 to 12 weeks of life, babies make cooing and gurgling noises, and will even engage in conversation like turn taking.
   • *Babbling* (involving consonant-vowel combinations) begins, for hearing children, at around 4 months of age, as a form of vocal play. Babies from all cultures babble in the same way until, at about 9 months, they begin to drop sounds that do not belong to the language they hear around them.
   • In *jargoning*, which begins around the end of the first year, babies imitate the stress intonations of the language they are learning while putting together long strings of syllables. In contrast to hearing children, deaf infants of a year of age rarely vocalize; instead, they begin to "babble" with their hands, using movements that become elements of sign language.
   • By 12 months of age, babies can understand about a dozen simple phrases and can say several words themselves.

V.   A New Bio-Social-Behavioral Shift

Advances in motor skills—particularly in locomotion—are coordinated with new developments in cognitive domains and in social relationships, creating a new bio-social-behavioral shift between 7 and 9 months of age. Infants are now able to move independently, to recall more of what they observe, and to grasp and explore objects more skillfully. Their social interactions change as they become more aware of the differences between familiar and strange adults, and their caretakers adjust their own behavior accordingly. These new patterns of adaptation will serve them until the next reorganization occurs, a year or so later.

Key Terms

Following are important terms introduced in Chapter 5. In the space on the right, write the definition of the term. In the space on the left, write the letter of the example that best illustrates the term.

_____ A-not-B error _____

_____ attachment _____

_____ babbling _____

_____ categorizing _____

_____ cognitive processes _____

_____ conceptual categories _____

_____ cross-modal percepton _____

_____ jargoning _____

_____ locomotion _____

_____ object permanence _____

_____ perceptual categories _____

_____ primary intersubjectivity _____

_____ secondary circular reactions _____

_____ secondary intersubjectivity _____

_____ social referencing _____

_____ zone of proximal development _____

a.   When a nurse enters the examination room and greets a 9-month-old girl, the infant glances at her mother's face, then smiles at the newcomer.

b.   Although she has just watched her dad hide his shiny watch under the sofa cushion, Jennifer searches for it behind the throw pillow, where she found it the last time.

c.   John's mother gets the applesauce on the spoon, then lets John guide it to his mouth.

d.   Becky, confronted with an array of toys, touches all the toy cars, one after another.

e.   A 7-month-old boy has learned to pull the ring his parents have dangled over his crib, causing a music box to play. He pulls it over and over again.

f.   A 10-month-old girl immediately whisks her mother's handkerchief off the rattle after her mother has covered it.

g.   A mother brings her face close to her baby's and smiles. The baby gazes at her and smiles in return.

h.   When Suzanne turns her gaze toward a large dog, Brian, her 8-month-old, also stares in that direction.

i.   An 11-month-old sounds as if he is explaining something to his family; however, no one can understand a bit of what he says.

j.   A baby plays with language sounds: "ba-ba-ba-ba-ba."

k.   Tim cries when his mother leaves the room, but gives her a big hug when she returns.

l.   To achieve this, babies must be able to integrate the movements of many parts of their bodies.

m.   Jody recognizes that the interlocking rings she feels under her blanket are the same ones she has seen hanging above her crib.

n.   These are formed when a 4-month-old recognizes the similarity of a group of pictures of dogs.

o.   Learning and memory are examples.

p.   These are based on an understanding that goes beyond perceptual features.

Fill-In Questions

Cover the list of answers next to the statements below and fill in each blank with the word or phrase that correctly completes the sentence.

faster   1.   Babies grow _____ during their first year than at any other time until adolescence.

ossify or harden   2.   Infants' bones _____, beginning with those of the hands and wrists.

cortex   3.   An important part of the brain to develop during the first year is the frontal _____, which plays a role in voluntary behavior.

reach   4.   By 9 months of age, babies can _____ for objects automatically, guiding their movements with a single glance.

5. Babies have the ability to reach for and explore objects by the time they can _____—their first effective form of locomotion.

crawl

6. Infants can learn some motor skills at earlier ages if given the opportunity to _____ them.

practice

7. Substage 3 of the sensorimotor period is called _____ circular reactions; during this time, infants learn to repeat actions which produce interesting results in their _____.

primary

environment

8. Piaget believed that, at birth, infants have no sense of the _____ of objects, behaving as if they no longer existed when out of sight.

permanence

9. During substage 4, infants learn to _____ secondary circular reactions in order to achieve a goal.

coordinate

10. It is not until stage 3 (4 to 8 months), Piaget thought, that infants react to an object's disappearance; at that time, they will search for a covered object so long as it is not completely _____.

hidden

11. Stage _____ children (8 to 12 months) will uncover a completely hidden object, but also make the _____ error when an object has been hidden in another place.

4
A-not-B

12. Renee Baillargeon and her colleagues have demonstrated that, under some conditions, infants as young as 3 1/2 months realize that _____ objects continue to exist.

hidden

13. Babies have more trouble searching for hidden objects when they have to wait to begin the search. This shows that part of their problem is limited _____.

memory

14. Studies with both kittens and human infants have demonstrated that experience with _____ leads to better understanding of spatial relations, as measured by performance on the visual cliff.

locomotion

15. Joseph Campos found that when babies who were not yet crawling on their own were given experience in walkers, their performance on a hidden object task was _____ than that of babies without comparable experience.

better

integrate

16. There is evidence that even very young infants are able to _____ the different sense impressions they receive from objects.

category

17. Between 6 and 9 months of age, infants begin to treat objects that are similar in some ways (though dissimilar in others) as though they belong to the same _____.

recall

18. By the time they are 9 months of age, infants are able to _____ events they have seen previously, even if they have not actively participated.

familiar

19. Once objects and situations can be categorized and remembered, infants begin to react with wariness to those that are not _____.

proximal

20. Only familiar adults can be trusted to fine-tune their actions to infants' needs, creating a zone of _____ development.

attachment

21. Between 7 and 9 months of age, infants form a new emotional bond, called _____, to their primary caretakers.

intersubjectivity

22. The face to face interactions between very young infants and their caretakers has been called primary _____.

secondary

23. In _____ intersubjectivity, older infants and their caretakers begin to interact in more complex ways, for example by following one another's gaze toward a third person.

social

24. Infants also begin to engage in _____ referencing, in which they look to their caretakers for clues about how to react in new situations.

babbling

25. At around 4 months of age, babies begin _____—vocalizing in consonant/vowel combinations.

jargoning

26. Later in the first year, babies engage in _____—reproducing the sound patterns and intonation of the language they are learning.

hands

27. Deaf babies "babble" using movements of their _____.

7
9

28. A new bio-social-behavioral shift takes place between _____ and _____ months of age.

Multiple-Choice Questions

Circle the letter of the word or phrase that correctly completes each statement.

1. What, if any, changes occur in infants' body proportions during the first year of life?
   a. The head becomes a larger proportion of total body length.
   b. The head becomes a smaller proportion of total body length.
   c. The head and body maintain the same relative proportions.
   d. The head and body each maintain the same overall size.

2. The _____—a part of the brain involved in voluntary behavior—undergoes a spurt in development between 7 and 9 months after birth.
   a. cerebellum
   b. brain stem
   c. frontal cortex
   d. hippocampus

3. In the long run, which of the following skills should benefit most from extensive early practice?
   a. sitting
   b. walking
   c. dancing
   d. crawling

4. According to Piaget, infants' development emerges from the interplay between

   a. perceptual and motor skills.
   b. assimilation and accommodation.
   c. self and society.
   d. memory and cognition.

5. According to Piaget, during the last few months of the first year infants are learning to
   a. modify their basic reflexes.
   b. make interesting experiences, centered on their own bodies, last.
   c. make interesting events in the outside world last.
   d. coordinate actions to reach a goal.

6. Infants in _____ of developing object permanence tend to search for hidden objects in places they have found them before, even when they have seen them being moved to another place.
   a. stage 1
   b. stage 2
   c. stage 3
   d. stage 4

7. Research has shown that 7 1/2-month-old babies are more likely to make the A-not-B error
    a. when they have had extensive practice in finding hidden objects.
    b. when they are kept from searching for an object for several seconds.
    c. when they are allowed to begin searching immediately after the object is hidden.
    d. when the object is only partially hidden.

8. Studies of the effects of locomotion on perceptual-motor skills have demonstrated that
    a. Experience with independent locomotion enhances performance on the visual cliff both in kittens and in human infants and leads to better performance by infants on hidden object tasks.
    b. Locomotion is beneficial to performance on the visual cliff and on hidden object tasks, but it does not matter whether the kitten or infant moves independently or is carried around by someone else.
    c. Experience with locomotion is beneficial to performance on the visual cliff by both kittens and human infants but has no effect on infants' performance on hidden object tasks.
    d. Experience with locomotion aids kittens in their performance on the visual cliff but has no effect on the performance of human infants.

9. Which is an example of primary intersubjectivity?
    a. A child turns her gaze toward the door when her mother looks that way.
    b. Seeing his mother's look of alarm, a child cries when approached by a large dog.
    c. A child takes turns smiling at her mother and being smiled at in return.
    d. A child is upset when he is left with a babysitter while his parents go out.

10. Between the ages of 7 and 9 months, infants begin to act _____ people and things that are unfamiliar.
    a. afraid of
    b. attracted to
    c. indifferent to
    d. attached to

11. With respect to parent-infant interaction, a "zone of proximal development" refers to
    a. the parent directly training the child to learn new skills.
    b. the parent allowing the child to learn new skills entirely on his or her own.
    c. the child following the parent around wherever the parent may go.
    d. the parent helping the child do things he or she cannot yet accomplish alone.

12. Which is not a sign of attachment to the mother during the first year of life?
    a. The child cries when his mother leaves the room.
    b. The child is perfectly happy to be left by his mother.
    c. The child follows his mother around the house.
    d. The child is happy when his mother returns after a separation.

13. Infants' earliest babbling sounds
    a.   may contain the sounds of any language.
    b.   contain only the sounds of the language they hear around them.
    c.   are no different in deaf babies than in hearing babies.
    d.   do not occur without reinforcement from parents.

14. Which is <u>not</u> part of the bio-social-behavioral shift that takes place between 7 and 9 months of age?
    a.   the ability to crawl
    b.   coordinating actions to reach a goal
    c.   greater acceptance of strangers
    d.   social referencing

Short-Answer Questions

1. How are improvements in memory and in locomotion related to infants' ability to search for hidden objects?

2. In what ways might the growth of memory and the ability to classify contribute to infants becoming wary of strange objects and people?

3. What do cross-cultural studies tell us about the roles of nature and nurture in the development of motor skills?

4. What evidence is there that infants may believe in the continued existence of hidden objects even though they fail to search for them?

Putting It All Together

Look back to Chapter 4 and find information about social smiling. Then, give examples of its importance during the first year of life.

Additional Resources

Brazelton, T. Berry. *Infants and Mothers: Differences in Development* (Rev.Ed.). New York: Dell, 1986.
The author follows the progress of an active baby, a quiet baby, and an average baby through the first 12 months of life.

Caplan, Frank (Ed.). *The First Twelve Months of Life*. New York: Bantam, 1984.
This is a month-by-month look at the physical, cognitive, and social changes taking place during an infant's first year.

McCall, Robert B. *Infants*. Cambridge, Mass.: Harvard University Press, 1979.
This book about infants covers physical growth and the development of personality, cognition, and attachment.

Walden, Tedra A. and Tamra A. Ogan. "The Development of Social Referencing." *Child Development*, 1988, *59*, 1230-1240.
This study examines the course of development of social referencing in infants from 6 to 22 months of age.

Zucker, Kenneth J. "The Infant's Construction of His Parents in the First Six Months of Life." In Tiffany Field and Nathan Fox (Eds.), *Social Perception in Infants*. Norwood, NJ: Ablex, 1985.
This chapter traces the development during the first 6 months of infants' ability to recognize their parents.

Answer Key

Answers to Key Terms: b, k, j, d, o, p, m, i, l, f, n, g, e, h, a, c

Answers to Multiple-Choice Questions: 1. b, 2. c, 3. c, 4. b, 5. d, 6. d, 7. b, 8. a, 9. c, 10. a, 11. d, 12. b, 13. a, 14. c.

The End of Infancy

Between 12 and 30 months of age, children develop in important ways—physically, cognitively, and in their social relations. During this time, they develop increasing control over their bodies, as reflected in "gross motor" skills such as walking and running, "fine motor" skills such as scribbling with crayons, and in the ability to feed, dress, and toilet themselves.

New developments in thought allow children to reflect on what has happened in the past and to set themselves goals for the immediate future. Being able to call objects and events to mind helps them avoid some of the trial and error on which younger infants depend when solving problems.

While older infants are still dependent on their caretakers for support when coping with unfamiliar situations, they are learning to predict and understand their caretakers' periodic absences and returns. Development in the ability to communicate with language helps infants make their needs better known.

The changes of late infancy—physical, cognitive, and social—allow children a greater degree of independence and self-direction. Their behavior begins to reveal a sense of "selfhood" at this time. These developmental charges complement one another; changes in one area help development in another. At about 2 years of age, developments in physical growth and coordination, thinking and language skills, and greater self-directedness will result in a new bio-social-behavioral shift and a transition to a new level of development.

Chapter Outline

I.   BIOLOGICAL MATURATION

During the second and third years of life, children raised in the United States continue to grow substantially; height increases, on the average, from 20 inches to 38 inches and weight from 20 pounds to 33 pounds.

Important changes are also taking place in children's brains. Fibers that connect the brain stem with the frontal and prefrontal areas of the cerebral cortex become covered with a coat of myelin, allowing them to transmit messages more efficiently. Individual neurons grow new branches, forming additional connections to other cells. And brain areas that had, until now, been maturing at different rates finally reach similar levels of development.

II.   PERCEPTUAL-MOTOR COORDINATION

The developments in their nervous systems give children much greater control over physical movement.

A.   Walking involves not only the development of motor skills but also increased sensitivity to perceptual input from the environment. Karen Adolph and her colleagues found that 14-month-old toddlers could adjust their movements to navigate slopes of different degrees of steepness; 8 1/2-month-olds who did not walk could also perceive the steepness of the slopes, although they did not adjust their movements. According to Esther Thelen and her colleagues, babies can make the leg movements needed for walking at 7 monthsof age, but cannot yet shift their weight and move their arms in a coordinated way.

B.   Between 12 and 30 months, infants develop greater coordination of fine hand movements, becoming able to string beads, use scissors, and feed and dress themselves.

C.   Voluntary control over elimination is not possible until at least 15 months of age. Waiting to teach toileting has advantages as 20-month-olds can be trained twice as quickly as 10-month-olds. Most children can remain dry during the day by the time they are 2 years old, though many do not achieve complete daytime control until 3 years of age. Nighttime dryness is more difficult and is not achieved until children are about 4 years old.

III. A New Mode of Thought

Children's increased ability to control their actions is accompanied by a new mode of thinking.

A.   Piaget described two additional substages that occur during later infancy and that mark the end of the sensorimotor period:
   • In substage 5 (*tertiary circular reactions*)—12 to 18 months—children explore the world in more complex ways by varying the actions they use to reach their goals. They are not yet able to imagine the consequences of actions, so these actions must still be performed physically.
   • In substage 6 (*representation*) 18- to 24-month-old children literally "re-present" the world to themselves mentally. This allows them to plan solutions to problems before carrying them out. They are now able to imitate past events, make use of language, and solve problems more systematically.

B.   Children master the remaining stages of what Piaget called object permanence during the second year of life.
   • Beginning at about a year of age (stage 5), they stop making the A-not-B error; that is, they will search for a toy in a place it has not previously been, so long as they see it being hidden there.
   • Between 18 and 24 months, they achieve stage 6; now they can find the toy in a new place even if they have not seen it hidden there, apparently reasoning that it must be somewhere nearby. They can also anticipate the path of a moving object.

C.   Developments in sensorimotor intelligence and in the ability to reason about the location of hidden objects are accompanied by changes in children's problem-solving behavior. They now become less dependent on trial and error and are better able to imagine the results of their actions before carrying them out.

D.   Increasingly complex forms of play reflect 12- to 30-month-old children's developing mental skills. Peter Smith has described four kinds of play—locomotor, object, social, and fantasy—which, he feels, provide practice in activities that are important in children's development. Although fantasy play seems to occur only in human children, the other three types can be seen in the behavior of young animals of many species. Twelve-month-olds begin to use objects as adults would use them—for example, banging a hammer on a block. Between 12 and 24 months, children begin to engage in *symbolic play*, making one object stand for another—for example, a rock for a baby. As children develop, their symbolic play becomes more elaborate.

• Lev Vygotsky's view was that play serves as a zone of proximal development that allows children to perform developmentally more advanced actions than they can perform on their own. Research has shown that children's play lasts longer and is more advanced whey they play with their mothers or siblings than when they play alone.

It is still not known to what extent play is beneficial to infants' development.

E.   Piaget felt that *deferred imitation*—imitation of events which happened in the past—did not occur until well into the second year of life and was closely related to symbolic play, which appeared at about the same time. However, more recent work has indicated that deferred imitation makes its appearance as part of the changes occurring toward the end of the first year of life. In late infancy, however, it can be seen in a wider range of contexts.

F.   One way of finding out more about children's mental representations is to observe how they categorize objects. As discussed in Chapter 5, younger babies can detect similarities between objects—first on the basis of perceptual features, then on the basis of conceptual features. During the second year of life, children begin to create categories from an array of objects. A study by Susal Sugarman explored classification in 12- to 30-month-old toddlers. Although 1-year-olds noticed similarities between objects, they did not yet place similar objects together. Eighteen-month-olds, on the other hand, created a "work space" and filled it with objects of a particular category—for example, all the boats in a collection of toys. Twenty-four-month-old toddlers divided the objects into two groups, and 30-month-olds divided their collections into subcategories—for example, red boats and blue boats.

G.   Research by Judy De Loache demonstrated that when 3-year-old children saw an adult hide a toy within a scale model of a room, they could use the information to find the toy in the room itself. In contrast, 2 1/2-year-olds were confused by the task. But when De Loache and her colleagues told the 2 1/2-year-olds that the room could be shrunk by a machine to become the model—highlighting the model's dual nature as symbol and object—the children were able to make use of information from the model to find an object in the room.

H.   Children's ability to use and understand language increases greatly during the second year of life; by 21 months, for example, they can follow fairly complex verbal directions. Language use is also linked to other expressions of mental representation such as deferred imitation and symbolic play. For example, when 18-month-olds are combining two words in speech, they also are able to combine two actions in play. There are also parallels between the growth of vocabulary and children's ability to search for hidden objects and to solve problems.

IV. THE DEVELOPMENT OF CHILD-CARETAKER RELATIONS

As babies begin to move around on their own, they need to be able to learn about the world while, at the same time, avoiding its hazards. The development of attachment, an emotional bond between children and their caretakers, helps provide a balance between security and opportunities to explore.

A. Because children in all cultures begin to resist separation from their caretakers at about the same age, it has been suggested that attachment is a universal feature of development. As discussed in Box 6.1, children generally become attached to their mothers first, but also form attachments to fathers, siblings, and other caretakers. Psychologists have suggested several different explanations for why attachment occurs.

• Freud's theory emphasizes the importance of *biological drives* (for example, hunger) and proposes that infants become attached to those who help them satisfy these drives. Children first become attached, during what Freud called the oral stage, to those who satisfy their hunger; during the second year of life, while in the anal stage, they will strive for independence and self-control. Freud believed that children's relationships with their mothers were models for their adult relationships.

• Erik Erikson emphasizes society's influence on development. He believes that, at each of eight stages of development, from birth through old age, people meet and resolve a particular conflict or crisis. Erikson's theory stresses that attachment is related to children's development of trust in their caretakers during the earliest stage and to the development of autonomy—control of their bodies and actions—during stage 2.

• In John Bowlby's ethological explanation, attachment serves to regulate the distance between infants and their caregivers. It progresses through four phases during the first 2 years of life. First comes "preattachment" (birth—6 weeks), then "attachment-in-the-making" (6 weeks to 6-8 months), during which infants show the first signs of wariness. At about 6-8 months is the phase of "clear-cut attachment", characterized by *separation anxiety* when the caregiver leaves. During the phase of "reciprocal relationships," (18-24 months and later), caregiver and child share the responsibility for maintaining the equilibrium of the system. According to Bowlby's view, the attachment relationship serves as an *internal working model* for guiding children's interactions with caregivers and others. In unfamiliar situations, the caregiver serves as a *secure base* from which the infant can explore, occasionally returning for reassurance.

• The studies of Harry Harlow and his colleagues using animal models suggest that bodily contact rather than drive-reduction is important in fostering attachment. Infant monkeys became attached to terry-cloth-covered "surrogates" in preference to wire-bodied ones even when only the wire "mothers" provided them with food. But, attachment—and the sense of security it brings—did not, by itself, ensure healthy social development; monkeys who became attached to nonliving surrogates did not learn how to behave with other monkeys. Under normal circumstances, two-way interaction with a responsive caregiver teaches the infant how to relate to others of its kind.

B.   Mary Ainsworth and her colleagues studied attachment in the *strange situation*, in which children were left alone in an unfamiliar room, approached by a strange adult, then reunited with their mothers.

• Several different behavior patterns emerged. *Securely attached* infants were upset when their mothers left, but were quickly reassured when they returned. *Anxious/avoidant* infants appeared indifferent to their mothers and ignored them when they returned. *Anxious/resistant* infants became upset when their mothers left, but struggled to resist comfort from them when they returned. Anxious children are sometimes labelled "insecurely attached."

• Some, though not all, studies show that infants of responsive mothers are more likely to behave in a securely attached manner in the "strange situation"; in contrast, it is more certain that infants of insensitive mothers are more likely to be rated as insecurely attached.

• Children's own characteristics can affect attachment. For example, unresponsiveness on the part of an infant can interfere with parent-infant attachment. Children's own temperaments may also affect their attachment behavior.

• Cultural differences in child-rearing practices result in differences in babies' behavior in the "strange situation." For example, Japanese children and communally raised Israeli infants are more often rated anxious/resistant, and a study of German children showed more anxious/avoidant infants than are usually found in American samples. The possible significance of these differences is not known, but they suggest that cultural factors are an important influence on child-caregiver relationships.

• Children's attachment patterns are likely to remain stable at least in the short term, but only so long as their life circumstances also remain the same. In particular, children whose families are under stress may move from secure to insecure attachment.

C.   There is conflicting evidence about the significance of the different attachment patterns for children's later development. What is clear, however, is that—in all parts of the world—infants follow a similar pattern: beginning at about 7 months, more and more become distressed when they are separated from their mothers; this trend reverses at about 15 months of age.

V.   A NEW SENSE OF SELF

Two-year-olds' capabilities in thinking, motor skills, language, and the ability to do things on their own combine to give them a greater awareness of themselves as people.

A.   Eighteen-to-24-month-old children begin to identify their own images in the mirror.

B.   Between 18 and 24 months, children begin to describe their own actions in their speech.

C.   Children become more sensitive to adult standards of "rightness"; they notice when toys are broken or clothing is soiled. They may even feel responsible for living up to adult standards—for example, by being able to imitate adults' behavior. They seem to set themselves goals—perhaps, making a tower of *all* the blocks—and to check their progress in achieving them.

D.   In addition to the six primary emotions displayed in early infancy (joy, fear, anger, surprise, sadness, and disgust), by 24 months of age, infants experience certain *secondary emotions* such as embarrassment, pride, shame, guilt, and envy. These emotions are linked to their emerging ability to evaluate their behavior in terms of social standards. So, toddlers may display pride in a new ability or shame at having done something "bad."

VI. THE END OF INFANCY

Children's growing abilities to do more things for themselves, tolerate temporary separations from their caregivers, express themselves in words and play, and to begin to follow adult standards combine to produce the stagelike transition characteristic of a bio-social-behavioral shift. The changes occurring at the end of the second and the beginning of the third year—listed in Table 6.3—mark the end of the period we call infancy.

Key Terms

Following are important terms introduced in Chapter 6. In the space to the right, write the definition of the term. In the space to the left, write the letter of the example that best illustrates the term.

_____ biological drives _____

_____ deferred imitation _____

_____ internal working model _____

_____ representation _____

_____ secondary emotions _____

_____ secure base _____

_____ separation anxiety _____

_____ strange situation _____

_____ symbolic play _____

_____ tertiary circular reactions _____

a.   A girl watches her mother apply lipstick. The next day, she tries to apply her mother's lipstick to her own lips.

b.   A boy places pebbles in a bowl, stirs them around, and serves "soup" to his teddy bear.

c.   Hunger and thirst are examples of these.

d.   A child, sitting in a high chair, repeatedly drops peas onto the floor. Sometimes holding his arm straight out, sometimes to the side, he varies the position from which each pea is dropped.

e.   A child is able to think about things that are not present to her senses.

f.   Pride and embarrassment are examples of these.

g.   A 1 -year-old plays by himself in the living room, but comes into the kitchen periodically to make contact with his mother.

h.   An infant takes part in an experimental study in which his mother leaves him alone in an unfamiliar room, and a strange adult tries to comfort him until she returns.

i.   A 1-year-old screams when he notices that his mother has left the room.

j.   A 2-year-old is able to predict her mother's coming and going on the basis of past experiences of being separated from and reunited with her.

Fill-In Questions

Cover the list of answers next to the statements below and fill in each blank with the word or phrase that correctly completes the sentence.

walking

1.   At about 12 months of age, babies have the neural connections necessary for independent _____.

elimination

2.   Children are usually unable to voluntarily control _____ until about 15 months of age.

tertiary

3.   In substage 5 of Piaget's period of sensorimotor development, infants begin to vary the action sequences they use to attain goals. These sequences are called _____ circular reactions.

representation

4.   The sensorimotor period comes to an end during substage 6, when infants become able to use _____ to act on objects mentally, rather than solely through physical manipulation.

5. Babies in stage _____ of object permanence will search for an object in a new location, provided they have actually seen the object being moved. Stage _____ infants do not need to see the change in order to search in a new location.

5

6

6. At about 12 months of age, babies begin to use objects similarly to the ways they are used by _____.

adults

7. Between 18 and 24 months, children begin to use one thing to stand for another as they engage in _____ play.

symbolic

8. Peter Smith described four kinds of play that provide practice for later activities. Three of these—locomotor, object, and social play—occur among the young of many species; however, _____ play appears to occur exclusively among human beings.

fantasy

9. Lev Vygotsky described play as providing a zone of proximal development that allows children to perform developmentally more _____ actions before they can do so independently.

advanced

10. During the second year, children also engage in _____ imitation, copying events that have occurred in the past.

deferred

11. While infants less than 1 year of age can recognize that an array of objects has a categorical structure, they do not begin to generate _____ until sometime in the second year.

categories

12. One clear indicator of representational thought is the use of _____ to stand for objects and events.

words

13. At about 18 months of age, children can combine two symbolic actions in their play; they can also combine _____ words to make a sentence.

two

14. According to Freud's explanation of attachment, babies become attached to those who satisfy their need for _____.

food

15. According to Erik Erikson, infants become attached to those whom they can _____ to minister to their needs. During their second year, toddlers are better able to tolerate separation as they develop a sense of _____ in their relations with the environment.

trust

autonomy

explore

drive-reduction

securely, anxious

responsive

child

temperaments

attachment

less

standards
goals

words

mirror

16. John Bowlby emphasized that, in unfamiliar situations, the mother provides a secure base from which the child can _____.

17. Harry Harrow's studies with baby monkeys who were raised with wire or cloth surrogates provided evidence against the _____ theory of attachment.

18. Mary Ainsworth found three basic patterns of infant response to the "strange situation": _____ attached, _____ avoidant, and anxious/resistant.

19. Mary Ainsworth and Sylvia Bell found that the infants of mothers who were rated as highly _____ when the infants were 1 to 3 months of age were found to be more securely attached several months later.

20. While parental responsiveness is important in forming attachments between children and parents, responsiveness on the part of the _____ is also important.

21. According to some studies, children's own _____ are a source of variation in their response to the strange situation.

22. Cultural factors provide an additional source of variation in patterns of _____.

23. In families under stress, there is often a change from more to _____ securely attached from one testing session to the next.

24. At about 1 1/2 years of age, children seem to develop a recognition of adult _____ for what is proper and improper. They also begin to set _____ for their own behavior and work to achieve them, alone or with adult help.

25. Between 1 1/2 and 2 years of age, children begin, for the first time, to use _____ to describe their own actions.

26. Starting at about 18 months, children show themselves able to use a _____ for self-recognition.

Multiple-Choice Questions

Circle the letter of the word or phrase that correctly completes each statement.

1. Brain development during the second year of life is characterized by
    a. an increase in myelination.
    b. growth in the length and complexity of neurons.
    c. balance between systems that before had been maturing at different rates.
    d. All of the above

2. Children younger than _____ are usually not able to voluntarily control their bladder and bowel functions.
    a. 5 months
    b. 15 months
    c. 3 months
    d. 3 years

3. In sub-stage 5, tertiary circular reactions, children begin to
    a. repeat interesting action sequences without variation.
    b. carry out actions in thought rather than physically.
    c. vary the action sequences they use to reach a goal.
    d. imitate objects and events that are not present.

4. At the end of infancy, children are able to _____ the world to themselves.
    a. assimilate
    b. accommodate
    c. represent
    d. explain

5. Which is an example of symbolic play?
    a. using a banana as a telephone
    b. making cookies out of playdough
    c. serving a doll a cup of sand coffee
    d. All of the above

6. According to Peter Smith, humans are the only species who are definitely known to engage in _____ play.
    a. locomotor
    b. fantasy
    c. object
    d. social

7. Because play with other children creates a zone of proximal development, it allows children to perform
   a. only those actions they can already perform independently.
   b. actions that their parents ordinarily do not allow.
   c. actions developmentally more advanced than those they can perform independently.
   d. less advanced actions than they can perform independently.

8. _____ imitation was formerly thought to appear in the middle of the second year of life; now there is evidence that it is present toward the end of the first year.
   a. Deferred
   b. Immediate
   c. Reflexive
   d. Assimilative

9. Children learn to _____ the categorical structure of a group of objects before they are able to _____ categories by themselves.
   a. make use of; recognize
   b. accommodate; assimilate
   c. rearrange; recognize
   d. recognize; generate

10. John Bowlby's explanation of attachment emphasizes the role of attachment in
    a. satisfying biological drives.
    b. building trust between infant and caretaker.
    c. balancing safety and exploration.
    d. promoting object permanence.

11. Harry Harlow found that his surrogate-raised infant monkeys
    a. became attached to the wire surrogate, whichever surrogate fed them.
    b. always became attached to the surrogate, wire or cloth, that fed them.
    c. always became attached to the cloth surrogate, whichever surrogate fed them.
    d. did not become attached to either kind of surrogate.

12. In Mary Ainsworth's "strange situation," _____ children calm down quickly and resume playing when their mothers return after a brief separation.
    a. securely attached
    b. anxious/avoidant
    c. anxious/resistant
    d. All of the above

13. Cross-cultural studies on patterns of attachment indicate that
    a. similar distributions of attachment patterns occur in all societies studied.
    b. different cultures produce varying patterns of attachment as measured in the "strange situation."
    c. good parenting practices produce the same distribution of patterns of attachment in any culture.
    d. attachment as we know it only exists in societies with "nuclear" families.

14. Which is an example of a *secondary emotion* ?
    a. embarrassment
    b. anger
    c. sadness
    d. All of the above

15. Children show signs of recognizing their mirror images
    a. starting shortly after birth.
    b. at about the time they develop separation anxiety.
    c. at about the time they begin to describetheir own actions in their speech.
    d. at about the time they begin preschool.

Short-Answer Questions

1. In what way does play serve as a zone of proximal development? Give an example.

2. Psychologists believe that, starting at about 18 months of age, children begin to set goals for themselves and to become more aware of adult standards. What are some indications of this change? What changes in children's language and problem-solving capabilities occur at about the same time?

3. What are some of the ways we can tell that children have begun to mentally represent things to themselves?

4. Why do psychologists say that there are different kinds of attachment relationships between parents and babies? Why might nature allow for a certain amount of variability in the characteristics of attachment?

Putting It All Together I

In this section, you will need to put together information from Chapters 4, 5, and 6 to get a more complete picture of development throughout infancy.

Reviewing Piaget's sub-stages of sensorimotor development

Here are some behaviors that Piaget observed in his own children during the sensorimotor stage. Match each behavior with the substage in which you would expect it to occur.

Substages
1. Reflexes
2. Primary circular reactions
3. Secondary circular reactions
4. Coordination of secondary circular reactions
5. Tertiary circular reactions
6. Representation

_____ Laurent strikes at a pillow to lower it, then grasps a box of matches.
_____ Laurent repeatedly brings his hand to his mouth in order to suck his fingers.
_____ Lucienne sees her father hide a chain inside a slightly open matchbox. She looks at the opening, opens and shuts her mouth several times, and finally reaches in a finger to open the box and grasp the chain.
_____ Laurent becomes quicker at finding the nipple when it touches him anywhere on his face.
_____ Laurent lifts toys and lets them fall, varying his arm position each time.
_____ Lucienne, lying in her bassinet, sees a doll hanging above her and kicks it. The doll sways, and Lucienne attempts to kick it again and again.

Try to think of another example of infant behavior that would illustrate each substage.

Putting It All Together II

Piaget's Observations of Object Permanence—A Review

Match each description of behavior with the appropriate stage.

Stage	Approximate ages	Behavior
1 & 2	Birth - 4 months	_____
3	4 - 8 months	_____
4	8 - 12 months	_____
5	12 - 18 months	_____
6	18 - 24 months	_____

a. The child does not search actively for hidden objects.
b. The A-not-B error appears.
c. The child will search for an object hidden in a new place if he sees the object being moved there.
d. The child will search for a partially hidden object.
e. The child will search for a hidden object in a new place, even if he has not seen the object moved there.
f. The child is not disturbed if the same object appears in two places at once.
g.. For the first time, the child will search actively for a completely covered object.

Additional Resources

Ames, Louise B. and Frances L. Ilg. *Your Two-Year Old: Terrible or Tender*. New York: Delacorte Press, 1976.
The authors describe typical 2-year-old behavior in the tradition of Gesell's maturational approach.

Brazelton, T. Berry. *Toddlers and Parents: A Declaration of Independence*, Rev. Ed. New York: Delacorte, 1989.
This book describes the individual differences seen among toddlers and discusses the developmental tasks facing children during later infancy.

Caplan, Frank and Theresa. *The Second Twelve Months of Life*. New York: Bantam Books, 1980.
This book describes the development of mental, motor, and language skills, month by month, during the second year.

Erikson, Erik. *The Life Cycle Completed: A Review*. New York: W. W. Norton and Co., 1982.
This is a compact discussion of Erikson's psychosocial theory of development.

Kaplan, Louise J. *Oneness and Separateness: From Infant to Individual*. New York: Simon & Schuster, 1978.
A discussion of Margaret S. Mahler's theories of development, this book chronicles infants' "second birth," in which, during late infancy, they develop individual identities.

Shatz, Marilyn. *A Toddler's Life: Becoming a Person*. New York: Oxford University Press, 1994.
A developmental psychologist describes a study in the tradition of Piaget's observations, in which her grandson, Ricky, is followed from 15 months to 3 years of age.

Sheridan, Mary D. *Spontaneous Play in Early Childhood*. Great Britain: NFER Publishing Co. (U.S. distributor: Humanities Press, Inc.), 1977.
This book presents information about play from birth through 6 years of age, and suggests ways of promoting and enhancing play experiences. Suggestions for handicapped children are included.

Smith, Helen Wheeler. *Survival Handbook for Preschool Mothers., Grandmothers, Teachers, Nursery School and Day-Care Workers*. Chicago, Ill.: Follett Publishing Co., 1977.
This book contains suggestions that should be helpful to anyone who works with young children. Suggestions for age-appropriate activities, books, and discipline techniques are included.

Answer Key

Answers to Key Terms: c, a, j, e, f, g, i, h, b, d

Answers to Multiple-Choice Questions: 1. d, 2. b, 3. c, 4. c, 5. d, 6. b, 7. c, 8. a, 9. d, 10. c, 11. c, 12. a, 13. b, 14. a, 15. c

Answers to Putting It All Together I: 4, 2, 6, 1, 5, 3

Answers to Putting It All Together II: 1&2: a; 3:d,f; 4:b,g; 5:c; 6:e.

Early Experience and Later Life

For thousands of years, philosophers have expressed the belief that children's earliest experiences have the greatest impact on their development—that "As the twig is bent, so grows the tree." Modern psychologists, for the most part, agree. But do early experiences invariably set the course of development? Chapter 7 explores this issue and the related question of what kinds of early experiences help or hinder normal development.

It seems clear that one of children's needs is a certain amount of stimulation from and interaction with other people. Babies raised in poorly staffed orphanages with little human contact have been found to be both mentally and socially retarded. The longer they live under these conditions, the less complete their recovery when moved to more favorable environments. On the other hand, children in well-staffed orphanages have fared much better, even when cared for by as many as 24 nurses during their first 2 years! Children who have been totally isolated become severely retarded; still, under certain circumstances, recovery is apparently possible even for them.

Children who live in environments in which a number of stress-producing factors combine are at risk for later psychiatric problems. However, some children are remarkably resilient because of counterbalancing circumstances such as good schools or supportive extended families. Psychologists cannot predict developmental outcome with certainty. There are enough discontinuities in development to make it difficult to know for sure how the circumstances of babies' lives help to shape the adults they will someday be.

Chapter Outline

Some theorists believe that children's earliest experiences are the most significant for their later development. This idea is called the *primacy* of infant experience.

I. OPTIMAL CONDITIONS FOR INFANT DEVELOPMENT

Optimal rearing conditions are generally thought to involve mothers' responsiveness to their babies' signals. However, mothers of different cultures have different strategies for raising children with the characteristics that are valued in their societies.

A. Parents often worry that overresponsiveness to their children's signals will "spoil" the children. However, as observed by Silvia Bell and Mary Ainsworth, mothers who respond slowly to their infants' cries have infants who cry more frequently than those who respond promptly.

B. Parents also worry that unresponsiveness to their infants will result in *learned helplessness*—that the infants will learn that their actions have no effect on the world and will be discouraged from acting in the future. John S. Watson demonstrated that infants who had teamed to control the movement of mobiles at home learned more quickly to control similar mobiles in the laboratory than infants who had previously observed the mobiles but were unable to control them. Neal Finkelstein and Craig Ramey showed that infants as young as 8 months of age generalize what they learn in one situation—in this case, pushing a panel to get an interesting result—to learning new behaviors—vocally activating a stimulus panel, for example. While infants are learning how actions are connected to outcomes, they also seem to be learning about their personal effectiveness in controlling their environment. The term *competence motive* is psychiatrist Robert White's expression referring to the tendency for human beings to want to control their environments.

II. EFFECTS OF SEPARATION

Children are separated from their parents for various reasons, ranging from short, temporary separations due to parental employment to long-term separations caused by war or natural disasters. Psychologists study the effects of these separations in an effort to learn how to counteract any adverse effects that may result.

A. A common form of temporary separation occurs when infants are placed in out of-home day care while their parents work. As discussed in Box 7.1, the effects on development of out-of-home care during infants' first year is still hotly debated. On one side, Jay Belsky cites findings that show less secure attachment on the part of children with extensive day care experience during the first year. On the other hand, other studies have shown that the quality of care children receive and the characteristics of their families are more important in determining adjustment than simply whether or not children receive out-of-home care.

• Children are sometimes separated from their parents for hospitalization. A study by Michael Rutter showed that, while a single hospitalization before age 5 had no long-term effect on children's emotional development, repeated hospitalization was associated with psychological problems. Because hospitalized children were somewhat more likely to come from disadvantaged families, the exact contribution of separation to their problems is not known.

• Children were evacuated from English cities during World War II bombing and were sent to live in the countryside. While the children found the separation distressing, their experiences did not cause them to develop mental illnesses or markedly abnormal behavior.

B. Children living in orphanages experience a much more severe form of separation. A well-known study by Wayne Dennis and his colleagues showed that normal infants placed in the unstimulating environment of a Lebanese orphanage shortly after birth were, by the end of their first year, developing at only half the normal rate. Those of the children who were adopted before age 6 eventually reached normal or near normal levels of development, depending on how young they were when adopted. At age 6, the girls who remained institutionalized were sent to live in another impersonal, unstimulating situation; by the time they reached their teens, they were severely retarded. The boys, sent to a more stimulating environment, made substantial intellectual recovery.

Children raised in better-equipped, more stimulating nurseries in England were studied by Barbara Tizard and her coworkers. Because they were cared for by large numbers of nurses, these children had no opportunity to form close attachments to their adult caregivers. Those who were adopted between 2 and 8 years of age formed attachments with their adoptive parents no matter how old they were when adopted. Those returning to their biological families fared less well, perhaps because their parents gave them less attention; still, they did better than the children who remained institutionalized. Interestingly, the formerly-institutionalized children tended to have problems with peer relationships, even when they had satisfactory relationships with their parents.

C. Occasionally, cases are discovered in which children have been separated, not only from their parents, but from all human company. Victor, the Wild Boy of Aveyron, is one example. In another case, twin boys, isolated in a closet until 6 years of age with only one another's company, eventually recovered normal intelligence. Genie, a girl who was severely isolated for 11 years, recovered somewhat but never developed normal language. We do not know exactly how long or how severe deprivation must be in order to cause lasting damage.

III. VULNERABILITY AND RESILIENCE

Michael Rutter and his colleagues discovered that children's behavior problems were strongly associated with four factors: family discord; criminal or psychiatric deviance on the part of a parent; social disadvantage; and a poor school environment. The combination of two or more of these factors affecting a child resulted in a greatly increased risk for developing a psychiatric disorder. Still, some children subject to these risk factors are *resilient*—they manage to develop normally in spite of adverse circumstances. Psychologists are searching for the source of this resilience.

A.   Study of a large group of low-income children on the island of Kauai by Werner and Smith highlights family factors as buffers contributing to children's resilience in the face of risks that might affect their development. In particular, children from cohesive families who received ample attention from their caretakers and had a network of relatives and friends to provide support were less likely to suffer developmental problems.

B.   Characteristics of the community in which children live are related to their likelihood of developing problems. Children from poor, inner-city areas are more at risk than those from poor, rural communities; children from affluent communities are less at risk. Social support networks provided by social service agencies and by friends and relatives can reduce the impact of negative community characteristics. Good experiences at school also seem to counteract stressful home circumstances.

C.   Personal characteristics associated with greater resilience include high intelligence, the capacity to plan, and a sense of humor. In addition, an "easy" temperament in infants is associated with resilience, while infants classified as "difficult" are more likely to have psychological problems. As discovered by M.W. de Vries, there are certain cultural circumstances in which a "difficult' temperament may contribute to an infant's survival. However, Werner and Smith's study revealed that children who were well-adjusted while growing up had been described by their mothers as "very active" and "socially responsive" in infancy.

As discussed in Box 7.2, infants whose mothers suffer from chronic depression are also at risk for developmental problems. Good relationships with peers and with non-depressed adults, competence in school, and having an engaging personality appear to offer some protection against the effects of maternal depression. Interventions that instruct depressed mothers in how to interact with their infants have also been helpful.

D. These influences on development work not in isolation, but in combination with one another. *Transactional models* trace these interactions over time as they influence developmental outcomes. For example, Michael Rutter and his colleagues found that, in their sample, the poor parenting practices of women raised in institutions in infancy were not a straightforward result of their early experience, but resulted from a chain of events which could be broken at various points by more favorable life circumstances.

IV. RECOVERY FROM DEPRIVATION

How might children best be helped to recover from early deprivation? Harry Harlow's research with monkeys tells us something about this.

A. Harlow demonstrated that, when infant monkeys were deprived of normal social contact and raised by inanimate mother surrogates, the duration and timing of deprivation affected the monkeys' long-term behavior. Monkeys isolated for their first 3 months developed normal social behavior when placed with a group of other monkeys. Monkeys isolated for their second 6 months after 6 months of normal interaction became aggressive and fearful when returned to the group, but recovered and later were able to mate normally. In contrast, those monkeys isolated for their first 6 months only partially recovered and later were unable to mate. Isolation for the first year of life produced monkeys who showed no tendency to recover spontaneously.

B. Was birth to 6 months of age a critical period for normal social development? Harlow and his colleagues tried several methods, all ineffective, for easing isolated monkeys' transition to group interaction. However, when previously isolated female monkeys had infants, they began to recover (assuming the infants survived their abusive behavior). The longer they interacted with their infants, the more normal their behavior became. The researchers found that, by giving them 2- to 3-month-old monkeys to interact with, they could reverse the abnormal social behavior of 12 month isolates to the point that researchers had difficulty telling them from non-isolated monkeys.

C. Both Harlow's monkey studies and research with human children suggest that interaction with younger children may be more therapeutic than interaction with peers in reversing the effects of social isolation. Wyndol Furman, Donald Rahe, and Willard Hartup found that socially isolated 2 1/2- to 5-year-olds who played, over a 6-week period, with 1- to 1 1/2-year-olds more than doubled their social interactions with peers, while those who played with peers showed much less improvement. This suggests that socially isolated children can be helped substantially by the proper arrangement of the environment.

V.   THE PRIMACY OF INFANCY RECONSIDERED

There is no doubt that the experiences of infancy have an effect on later development. But this effect is modified by changes in children's capacities and in their environments. In addition, as children develop new capacities during the course of infancy, they experience their environments in different ways. Therefore, instead of speaking of the primacy of infant experience, many psychologists instead focus on continuities and discontinuities between infancy and later periods of development, and the mechanisms by which the characteristics evident in early life are transformed or remain the same as children make the transition from infancy to early childhood.

A.   Studies of long-term effects of different patterns of attachment have yielded mixed results. For example, Leah Matas, Richard Arend, and Alan Sroufe found that children rated "securely attached" earlier in infancy were more successful in working with their mothers on a problem-solving task than children rated as anxious/ avoidant or anxious/resistant. Follow-up work showed that differences between the groups were still evident in middle childhood and adolescence. However, John Bates, Christine Maslin, and Karen Frankel reported no relationship between attachment behavior at 12 months and behavior problems at 3 years. Inge Bretherton hypothesizes that early attachments affect later development through their effect on an *internal working model* of the way to behave toward other people. Later behavior will not be entirely predictable, however, because effects of the environment may either strengthen or modify the internal working model.

B.   Studies of the predictive reliability of measures of infant psychological functioning have produced conflicting evidence. For example, standardized developmental tests given during infancy do not predict children's later IQ scores. This makes cognitive development seem discontinuous between infancy and later childhood. However, studies have shown that some continuity is revealed when similar behaviors are measured at each age. For example, it has been found that infants who habituate rapidly to repeated events are likely to display signs of advanced intellectual development during early childhood.

C.   Freud noted that when we trace development backward—from outcome to origins— the steps seem to have led, one to another, in an inevitable sequence. He also pointed out, however, that when we trace development forward, the sequence no longer appears inevitable. We see alternatives that might have occurred. It is just as well that development is not perfectly predictable; otherwise, parents would have no opportunities to influence and enhance the development of their children.

Key Terms

Following are important terms introduced in Chapter 7. In the space to the right, write the definition of the term. In the space to the left, write the letter of the example that best illustrates the term.

_____ competence motive _____

_____ learned helplessness _____

_____ primacy _____

_____ resilient _____

_____ transactional models _____

a. The idea that, for example, children's earliest attachments have the greatest effect on their later love relationships.
b. Children who learn that their actions have no effect on the environment are slower to learn actions which do have effects.
c. The characteristics of individual children interact with changes in the caregiving environment; these interactions can be traced through time.
d. The tendency for people to want to have control over their environments.

Fill-in Questions

Cover the list of answers next to the statements below and fill in each blank with the word or phrase that correctly completes the sentence.

1. The idea that children's earliest experiences have the greatest effect on their development is called _____.   **primacy**

2. Parents sometimes worry that, if they are too responsive to their infants' signals, their babies will become _____.   **spoiled**

3. According to one study, babies whose mothers respond promptly to their cries tend to cry _____ often than those whose mothers respond slowly.   **less**

4. Babies whose signals are ignored may develop "learned _____."   **helplessness**

control or influence

5. By observing that their actions have effects, infants learn that they can, to some extent, _____ their environments.

short

6. Babies resist being separated from their parents, but _____ separations seem to have no negative consequences.

7. Some studies show that extensive day care experience before 1 year of age has negative effects on the quality of children's

attachment

_____ to their parents; other studies show no effect.

quality

8. The _____ of out-of-home care which infants receive is important in determining its effect on them.

9. Studies of children raised in institutions indicate that children

stimulation

cannot develop properly unless they receive sufficient _____ from the environment.

10. It appears that even children 8 years of age who have never

attached

formed a primary attachment can still become _____ to adoptive parents.

isolation

11. Even children who have lived under conditions of _____ from other humans may show substantial recovery.

resilient

12. Children from supportive families are more likely to be _____ in the face of risks to their development.

difficult

13. Infants classified as temperamentally _____ are more likely to have later psychological problems.

Transactional

14. _____ models of development trace, over time, the interactions of factors that influence development.

15. Harry Harlow discovered that a good therapy for formerly isolated monkeys was placing them with monkeys who were

younger

much _____.

16. A study by Leah Matas, Richard Arend, and Alan Sroufe found

securely

that children rated as _____ attached were later more successful at working with their mothers on a problem-solving task.

attachments

17. Some psychologists have proposed that children's early _____ serve as models for their later relationships with others.

18. Developmental tests given during _____ are not very   **infancy**
    predictive of children's later IQs.

19. More continuity in development is revealed when the tests given
    at each age measure _____ behaviors.   **similar**

20. As Freud pointed out, developmental outcomes always look more
    inevitable when we trace their steps _____.   **backwards**

Multiple-Choice Questions

Circle the letter of the word or phrase that correctly completes each statement.

1. Infants whose mothers respond quickly to their cries
    a. are usually spoiled.
    b. cry more than those whose mothers respond slowly.
    c. feel helpless to influence the environment.
    d. cry less than infants of slowly responding mothers.

2. When confronted with mobiles in the laboratory, infants who had learned to control
    similar mobiles at home
    a. were afraid of them.
    b. quickly learned to control them.
    c. were not able to learn to control them.
    d. behaved similarly to infants who had seen mobiles before without learning to
        control them.

3. Some studies have shown that infants with extensive day care experience during the
    first year of life
    a. are less intelligent than children cared for at home.
    b. are more securely attached to their mothers than children cared for at home.
    c. are less securely attached to their mothers than children cared for at home.
    d. are more cooperative than children cared for at home.

4. Children reared in unstimulating Lebanese orphanages
    a. became severely retarded unless removed before about 6 years of age.
    b. were not affected intellectually, but failed to develop secure attachments.
    c. developed slowly during infancy but recovered later, even if they remained in the
        same environment.
    d. were not distinguishable in their development from children raised in families.

5. Children who come from cohesive, supportive families are more likely to be _____
    in the face of risk factors for developmental problems.
    a.   vulnerable
    b.   indifferent
    c.   logical
    d.   resilient

6. In a _____ model, the interaction between children's characteristics and their
    environments is traced over time.
    a.   stage
    b.   environmental-learning
    c.   transactional
    d.   biological-maturation

7. For Harry Harlow's formerly isolated monkeys, the best therapy leading to normal
    social behavior was
    a.   interacting with humans.
    b.   interacting with other formerly isolated monkeys.
    c.   interacting with younger monkeys.
    d.   interacting with a mate.

8. The primacy of infant experience refers to the notion that the experiences of infancy
    are
    a.   the earliest experiences people remember.
    b.   more important for development than later experiences.
    c.   the only experiences with any importance for development.
    d.   qualitatively different from later experiences.

9. Research shows that infants' attachment classifications are
    a.   inconsistent in predicting their later behavior.
    b.   good predictors of their later behavior.
    c.   useless in predicting their later behavior.
    d.   nearly perfect predictors of their later behavior.

10. A major objection to using infant tests to draw conclusions about continuity in
    development is that
    a.   the degree of continuity is likely to appear exaggerated.
    b.   continuity in development is, by definition, impossible.
    c.   the infant tests do not measure the same psychological processes as the later
         measures.
    d.   infants' psychological characteristics cannot be measured.

Short-Answer Questions

1. Discuss how optimal mothering strategies may differ between cultures whose life circumstances are very different. Give examples of this.

2. What do studies of orphanage-raised children tell us about the importance of early experience?

3. What characteristics of children and their environments put them at risk for later psychiatric problems? What factors make children resilient in unfavorable environments?

4. What do animal studies of recovery from isolation tell us about how effective recovery programs for isolated children might be designed?

Putting it All Together

The question of the importance of early experience is related to questions about continuities and discontinuities in development, introduced in Chapter 1. Look back to the material on critical periods in Chapter 1. How does the material on early experience presented in Chapter 7 support or refute the idea that human development is affected by critical periods?

What were philosopher John Locke's views on the importance of early experience?

Sometimes, experiences during infancy interact with experiences during the prenatal period. Chapter 3 includes material on the later effects of prenatal undernutrition. Under what circumstances are these effects counteracted? Under what circumstances not? What similarities exist between the developmental insults of prenatal undernutrition and postnatal social isolation?

Additional Resources

Dennis, Wayne. *Children of the Creche*. New York: Appleton-Century-Crofts, 1973.
A description of the author's well-known study of children raised in a Lebanese orphanage.

Dynerman, Susan B. *Are Our Kids All Right? Answers to the Tough Questions About Child Care Today*. Princeton, N.J., Petersons, 1994.
The author combines an analysis of research on child care and interviews with parents and daycare providers. She presents useful information to guide parents in their search for high-quality child care.

Harlow, H., M. Harlow, and S. Suomi. "From Thought to Therapy: Lessons From a Primate Laboratory." *American Scientist*, 1971, *59(5)*, 538-549.
A discussion of the work of Harlow and his colleagues with infant monkeys including their work on rehabilitation.

Leiderman, P., S. Tulkin, and A. Rosenfeld. *Culture and Infancy: Variations in the Human Experience*. New York: Academic Press, 1977.
This volume contains several cross-cultural studies of infancy that illustrate how infant care practices prepare children to become culturally socialized members of their particular societies.

Thompson, Angela M. "Adam—A Severely-Deprived Columbian Orphan: A Case Report." *Journal of Child Psychology and Psychiatry*, 1986, *27*, 689-695.
A demonstration of a child's progress after intervention to counteract severe deprivation resulting from poverty.

Wachs, T., and G. Gruen. *Early Experience and Human Development*. New York: Plenum, 1982.
The authors explore the ways that biological and environmental influences interact to influence development.

Werner, Emmy E. "Children of the Garden Island." *Scientific American*, April 1989, 106-111.
Emmy Werner reports on the "resilient" children, now adults, whom she has been following since their births.

Answer Key

Answers to Key Terms: d, b, a, e, c

Answers to Multiple-Choice Questions: 1. d, 2. b, 3. c, 4. a, 5. d, 6. c, 7. c, 8. b, 9. a, 10. c

Language Acquisition

One of the most amazing accomplishments of children's preschool years is the rapid acquisition of language. With language, children can make their needs known more clearly and can state their opinions; they also become able to learn more easily from the experiences of others, including those of people who lived generations earlier.

Despite its importance for human beings, language development has yet to be thoroughly explained by psychologists and linguists. No single theory is able to account for all the known facts; however, learning, nativist, and interactionist theories can each explain certain aspects of language acquisition.

As Elizabeth Bates has expressed it, language acquisition can be thought of as learning "to do things with words." In order to be able to do things with words, children must learn to produce the sounds and master the grammatical rules of the language they are learning; they must also learn to select words and constructions that will best express what they want to say.

What experiences must children have in order to learn a language? Certainly they must be exposed to the language itself. Adults provide children with informal language instruction in the course of socializing them as members of the family and community. And while adults in some cultures engage in more deliberate teaching, this is apparently not necessary for children to learn to communicate in this uniquely human way.

Chapter Outline

While the blossoming of language was part of the bio-social-behavioral shift at the end of infancy, children's language abilities undergo explosive growth during the period from 2 to 6 years of age.

I.   PRELINGUISTIC COMMUNICATION

While newborns are predisposed to pay attention to language and quickly learn to distinguish the sounds of their native language, their only means of vocal communication is crying. Their repertoire is supplemented by social smiling at about 2-1/2 months of age, and is eventually expanded to include cooing, followed by babbling and jargoning. *Primary intersubjectivity*, the face to face interaction that appears at about 3 months of age is followed, at about 9 months by *secondary intersubjectivity*, in which the attention of both participants is focused on a third person, or on an object or activity. Social referencing is an example of this. Communication oftentimes also is enhanced by pointing. Thus, a great deal of communication takes place before children are able to make much use of conventional language.

II.   THE PUZZLE OF LANGUAGE DEVELOPMENT

While a great deal is known about language, much about its acquisition remains poorly understood.

A.   It is still not known how children learn which objects or relations words refer to.

B.   Children do not learn *grammar*—the rules governing a languag—solely by imitating adult speech, and *recursion*—the ability to embed sentences within one another—does not appear to be consciously taught. How, then, do these properties of language appear in children's speech?

III.   THE FOUR SUBSYSTEMS OF LANGUAGE

Language is composed of four distinct subsystems that work together as a unified, organic whole.

A.   Although adults can talk at rates of 12-1/2 sounds per second, it takes children several years to master the pronunciation of the sounds of their native language. In the meantime, they compensate for difficulties in pronunciation through substitution and simplification.

• Newborns can perceive the differences among the sounds, or *phonemes*, of their language. But in order for children to attend to and pronounce the sounds, the sound differences must be associated with meaning differences, as /l/ and /y/ are in "lard" and "yard." Children must also learn to cope with the fact that words often contain more than one *morpheme*, or meaning-bearing part. For example, the word "transplanted" is made up of three morphemes.

B. The first real words appear late in the first year and acquire meaning through a joint effort between children and their adult listeners.

• As children notice that adults react to the sounds they make, their speech comes to anticipate, guide, and stimulate action. Now, children can operate on the world indirectly through language—that is, in a *mediated* manner.

• Children's first words tend to name familiar objects ("ball," "juice") or persons ("Mommy," "Daddy"), and to be closely linked to actions that the child can accomplish. Words naming objects that change and move ("car") or that communicate change in state or relation ("gone") are frequently used. Another frequently used word is "No!" And, beginning at about age 2, children use words ("Hooray!" or "uh-oh") to comment on their successes or failures.

• The meanings of words are not fixed. Still, as children become familiar with the ways words are used in their cultural group, their own word usage comes more into conformity with that usage. *Overextension* occurs when children apply a word too broadly; for example, by calling all animals "doggie." *Underextension* refers to too-narrow application of a word, for example, using the word "animal" only for mammals. Children must also learn to use words at an appropriate level of abstraction. Their first words tend to refer to objects at an intermediate level of abstraction ("dog"), although they are able to recognize examples representing other levels ("poodle" or "animal").

• Children's first words and phrases are tied to specific experiences. But as they accumulate experience with objects and events they have learned to label, the organization of their vocabularies changes. Words acquire meanings that no longer depend on particular situations.

• Some investigators believe that each of a child's first words expresses a whole idea—a *holophrase*. Others believe that children's one-word utterances are part of a complex that includes gestures and expressions as well.

C. Toward the end of infancy, grammatical expression appears in children's speech as they begin to form utterances of tw or more words.

• Two-word utterances are more explicit and therefore easier to interpret than one-word utterances. Word order aids in this interpretability. Still, early multiword utterances are telegraphic; it is often necessary to know the context in order to choose between possible interpretations.

- The length of 2-year-olds' sentences in terms of "mean length of utterance" (MLU) measured in morphemes, increases rapidly. Children come to make greater use of *grammatical morphemes* (such as "a" and "ing"), which create meaning by showing the relations between sentence elements. The sequence in which these appear in the speech of English-learning children is roughly constant. By 5 or 6 years of age, children are using the standard parts of speech they will use as adults. Carol Chomsky has studied the difficulties they may continue to have with subtle syntactic constructions. "Tag questions" (for example, "It's your birthday, *isn't it?*") are mastered by 8 or 9 years of age.

D. While learning words and the rules for putting them together, children also master the *pragmatic uses of language*—how to use speech in ways appropriate to their actions in different contexts.
    • Utterances can be thought of as *conversational acts*, actions that accomplish goals through language. Such acts can be *proto-imperatives*, intended to engage another person to achieve a goal, or *proto-declaratives*, which serve as ways of referring. Even 2-year-olds are able to understand and respond to indirect commands ("Is the door shut?") as requests for action rather than information.
    • In order to use language to accomplish goals, children need to learn the rules of basic conversation, such as the *cooperative principle*—that is, they must make contributions at the required time, and for the accepted purpose of the exchange. Sometimes, children and adults deliberately violate conversational rules, for example, when they use *figurative language*, as discussed in Box 8.2. Also, the social conventions regulating the use of language vary among cultures.
    • Children's early language is not fully communicative because it often does not take account of the listener's point of view. This improves gradually between 2 1/2 and 8 years of age. For example, it has been found that 4-year-olds will simplify their speech when speaking to 2-year-olds, making it easier for the younger children to understand.

IV. EXPLANATIONS OF LANGUAGE ACQUISITION

Theories about language acquisition correspond roughly to the explanations of human development proposed by the various theoretical approaches discussed in Chapter 1.

A. According to the learning-theory explanation, language is learned in the same way as other forms of behavior.
    • Children can learn to understand language—that is, to associate words with particular referents—through classical conditioning.
    • Children's repertoires of vocalizations can be shaped into the words of the language they are learning through operant conditioning.
    • Imitation obviously plays a role in learning language, especially in adding new words to the vocabulary. Explaining how more complex grammatical constructions are learned requires an additional explanatory principle such as *abstract modeling*—

proposed by Albert Bandura—in which it is assumed that, as children imitate specific utterances, they abstract the underlying linguistic principles from them.

B.   A nativist explanation has been proposed by linguist Noam Chomsky, who has suggested that the ability to acquire language is innate and that language is not learned in the same way as other kinds of behavior. Instead, he likens the capacity to comprehend and generate language to a special human organ. In order to discover the conditions for language acquisition, Chomsky has examined grammatical rules that remain the same no matter what topics people talk about. He calls the sentences people produce the *surface structure* of language; *deep structure* is his name for the set of rules from which the surface structure can be derived. To test his ideas, Chomsky asks native speakers whether particular sentences are grammatical. In this way, he can find out what rules are part of any person's linguistic competence.
• When young children are acquiring language, they often are very resistant to grammatical correction, supporting the nativist position that specific teaching is not important for language learning. Chomsky has hypothesized that children are born with a *language acquisition device (LAD)*, programmed to recognize rules of whatever language they might hear and trigger their innate ability to learn that language.

C.   Interactionist explanations consider language acquisition to be closely linked to children's basic cognitive development and to support from the social environment. They note a link between the appearance of deferred imitation and children's ability to talk about possible rather than actual experiences, and a parallel between categorization and category use in speech. The acquisition of grammatical structures can be explained as a by-product of using language to get things done, according to Elizabeth Bates and her colleagues. A cultural-context version of the interactionist explanation emphasizes the role of the social environment in shaping children's language acquisition. Jerome Bruner emphasizes the importance of *formats*—socially patterned adult-child activities such as peek-a-boo and bedtime routines. These formatted activities constitute a *language acquisition support system (LASS)*, which complements Chomsky's LAD.

V.   ESSENTIAL INGREDIENTS OF LANGUAGE ACQUISITION

While none of the theories provides a complete explanation, each helps to explain certain elements of language acquisition.

A.   What biological features are necessary for the production and comprehension of language?
• To what extent is the ability to learn language unique to humans? Chimps raised in families do not learn speech, though they learn to comprehend many spoken words. Chimps have been taught to use manual language and to communicate through symbols on a keyboard. Primates have learned to use language to make requests and

comments, and can construct two word utterances. However, their language abilities are soon surpassed by human children with no special training.

• Evidence from children with severe biological handicaps such as Williams syndrome suggests that at least some aspects of language develop separately from general cognitive ability. However, normal linguistic functioning needs a minimum level of growth and ability.

B.   What kinds of environmental input are necessary for normal language development?

• Interaction with other people appears crucial for normal language acquisition. For example, children do not learn language from exposure to television alone. Deaf children in hearing homes, who have restricted language experience but who participate in culturally formatted activities, do learn to communicate in "home sign," a pantomime they develop themselves. Children raised in linguistically impoverished environments develop language at a basic level, but their language is not fully developed, lacking, for example, such subtle features as grammatical morphemes.

• Children learn language as part of family or community activity. For example, as mentioned in Chapter 1, Elsa Bartlett and Susan Carey found that preschool children learned the name of an unfamiliar color after one experience in which their teacher introduced the color name into classroom conversation. This process—in which children form a quick idea of a word's meaning—is called *fast mapping*. Fast mapping can be explained by several cognitive principles used by children, such as the *whole object principle* (a new word appearing in connection with an object refers to the whole object) and the *categorization principle*, (object labels extend to classes of similar objects). Interactions with adults also help children learn word meanings. For example, Michael Tomasello and his colleagues found that mothers talking to 1-1/2 to 2-year-olds tended to label objects that were already the focus of the child's actions or attention. Children's reward for using new words is their greater ability to communicate.

• What role does deliberate instruction by adults play in language acquisition? In some cultures, adults use special teaching strategies; even in societies in which this is not done, adults talking to children may use a high-pitched voice, simplified vocabulary, and emphasize boundaries between idea-bearing clauses. This type of speech has been called *motherese*. Adults simplify all aspects of their speech when talking to children; they also expand children's utterances into grammatically-correct adult versions. However, there is no conclusive evidence that explicit tutoring affects children's language development. Children in all cultures become competent language users, regardless of specific teaching practices.

VI. LANGUAGE AND THOUGHT

How are the development of language and the development of thought related?

A.   According to environmental-learning theorists such as Bandura and Skinner, language serves as a symbolic system that can be substituted, in thought, for external events.

Thus, for example, problems can be solved in thought rather than only in action. Acquiring language, in this view, should enhance the development of children's thinking.

B.   According to Piaget's interactionist perspective, children's language abilities *reflect* their cognitive abilities rather than determining them. Piaget emphasized the egocentric nature of preschoolers' speech; for example, *collective monologues*— conversations in which no actual communication takes place—appear to mirror egocentrism in their thinking.

C.   Nativist theorist Noam Chomsky has explained language acquisition as the activity of a *mental module*, a highly specific mental faculty that is tuned to particular kinds of environmental input. In this view, language and thought do not depend on one another, though language is used in the expression of thought.

D.   In a cultural-context view of the relationship between language and thought, Soviet psychologist Lev Vygotsky regarded early language as primarily a social and communicative activity. Egocentric speech, he believed, is a form of self-regulation. In this view, thought and language develop separately until children are about 2 years of age; then they begin to intermingle, with the result that thinking becomes verbal and language becomes intellectual.

VII. THE BASIC PUZZLES OF LANGUAGE ACQUISITION RECONSIDERED

The questions of how children learn the meanings of words and how they learn the sequences in which words must be placed to express meanings are still only partially answered. Perhaps, as Jerome Bruner has suggested, language results from the union of the LAD and the LASS. And while explicit instruction appears unnecessary for early language acquisition, it plays an important role as children grow older and receive specialized instruction in the specific skills that will prepare them for adult life in their culture.

Key Terms

Following are important terms introduced in Chapter 8. In the space to the right, write the definition of the term. In the space to the left, write the letter of the example that best illustrates the term.

_____ collective monologues _____

_____ conversational acts _____

_____ cooperative principle _____

_____ deep structure _____

_____ fast mapping _____

_____ format _____

_____ grammar _____

_____ grammatical morphemes _____

_____ holophrase _____

_____ language acquisition device (LAD) _____

_____ language acquisition support system (LASS) _____

_____ mental module _____

_____ motherese _____

_____ overextension _____

_____ pragmatic uses of language _____

_____ recursion _____

_____ surface structure _____

_____ underextension _____

a.   The belief that a baby's one-word utterances each carry the meaning of a whole sentence.
b.   The way children form a quick idea of a word's meaning when they hear it in a structured situation.
c.   An 18-month-old does this when he applies the word "doggie" to all four-legged animals.
d.   The sentence "The boy who petted the dog was bitten" illustrates this property of language.
e.   "Proto-imperatives" and "proto-declaratives" are examples.
f.   Piaget gave this name to speech by preschoolers in which remarks are made in the presence of others but with no apparent intent to communicate.
g.   A hypothetical structure, similar to an organ, that underlies children's ability to acquire language, according to linguist Noam Chomsky.

h. A child is doing this when she uses the word "dog" only for pictures of dogs but not for live dogs.

i. Some examples are ing, the, and ed.

j. The rules that determine the ordering of words in sentences and the ordering of parts within words.

k. We violate this if we interrupt others during a conversation or make irrelevant remarks.

l. An example is saying "Who left the window open?" when you mean "Please shut the window."

m. Jerome Bruner uses this term to refer to the totality of the events within which children are led to acquire language.

n. All the grammatically correct utterances formed by speakers of a language are derived from this.

o. The ritualized routines of bedtime are an example of this.

p. This term emphasizes the idea that language is a highly specific human faculty that is not dependent on other intellectual abilities.

q. A person using this speaks in a high-pitched voice and simplifies his or her speech in many ways.

r. This is observed simply by listening to the things people actually say.

Fill-In Questions

Cover the list of answers next to the statements below and fill in each blank with the word or phrase that correctly completes the sentence.

1. One part of children's prelinguistic communication involves _____ at objects. **pointing**

2. Psychologists and linguists still do not know how children figure out that words _____ to objects and relations. **refer**

3. The _____ of a language governs the ordering of words in sentences and the ordering of parts within words. **grammar**

4. _____ are the categories of sound that are meaningful in a language. **Phonemes**

5. The word "implanted" is made up of three meaning-bearing parts called _____. **morphemes**

6. Language allows children to act on the world and to be influenced by others in an indirect or _____ manner. **mediated**

overextensions   7.   Children's early speech often contains _____; for example, calling a skunk "kitty."

intermediate   8.   In general, children's early words tend to refer to objects at an _____ level of abstraction.

holophrase   9.   The term _____ refers to the idea that children's single-word utterances express the meaning of whole sentences.

telegraphic   10. Because of the _____ nature of children's two-word utterances, they must be interpreted in context.

grammatical   11. All children master _____ morphemes, such as "ed" to indicate past tense or "'s" to indicate possession, in much the same order.

                         12. The sentence "Jane's hair is long, isn't it?" is an example of a
tag   _____ question.

pragmatic   13. When children master the _____ uses of language they learn to select words and word orderings that are appropriate to their actions in particular contexts.

acts   14. Children's earliest conversational _____ are proto-imperatives
declaratives   and proto-_____.

figurative   15. Children purposely violate the rules of conversation when they use language in _____ ways.

learning-theory   16. According to the _____ explanation of language development, children learn language through imitation and through classical and operant conditioning.

                         17. Noam Chomsky's nativist explanation of language development
language acquisition   hypothesizes a _____ _____ _____ programmed to
device   recognize the universal rules that underlie language.

                         18. One interactionist hypothesis assumes that language is associated
cognitive   with the development of basic _____ processes.

support system   19. A language acquisition _____ _____ is a feature of the cultural-context version of the interactional explanation of language development.

20. Chimpanzees are capable of learning the rudiments of a gestural
    _____.   **language**

21. Deaf children raised by hearing, non-signing parents often
    spontaneously develop a kind of " _____ sign" as a means of   **home**
    communication.

22. In order to acquire language beyond a rudimentary level,
    children must experience language as part of the
    _____.   **environment**

23. Psychologists have suggested that children form partial
    understanding of the meanings of new words through a process
    called "fast _____."   **mapping**

24. When adults talk to young children, they _____ their speech   **simplify**
    to make it easier for the children to understand and _____ the   **expand**
    children's utterances into grammatically correct adult versions.

25. Piaget observed that preschool children sometimes engage in
    _____ monologues, in which they talk to one another but do   **collective**
    not really respond to what their conversational partners are
    saying.

26. Noam Chomsky has described human language-using capacity as
    a "mental _____."   **module**

27. Lev Vygotsky asserted that the relationship between language
    and _____ undergoes a fundamental change at about 2 years   **thought**
    of age.

Multiple-Choice Questions

Circle the letter of the word or phrase that correctly completes each statement.

1. The aspect of language that deals with the ordering of words in sentences and the
    ordering of parts within words is called
    a. pragmatics.
    b. phonetics.
    c. semantics.
    d. grammar.

2.   Learning theorists use the classical conditioning model to account for
     a.   how children learn to produce language.
     b.   how children learn the meanings of words.
     c.   the relationship between thought and language.
     d.   how children learn the rules of syntax.

3.   Which theorist has hypothesized a language acquisition device (LAD) that is
     programmed to recognize universal linguistic rules?
     a.   Jean Piaget
     b.   Lev Vygotsky
     c.   Elizabeth Bates
     d.   Noam Chomsky

4.   The sounds that are meaningful in a particular language are called
     a.   morphemes.
     b.   graphemes.
     c.   phonemes.
     d.   semantics.

5.   Which utterance contains five morphemes?
     a.   "Doggie!"
     b.   "John is eating an apple."
     c.   "She jumps rope fast"
     d.   "Bobby, have some gum."

6.   An example of a "tag question" is
     a.   "He wore his new jacket today, didn't he?"
     b.   "Where is my pencil?"
     c.   "When did you say you were going?"
     d.   All of the above are examples

7.   Which is an example of an "overextension"?
     a.   Using the word "bird" for both a parakeet and a baby chick.
     b.   Calling a cow "doggie."
     c.   Using the word "eeow" to refer to all cats.
     d.   Saying "fis" instead of "fish."

8.   The term "holophrase" refers to
     a.   the idea that children's one-word utterances may carry the meaning of entire
          sentences.
     b.   adults' expansions of children's one-word utterances.
     c.   children's belief that all words refer to "things."
     d.   one-word exclamations used by children and adults.

9. Grammatical morphemes
   a. are the same in all languages.
   b. appear in all children's speech in about the same order.
   c. are the rules for ordering words in sentences.
   d. do not appear in children's speech until the end of the preschool period.

10. Marilyn Shatz and Rochel Gelman found that, when talking to 2-year-olds, 4-year-olds
    a. simplify their speech to make it easier for the 2-year-olds to understand.
    b. use a larger vocabulary in order to teach new words to the 2-year-olds.
    c. speak just as they would to other 4-year-olds but louder.
    d. speed up their speech to make it more difficult for the 2-year-olds to understand.

11. According to _____ theory, language is a verbal reflection of children's nonlinguistic understanding.
    a. Chomsky's nativist
    b. Piaget's interactionist
    c. the environmental-learning
    d. the cultural-context

12. Lev Vygotsky believed that children's egocentric speech
    a. is a reflection of their egocentric thought.
    b. serves no communicative function.
    c. helps them to regulate their behavior.
    d. occurs more frequently in the presence of "listeners" who cannot understand (because, for example, they are deaf).

13. Chimpanzees in captivity
    a. communicate with sounds but not with gestures.
    b. have successfully learned the rudiments of human vocal language.
    c. have learned to communicate in simple ways using nonvocal languages.
    d. have demonstrated language development comparable to that of 3-year-old children.

14. Which of the following is sufficient for children to acquire full use of language?
    a. Hearing language on the radio.
    b. Hearing language on television.
    c. Being in an environment where others are communicating with one another, even if not directly with the child.
    d. Participating in activities of which language is a part.

15. The speech of American adults to young children
    a.   is not significantly different from their speech to adults.
    b   is more repetitive, but otherwise similar to their speech to adults.
    c.   is slower, but is otherwise similar to their speech to adults.
    d.   is adjusted according to the level of complexity of the children's speech.

Short-Answer Questions

1.   Why is it difficult for psychologists and linguists to explain how children acquire language?

2.   Discuss the factors that influence how adults interpret the utterances of 1-and 2-year-old children.

3.   In what ways does language appear to be a reflection of thinking? In what ways does it seem unique?

4.   To what experiences must children be exposed in order to acquire language? What happens if these requirements are not met?

Putting It All Together I

Match each milestone in language development with the age at which it occurs. You may need to refer back to material in earlier chapters.

_____ Children can perceive the categorical sound distinctions used in all the world's languages.

_____ Children's language typically contains overextensions.

_____ Children simplify their speech when talking to younger children.

_____ Children begin to practice consonant-vowel sound combinations.

_____ Children's vocalizations take on the intonation and stress patterns that characterize the language they are learning.

a.   At birth
b.   At about 4 months of age
c.   Toward the end of the first year
d.   At 2 years of age
e.   By 4 years of age

Putting It All Together II

Match up the facts about language development with the theories that are strongest at explaining them. Refer back to previous chapters when necessary.

_____ Babies can distinguish categorical differences between phonemes.

_____ Children's earliest "words" usually do not have clear meanings and must be interpreted by adults.

_____ Children acquire much of their early vocabularies by repeating the names they hear others give to objects.

_____ Deaf babies begin to babble at about the same time as hearing babies.

_____ Changes in some of children's early sensorimotor accomplishments—for example, delayed imitation—appear to be related to changes in the ways they use words.

_____ Children engage in less egocentric speech when playing with children who cannot hear.

_____ Compared with nonhuman primates, children pick up human language quite easily.

_____ Children who are able to put together two-word utterances usually are also able to combine two symbolic actions in play.

a.   Biological-maturation theories
b.   Environmental-learning theories
c.   Cognitive interactionist theories
d.   Cultural-context theories

Additional Resources

Berk, Laura E. "Why Children Talk to Themselves." *Young Children*, July 1985, 46-54.
This article discusses Piaget's and Vygotsky's ideas about the nature of children's private speech and attempts to resolve the conflict between these views.

de Villiers, Peter A., and **Jill G. de Villiers**. *Early Language*. Cambridge: Harvard University Press, 1979.
This is an informative and entertaining discussion of children's early language development by two experts in the field.

Lenneberg, Eric H. "On Explaining Language." *Science*, 1969, <u>164</u> (3880), 635-43.
A discussion of the biological underpinnings of language development which demonstrates that varying approaches to the study of language acquisition need not be antagonistic.

Pepperberg, Irene M. The Importance of Social Interaction and Observation in the Acquisition of Communicative Competence: Possible Parallels Between Avian and Human learning. In Thomas Zentall and G. Galef Bennet, Jr. (Eds.), *Social Learning: A Comparative Approach*. Hillsdale, N.J.: Erlbaum, 1988.
The subject of this study is an African Grey parrot named Alex, but the topic is how language might be acquired by interacting with others and by watching others interact with one another.

Piaget, Jean. *The Language and Thought of the Child*, trans. M. Gabain. London: Routledge and Kegan Paul, 1926.
In this volume, Piaget presents his work on children's language, including egocentric speech.

Answer Key

Answers to Key Terms: f, e, k, n, b, o, j, i, a, g, m, p, q, c, l, d, r, h.

Answers to Multiple-Choice Questions: 1. d, 2. b, 3. d, 4. c, 5. c, 6. a, 7. b, 8. a, 9. b, 10. a, 11. b, 12. c, 13. c, 14. d, 15. d.

Answers to Putting it All Together I: a, d, e, b, c.

Answers to Putting it All Together II: a, d, b, a, c, d, a, c.

Early Childhood Thought: Islands of Competence

Because of their lack of knowledge about the world, preschoolers expend great effort to understand some of the situations they experience each day. Their lack of experience also results in uneven thinking abilities that may appear remarkably sophisticated when applied in familiar contexts, startlingly illogical in less familiar domains.

Piaget's account of thinking during early childhood is the starting point for several explanations of preschoolers' development, and the phenomena he observed, including egocentrism, precausal reasoning, and appearance/reality confusions, continue to be of interest to contemporary developmental psychologists. Today, neo-Piagetians are developing ways to adapt Piaget's theory to better explain the unevenness of preschoolers' thought while information-processing theorists use computer models to understand these phenomena. Theorists who explain cognition in terms of mental modules search for the roots of development in the maturation of brain structures, while psychologists using the cultural-context approach look for sources of unevenness in the ways adults arrange the occurrence of basic contexts in which cognitive development takes place. While none of the theoretical approaches provides a complete explanation for development during early childhood, each contributes something to our understanding.

Chapter Outline

The performance of preschool children on tasks measuring memory, logic, or problem-solving are like a patchwork of logic and illogic, insight and ignorance. Is this inconsistency the result of inexperience or is it due to lack of reasoning ability?

Whether or not they agree with Piaget's explanations of devlopment, many psychologists base their work on his observations of young children's thinking.

I.   PIAGET'S ACCOUNT OF MENTAL DEVELOPMENT IN EARLY CHILDHOOD

According to Piaget's theoretical framework, preschool children are able to engage in representational thinking. However, after observing the many inconsistencies in their thinking, Piaget concluded that they were not yet capable of *mental operations* such as logically combining, separating, and transforming information. Thus, he referred to this period of development as the *preoperational stage*. A key to preoperational thinking, he hypothesized, is the tendency to *center*, or focus the attention on one aspect of a problem while ignoring others. As a result of this, a child might say that when a glass of milk is poured into a taller, thinner glass, the amount of milk has increased.

A.   Piaget believed that 3-, 4-, and 5-year-old children interpret the world from the point of view of the self, or ego, and that this *egocentrism* is the cause of some of their difficulties in problem solving.
• One manifestation is lack of spatial perspective taking. For example, in the "three mountains problem," when asked to select the view that would be seen by a doll placed at the opposite side of the table, preschoolers tend to choose a picture showing the scene from their own viewpoint.
• Young children's speech also has an egocentric quality. This may result in children failing to include information their listeners need to know.
• It may also be difficult for young children to reason about how other people think. As children begin to overcome egocentrism, they also become more skilled in reasoning about what others are thinking. The ability to think about other people's thoughts is referred to as a *theory of mind*.

B. Their tendency to focus attention on the perceptual attributes of a stimulus may make it difficult for preschoolers to separate appearance from reality. Rheta De Vries showed children a picture of a cat wearing a dog mask. Most of the 3-year-olds believed that the cat had become a dog, while the 6-year-olds were more confident that such a transformation was impossible. John Flavell believes that appearance/reality confusion is a genuine feature of young children's thinking; it appears in children from a variety of cultures and persists in spite of training or attempts to simplify the tasks.

C. When engaging in *precausal thinking*, preschoolers confuse cause and effect. For example, one child believed that graveyards caused people to die and that, by avoiding graveyards, one could avoid death.

II. THE STUDY OF YOUNG CHILDREN'S THINKING AFTER PIAGET

Piaget's view of young children's thinking won wide acceptance because it was comprehensive and because it was supported by vivid examples of his interviews with many children. In recent years, however, some studies have suggested that preschool children have more advanced reasoning capabilities than Piaget's methods give them credit for.

A. Variations in children's performance from one problem to another—what Piaget called *horizontal decalage*—is a challenge to his account of this period of development. For example:
 • When Helen Borke modified the "three mountains problem" to a more familiar scene, even 3-year-olds demonstrated that they could imagine perspectives other than their own.
 • Michael Chandler and his colleagues showed that, in the context of a treasure hunt game, 3-year-olds can reason about other people's beliefs. And, according to work by Andrew Meltzoff, even 18-month-olds have some understanding of adults' intentions.
 • Michael Siegal found that when appearance-reality problems were presented by asking each child only a single question rather than questioning them over and over (the standard procedure), 3-year-olds were able to distinguish between reality and pretending.
 • Merry Bullock and Rochel Gelman demonstrated that even 3-year-olds grasped the working of an apparatus which caused a Snoopy doll to pop up when a marble was dropped into one of two slots, although 5-year-olds had more adequate verbal explanations of the task.
 • Performing non-verbal tasks, preschool children have demonstrated understanding of some cause and effect relationships, even though their ability to verbalize these relationships is limited. Because Piaget's tasks are highly dependent on verbal explanations and because, as discussed in Box 9.1, young children can be confused by the suggestions of those who question them, these tasks may underestimate

preschoolers' competence. Seeking alternative explanations of preschoolers' thinking, psychologists have adopted neo-Piagetian, information-processing, biological, or cultural-context approaches.

B.   *Neo-Piagetian* theorists, refining Piaget's theory to account for new evidence, tend to take one of two major approaches. One is to keep the theory in its original form, but refining the ways observations are made and levels of performance are identified for particular tasks. Another approach tackles the problem of within-stage variability. Some researchers assume that children acquire knowledge within narrow domains, so that there may be little correspondence between their levels of performance on unrelated though seemingly similar problems. Others conceive of a child displaying a range of performance, with the context of the task determining the specific level achieved. Robbie Case and his colleagues take the view that, when the logical structure of problems from different domains is equated, performance levels on the two problems will be the same or similar.

C.   *Information-processing* theorists view people's thought processes as analogous to the workings of a computer. In one kind of information-processing model, information is seen as first entering a sensory register, then *short-term memory*, where it is combined with information about past experiences from *long-term memory*. According to this perspective, young children's cognitive difficulties are caused by limitations on their ability to process information. These limitations include distractibility, incomplete and unsystematic examination of stimuli, inability to hold several items in mind at once, difficulties in focusing on relevant features, and lack of strategies for dealing with the information they take in. Children's information-processing abilities improve with maturation and the development of more efficient strategies. Also, when tasks are arranged to reduce the load on children's information-processing systems, their cognitive performance is enhanced.

D.   Biological theories view the limitations of preschoolers' thinking as a reflection of physical immaturity, to be overcome by the processes of growth.
     • There is some evidence that developmental changes in preschoolers' brains correspond to changes in their behavior. Rapid growth in the auditory area may be related to language development; additional connections between the temporal, occipital, and parietal areas are associated with faster processing of temporal, visual, and spatial information. Myelination within the hippocampus is associated with improvement in short-term memory, and myelination of fibers connecting the cerebellum with the cortex allows better coordination of fine motor movements.
     • Noam Chomsky's theory of language development has inspired some psychologists to propose a mental module explanation of cognitive development—*modularity theory*— which hypothesizes highly specific mental faculties, tuned to particular kinds of environmental input. Modules are thought to be domain-specific, to have innately specified organizing principles, and to be only loosely connected to one another. The concepts of number, music perception, face recognition, and perception of causality have been suggested as examples of mental modules. Alan Leslie and his colleagues

have applied the concept of modularity to perception of causality, demonstrating that even 6-month-old infants have some understanding of cause-effect relationships. The modularity approach is also useful in explaining the performance of children who, like Mozart, are extraordinarily accomplished in one area of development while having normal abilities for their age in other areas.

• Modularity theory has also been applied to the study of *autism*, a condition involving inability to relate to other people. Autistic children have been found to have difficulty with tasks that measure the ability to predict other people's thoughts and feelings. This has been interpreted as evidence that there is a "theory of mind" module, which is impaired in autistic children.

• While mental modules almost certainly play some role in causing unevenness of cognitive development in preschoolers, modularity theory does not provide a full explanation of preschool mental development.

E. The cultural-context view emphasizes the way that parents promote development by arranging the environment in which their children grow up. Thus, children and the environment are both active agents in development, resulting in a process of *social co-construction*. In this approach, *context* refers to the relationship between behavior, the event of which the behavior is a part, and the setting in which they take place. Cultural contexts differ between societies and even sometimes between generations.

• Children construct generalized representations—or *scripts*—for routine events such as birthday parties, taking a bath, or going to restaurants.

• Scripts are guides to action that tell children what to expect. Scripted knowledge frees them to attend to more than the superficial details of an activity; it also helps them coordinate their activities with others who share the same scripts. In addition, scripts help children acquire abstract concepts—for example, playing house—by providing a framework into which specific examples can be fitted. As discussed in Box 9.2, preschoolers frequently engage in *sociodramatic play*, in which they enact, with other children, scripts they have encountered in stories, on television, or in real life. Piaget viewed this kind of play as a manifestation of egocentric thought that would give way to rule-bound play in middle childhood. Pretend play does in fact peak during the preschool period; however, fantasy does not disappear, even in adulthood. Lev Vygotsky viewed pretend play as a mental support system—a *zone of proximal development*—that allows children to perform more advanced behaviors than they are ordinarily capable of. An example is a study by M. G. Dias and Paul Harris in which 4- to 6-year-old children were able to perform a fairly advanced logical reasoning task when it was presented in a "let's pretend" format.

• Culture contributes to the unevenness of development by arranging the occurrence of activities, by arranging the frequency of activities, by shaping the relationships among activities, by regulating the level of difficulty of children's roles in activities, and by emphasizing activities that promote cultural values.

Barbara Rogoff has given the name *guided participation* to the process by which adults shape children's development.

• The Piagetian view of development is that the more sophisticated thinking of older children and adults is a product of generalized transformation of cognitive structures. Cultural-context theories differ from Piaget's approach in viewing these changes as context-specific, depending on the events in which children have participated. Like biological modularity theorists, they recognize the importance of maturation; however, they believe that normal development cannot occur without accompanying socio-cultural experiences.

III. APPLYING THE THEORETICAL PERSPECTIVES

Drawing is an activity in which the various approaches to preschoolers' cognitive development can be compared.

A.   In all cultures in which children are given opportunities to draw, their drawing passes through similar stages, much as Piaget would predict. Children progress from scribbling to, at about age 3, representational drawing; between the ages of 7 and 11, their drawings become more and more realistic.

B.   As predicted by the information-processing approach, children gradually learn to represent three dimensions in their drawings as they master drawing rules and become better able to remember to represent all three spatial coordinates.

C.   Lorna Selfe has observed a number of children who had exceptional drawing skills despite low language and general mental abilities. These cases can be interpreted within a mental module view of the development of drawing.

D.   The cultural-context approach emphasizes the fact that the process by which children's drawings become meaningful representations is culturally organized. For example, preschoolers are often asked, "What are you drawing?" This gives them the idea that drawings represent things. Children then begin to talk about their drawings as representations of things ("I made a mountain") even if they do not name their pictures until after they are completed. Instruction in drawing is organized so that children and adults come to share an idea of what "drawing a picture" means.

IV. RECONCILING ALTERNATIVE PERSPECTIVES

None of the theoretical approaches—Piagetian, neo-Piagetian, information-processing, biological, or cultural-context—provides a complete explanation of preschoolers' cognitive development. However, the theories can be viewed as complementary; in any case, the phenomena best explained by each would all need to be included in any comprehensive theory of preschool development.

Key Terms

Following are important terms introduced in Chapter 9. In the space to the right, write the definition of the term. In the space to the left, write the letter of the example that best illustrates the term.

_____ autism _____

_____ egocentrism _____

_____ guided participation _____

_____ horizontal decalage _____

_____ information-processing approach _____

_____ long-term memory _____

_____ mental operation _____

_____ modularity theory _____

_____ precausal thinking _____

_____ preoperational stage _____

_____ scripts _____

_____ short-term memory _____

_____ social co-construction _____

_____ sociodramatic play _____

_____ theory of mind _____

a.   Generalized event representations that specify the people, objects, and behaviors involved in, for example, birthday parties or visits to the dentist.

b.   A 3-year-old's speech is egocentric when he is answering a difficult question; when the question is changed somewhat, however, he is able to take account of his listener's knowledge.

c.   A preschooler points to a picture in a book and asks, "What's this?" not understanding that her mother can only see the outside cover of the book and not the picture she is indicating.

d.   This involves mentally combining, separating, or transforming information within a logical system.

e.   Preschoolers playing "mommy, daddy, and baby" are engaged in this.

f.   The behavior of children with this disorder is ritualized and compulsive, with retarded language development and a lack of normal social interactions.

g.   Psychologists using this approach view children's thinking processes as analogous to the workings of a computer.

h.   Children make use of this when they recall experiences from the past.

i.   John tells his nursery school teacher, "when the trees outside move, it makes the wind."

j.   We make use of this when we hold a phone number in mind long enough to write it down.

k.   According to Piaget, this is a period during which children's thought is representational but not yet logical.

l.   Laurie's mother lets her cream the butter and sugar together while making oatmeal cookies.

m.   Both environment and child are active agents in this process.

n.   Support for this approach comes from observations of "islands of brilliance" in children whose overall functioning is very low.

o.   This ability to think about the mental states of others develops during the fourth year of life.

Fill-In Questions

Cover the list of answers next to the statements below and fill in each blank with the word or phrase that correctly completes the sentence.

preoperational   1.   Piaget used the term _____ stage to describe children's thinking during the preschool period.

egocentric   2.   Preschool children, according to Piaget, are _____—that is, they have difficulty adopting others' points of view; because they sometimes confuse causes and effects, he called their reasoning

precausal   _____.

appearance   3.   In Rheta De Vries's study, 3-year-olds were likely to believe that a cat could actually become a dog; this illustrates a confusion between _____ and reality.

uneven   4.   Researchers have found that preschool children's thinking is _____—that is, sometimes it is logical and sometimes quite primitive.

5. _____ are psychologists who are trying to adapt Piaget's approach to take into account current findings about children's thinking abilities.

Neo-Piagetians

6. Robbie Case and his colleagues found that children performed equally well on two different tasks when the tasks were _____ equivalent.

logically

7. Information-processing theorists understand children's thought by analogy with the workings of _____.

computers

8. According to one information-processing approach, stimulation is first read into the system's _____ register; it is then stored in _____ memory.

sensory
short-term

9. One limitation on preschoolers' ability to process information is a tendency to explore stimuli in a haphazard rather than a _____ way.

systematic

10. Generally, older children and adults have developed more effective _____ for dealing with problems than have preschoolers.

strategies

11. Biological accounts of preschoolers' cognitive development emphasize developmental changes in the _____.

brain

12. A theoretical approach inspired by Noam Chomsky's theory of language development views the mind as a collection of mental _____.

modules

13. The difficulties experienced by _____ children in imagining the mental states of others lend support to the modularity approach.

autistic

14. The cultural-context approach looks at the way _____ support children's development through the contexts they create.

adults or parents

15. According to Katherine Nelson, contexts are represented mentally as generalized event schemas or _____.

scripts

16. Lev Vygotsky believed that _____ serves as a mental support system to help children control their behavior.

play

17. Culture contributes to the unevenness observed in children's development by regulating exposure to particular _____.

activities

guided
18. According to Barbara Rogoff, adults shape children's development through _____ participation in everyday activities.

scribbling
19. Children's earliest drawing takes the form of _____.

represent
20. At about 3 years of age children recognize that their drawings can _____ things.

rules
21. In the information-processing view, the developmental sequence children go through in learning to draw follows from their acquisition of drawing _____.

module
22. The mental _____ approach is best able to explain the extraordinary artistic ability of some otherwise developmentally disabled children.

cultural-context
23. The _____ approach has examined the ways that adults talk to children about their drawings, helping them discover the representational nature of art.

complementary
24. The various approaches to understanding preschoolers' development are best viewed as _____.

Multiple-Choice Questions

1. In Piaget's framework, the preschool period is associated with the _____ stage of development.
   a. sensorimotor
   b. preoperational
   c. concrete operational
   d. postsymbolic

2. Which of the following characterize(s) preschool thought, according to Piaget?
   a. egocentrism
   b. autism
   c. logical thinking
   d. All of the above

3. In studies designed to evaluate their thinking, preschoolers are often led astray by
   a. inability to understand language.
   b. difficulties making the required motor responses.
   c. having to keep their minds on one thing at a time.
   d. changes in surface appearance that contradict underlying reality.

4. _____ are psychologists who are working to apply Piaget's basic   assumptions to new evidence about children's thinking abilities.
   a. Neo-Piagetians
   b. Neuropsychologists
   c. Information-processing theorists
   d. Modularity theorists

5. Under which circumstance(s) may preschoolers have difficulty in reporting accurately on things they have experienced?
   a. they are asked for specific examples of events that occurred many times.
   b. they are pressed to answer questions to which they do not know the answers.
   c. they are allowed to give their accounts and then are probed for more information.
   d. All of the above cause preschoolers to have problems in accurately recalling events.

6. Which occurs in short-term memory?
   a. Information is stored for several seconds.
   b. Information is combined with information from long-term memory.
   c. Both a and b.
   d. Information is stored for several weeks; if not retrieved by then, it is forgotten.

7. Which of the following occurs in children's brain development during the course of the preschool period?
   a. The brain attains 50 percent of its adult weight.
   b.   Specific mental modules develop their physical structures.
   c. Excess myelin is dissolved from the hippocampus and cerebellum, allowing these areas to function more efficiently.
   d. New connections among different cortical centers allow better syntheses of information about different aspects of a problem.

8. Children's mental representations of routine events such as eating in a restaurant have been called _____ by psychologist Katherine Nelson.
   a. long-term memory
   b. scripts
   c. cultural contexts
   d. modules

9. According to Lev Vygotsky, in play children perform activities
    a.   at lower developmental levels than their usual behavior.
    b.   at the same developmental level as their usual behavior.
    c.   at higher developmental levels than their usual behavior.
    d.   that are more highly rule-bound than their usual behavior.

10. At about _____ of age, children begin to recognize that the lines they draw can
    represent things.
    a.   1 year
    b.   3 years
    c.   5 years
    d.   7 years

11. The unusual artistic ability of Nadia, an autistic child studied by Lorna Selfe, supports
    the _____ explanation of the development of drawing.
    a.   mental module
    b.   cultural-context
    c.   information-processing
    d.   All of the above equally

12. The view of the development of drawing that emphasizes the way adults talk to
    children about the things they draw.
    a.   mental module
    b.   environmental-learning
    c.   information-processing
    d.   cultural-context

Short-Answer Questions

1. In what ways can preschoolers' thinking be characterized as uneven? Why is this a
    problem for some theories of development?

2. What are the strengths and weaknesses of biologically-oriented explanations of
    cognitive development during early childhood?

3. Develop a script, from a preschooler's point of view, for "eating in a restaurant." Develop the same script for a college student. How do these scenarios differ? Note particularly how the supportive roles played by other people differ between the two.

4. What are the characteristics of play during early childhood? How does play serve to promote development?

5. Show how the different theoretical perspectives discussed in the chapter can each contribute to our understanding of the development of drawing.

Additional Resources

Caplan, Theresa, and Frank Caplan. *The Early Childhood Years: The 2 to 6 Year-old*. New York: Bantam, 1983.
This book gives an overview of development during the preschool years, covering motor and cognitive development, social development, early literacy experiences, sexuality, and family situations.

Flavell, John H. "Really and Truly." *Psychology Today*, January, 1986, 38-39,42-44.
The author discusses the problems of understanding appearance/reality distinctions among preschoolers of several cultures.

Goodnow, Jacqueline. *Children Drawing*. Cambridge: Harvard University Press, 1977.
An exploration of the development of children's drawings, from scribbles through representation.

Paley, Vivian. *Wally's Stories*. Cambridge: Harvard University Press, 1981.

Paley, Vivian. *Mollie Is Three*. Chicago: University of Chicago Press, 1986.
The subtle changes in children's behavior that occur between the end of infancy and the onset of middle childhood are poorly documented in standard research on early childhood. In these case studies of preschool children, the author vividly describes the unevenness of their thinking and the enormous amount of work that small children put forth daily in their efforts to understand the world around them.

Selfe, Lorna. *Normal and Anomalous Representational Drawing Ability in Children*. New York: Academic Press, 1983.
In this monograph, the psychologist who studied Nadia provides a wealth of examples of extraordinary drawing ability by children, illustrating the kind of phenomena emphasized by modularity theories of development.

Answer Key

Answers to Key Terms: f, c, l, b, g, h, d, n, i, k, a, j, m, e, o.

Answers to Multiple-Choice Questions: 1. b, 2. a, 3. d, 4. a, 5. d, 6. c, 7. d, 8. b, 9. c, 10. b, 11. a, 12. d.

Social Development in Early Childhood

Socialization begins at birth with infants' first interactions with their parents, and throughout infancy the values, standards, and knowledge of their society help to organize children's experiences. But it is not until the preschool period that children are able to actually construct an understanding of the workings of their families and their communities. At first, children follow the rules of their societies under adult constraint; eventually, though, they internalize standards and follow them on their own. Psychologists believe that a process called identification, in which children mold themselves after important people in their lives, is helpful in socialization, but they differ in their ideas of how identification comes about.

Preschool children face many important developmental tasks in addition to making sense of the rules that govern their environment. They are expected to learn to control their own behavior, including their impulses to hurt others, and to be helpful and cooperative when it is appropriate. They may need to cope with the addition of younger siblings to their families, and they must come to terms with their identities as males or females and master the sex-typed behaviors appropriate to their society.

The task of socialization is by no means completed at the end of the preschool period, but by then children understand their society's rules and expectations well enough to be ready for the increased responsibilities that accompany middle childhood.

Chapter Outline

Social development is a two-sided process. *Socialization* is the process by which children acquire the standards, knowledge, and values of the society in which they live. *Personality formation* refers to their development of *personality*, of which a distinctive *self-concept* and the characteristic ways of thinking and feeling that are called *temperament* are important parts. These two processes are closely intertwined but there is also tension between them, as children experience conflict between their desires and the rules of their society.

I.   ACQUIRING A SOCIAL AND PERSONAL IDENTITY

According to psychologists, socialization requires *identification*, a process in which children seek to be like important people in their social environment.

A.   Much of the research on identification focuses on how children acquire *sex roles*. Acquiring a sex-role identity involves identifying with the parent of the same sex.
• According to Freud, *primary identification* occurs during infancy, when babies recognize that some things in the external world are like them; *secondary identification*, which develops during the third year, involves molding oneself in some way after a particular other person.
• Freud's theory of development, discussed in Box 10.1, emphasizes the changing forms of sexual gratification during different periods. Children pass through the *oral stage*, *anal stage*, and the *phallic stage* before sexual desires are suppressed during the *latency stage* at about age 6 or 7. Puberty marks the beginning of adult sexuality—the *genital stage*.
• Freud viewed the personality as being made up of three mental structures: the *id*, source of basic desires and mental energy; the *ego*, intermediary between the id and the social world; and the *superego*, representing the authority of the social group. The superego begins to form during the preschool period and takes on an important role during middle childhood. Freud believed that, during development, dominance among the structures of the personality shifts frequently as id and superego battle for control. *Ego development* occurs in the process of resolving these conflicts.
• According to Freud, boys come to identify with their father though a process of *differentiation* from their mother, the parent with whom they had the closest relationship in infancy. During the phallic stage, Freud believed, a boy wants to take his father's place with his mother (the *Oedipus Complex*); he then relieves the guilt these feelings evoke by distancing himself emotionally from his mother and becoming closer to his father. Psychologists have viewed girls' identification with their mothers as a

process of *affiliation*, in contrast to the differentiation that characterizes the formation of boys' sex-role identities. Girls, Freud thought, blamed their mothers for their lack of a penis. In response to their guilty feelings over rejecting their mothers and competing for their fathers' affection, girls repressed their feelings for their father and identified with their mothers.

• In contrast to Freud's view, psychologist Nancy Chodorow, points out that parents themselves play significant roles in their children's sex-role identification. For example, mothers experience daughters as being like themselves and sons as representing a male opposite. And, whereas Freud equated development with differentiation (and thus viewed girls as less developed than boys), Chodorow views male and female development as having different strengths and weaknesses. In any event, researchers have demonstrated that the basis of sexual identity is present long before the resolution of the Oedipus complex.

• Social-learning theorists believe that all behavior, including sex-role behavior, is shaped by the environment. According to their view, children observe and imitate sex differences in behavior; they are also rewarded by adults for sex-appropriate behavior. Researchers have found that adults do, in fact, differentially reward children for sex-appropriate behavior; however, children's ideas about appropriate rewards are themselves sex-typed, and social learning theory does not explain where these preferences come from in the first place.

• Cognitive theorist Lawrence Kohlberg viewed sex-role identification as a result of children's structuring of their own experience. First, they are able to label themselves as boys or girls. Next, they become aware that boys grow up to be men and girls grow up to be women. Finally, they understand that sex remains the same in all situations. This theory describes the stages of children's understanding; however, they display sex-typed behavior well before they have achieved sex-role constancy, contrary to Kohlberg's prediction.

• An aternative view of sex-role acquisition, *gender schema theory*, hypothesizes children acquire a gender schema that guides their behavior and structures their perceptions. Children form gender schemas for people, objects, and familiar events. In any situation, they will be more likely to select and remember information relevant to their own sex.

• From early in life, male and female children are different in activity level and have distinctive styles of play. By age 3, they can accurately label pictures as showing boys or girls. Between 3 and 5 years of age, children's sex-typed behavior increases greatly. Researchers still have an incomplete understanding of how these things come about.

• To what extent do parents and teachers influence children's conception of masculine and feminine behaviors? Evidence suggests that their influence is limited; the prevailing culture provides so many examples of "sex-appropriate" behaviors that family and preschool have less influence by comparison.

B. The development of children's sense of racial or ethnic identity and their attitudes toward their own and other groups are important social issues. Children seem to be aware of, and to form judgments about, their race and ethnicity by 4 years of age. Several decades ago, when Kenneth and Mamie Clark asked children 3 years of age and older to indicate preferences for black or white dolls, they found that African American children seemed to prefer the white dolls. This was interpreted as indicating that minority children define themselves in terms of majority culture and have a negative self-concept. While later research has supported the findings, it has not supported the interpretations. Children's choices change with circumstances; for example, one study found that Native American children tested in their own language preferred dolls representing their own group. African American children's preference for white dolls has decreased over the years, according to more recent studies. Other studies show that the environment can affect preference. Both black and white children developed preferences for pictures of black people and animals over white ones when they were praised or given rewards for choosing them.

II. DEVELOPING THE ABILITY TO REGULATE ONESELF

As children acquire a sense of identity, they also learn what behavior their parents expect of them. At first, children's ideas of bad and good are strongly influenced by adults' reactions to their behavior. Piaget called this *heteronomous morality*, or "the morality of constraint." In heteronomous morality, Piaget believed, intentions play little role and the objective consequences of an act—the amount of damage done, for example—are the basis for judging the seriousness of an offense. During middle childhood, according to Piaget, children develop an *autonomous morality* in which rules are seen as agreements among people, not as decrees handed down by adults.

A. When children can anticipate adult reactions to their behavior and want to behave in ways that will bring adult approval they are said to have achieved *internalization* of adult standards. A new quality of personality—*conscience*—develops and children then feel guilt when they fail to live up to these standards. According to Erik Erikson's theory of psychosocial development, described in Box 10.3, the main conflict faced by children during the preschool period is that between the need to take initiative in their behavior and their negative feelings when the results of that initiative work out badly.

B. Children need to develop self-control in order to balance their desires with the social standards they have internalized. *Self-control* involves regulating one's own behavior in the absence of direct adult supervision. Frequently, it involves inhibiting behavior that would otherwise automatically occur; for example, a child who has been hit would refrain from hitting back. According to Eleanor Maccoby, young children must master inhibition of movement, emotions, conclusions, and, finally, choice. According to Claire Kopp, children's compliance with adult standards develops in three phases: situational compliance (1-2 years of age), in which a parent needs to be present to exert control; internalized knowledge of rules and expectations (2-3 years); and committed compliance, in which children cooperate without prompting. Grazyna Kochanska and Nazan Aksan found older children to be more compliant than younger ones and that greater compliance in the presence of children's mothers was associated with following prohibitions in their mothers' absence. Children's self-control improves as they internalize rules and expectations and as they become able to plan ahead and reason systematically.

III. AGGRESSION AND PROSOCIAL BEHAVIOR

The rudiments of both *aggression* and *prosocial behavior* are thought to be present during the newborn period. For example, infants may cry angrily when their sucking is interrupted. Newborns also cry in response to another infant's cry. This is thought to be the beginning of *empathy*, the sharing of another's feelings, which is the basis for prosocial behaviors.

A. Aggression is generally defined as an action intended to hurt another. As children develop, they begin to exhibit first *instrumental aggression*, in which aggressive behavior is aimed at getting something they want, and later person-oriented or *hostile aggression*, performed for revenge or to gain dominance. Judy Dunn observed an increase in instrumental aggression between siblings during the second year. Wanda Bronson, studying children's play in the laboratory, found that at about 2 years of age children began to worry about "ownership rights," engaging in struggles over toys they were not otherwise interested in. Between 3 and 6 years of age, children have fewer physical tussles, but they now exchange more verbal threats and insults, and hostile aggression makes an appearance. In general, boys are more aggressive than girls; as girls approach their second birthdays they become less aggressive while boys of the same age become more aggressive. Girls, however, engage in more *relational aggression*—which involves harming other children's friendships or excluding them from a group—than boys do.

B. Discovering the causes of aggression is one of the most important questions about human social relations.
• Charles Darwin pointed out that members of a species are essentially in conflict with one another to survive and that they pass on their inborn characteristics to the next generation. According to this view, aggression is natural and necessary, and automatically accompanies biological maturation.
• According to the social-learning view, aggressive behavior is learned. Gerald Patterson and his colleagues found that aggression by preschool children was generally followed by rewarding consequences for the aggressor.
• Sometimes parents unknowingly engage in modeling of aggressive behavior for their children in the very act of disciplining them. Support comes from the work of Albert Bandura and his colleagues, who found that children who saw an adult punch and otherwise abuse an inflatable "Bobo" doll would imitate the actions when they had the opportunity to play with the doll. Further evidence that children learn to be aggressive by observing adults comes from a cross-cultural study by Douglas Fry, carried out in two towns in Mexico. Children who lived in one town, noted for the violence of its adults, performed twice as many aggressive acts as children from a town with in which adults discouraged aggression.

C.   Theories explaining the causes of human aggression also suggest ways of controlling it.
•   Evolutionary theories suggest that once a *dominance hierarchy* is formed within a group the frequency of hostile interactions should diminish. There is some evidence that dominance hierarchies take shape among nursery school children.
•   It is widely believed that *catharsis*—the opportunity to vent aggressive tendencies in harmless behavior—will reduce the incidence of actual aggression; however, research demonstrates that this is not the case. Shahbaz Mallick and Boyd McCandless found that helping boys to sympathetically reinterpret a peer's obtrusive behavior was more effective in diffusing hostility than letting the boys "blow off steam" by shooting at targets.
•   Efforts to eliminate aggressive behavior through punishment have mixed results at best. Coercive child-rearing behaviors may develop when children inadvertently train their parents to use physical punishment; this may make the children themselves more aggressive as a result. If punishment is to be used to suppress aggressive behavior, it should be administered consistently and by a person with whom the child strongly identifies. According to Kenneth Dodge and his colleagues, excessive use of physical punishment by parents leads to higher levels of aggression by the children. This aggression is mainly reactive, involving retaliation for other children's real or imagined hostility; the aggressive children also tended to misinterpret other children's behavior as being intentionally hostile to them.
•   Teachers often find that the level of aggression in their classrooms declines significantly when they ignore aggressive behavior and only attend to and reward children's cooperative behavior. Allen, Turner, and Everett found similar benefits when teachers gave attention and advice to the victim of aggression but ignored the aggressor.
•   Reasoning with children about aggression—cognitive training—is sometimes effective even with preschoolers. Shoshana Zahavi and Steven Asher found that children were better able to control their aggression when their nursery school teachers made them aware of the feelings of the children they aggressed against.

D.   *Prosocial behaviors* such as altruism, cooperation, helping, and empathy develop during infancy and early childhood. Why do they occur?
•   Evolutionary explanations emphasize that prosocial behavior, like aggression, is also characteristic of other organisms. However, human altruism, unlike that of animals, often extends beyond the kin group to total strangers. While humans obviously have a biological potential for prosocial behavior, it is also influenced by socialization.
•   *Empathy*—sharing another's emotional response—is an important stimulus for prosocial behavior . Martin Hoffman has traced the development of empathy through four stages. During the first year, babies cry at the sound of another infant's cry; this empathy is reflexlike, occurring even before infants have any real awareness of other people. During the second year, babies actively attempt to comfort a person in distress. Preschoolers can empathize with a wider range of feelings and, through the media, with people they have never met or with story characters. Finally, between 6 and 9 years of age, children begin to emphasize with the social conditions of groups of people.

• Carolyn Zahn-Waxler and Marion Radke-Yarrow found that, based on mothers' observations, between 10 months and 1 1/2 to 2 years of age, children's responses to another person's distress develop from diffuse emotional reactions such as crying to active caregiving and comforting behaviors such as offering Band-Aids and blankets. These changes coincide with children's abilities to recognize themselves in the mirror and refer to themselves in speech. Similarly, Judy Dunn found an increase between 15 and 36 months of age in the tendency of children to comfort a sibling in distress. Harriet Rheingold found that all the 2-year-olds she studied spontaneously helped their mother with household chores in a laboratory situation and that most of them even helped an unfamiliar woman.

• Explicitly rewarding children for prosocial behaviors does not seem to be effective in increasing these acts. Two less direct but effective methods are *explicit modeling*, in which adults behave in ways they want the child to imitate, and *induction*, in which explanations are used. Marion Yarrow and her colleagues found that when explicit modeling was carried out in a nurturing, loving way, the effects on preschoolers' behavior lasted for some time. Induction has more generally been used with older children.

IV. THE DEVELOPMENT AND REGULATION OF EMOTIONS

A. Six or 7-month-old infants can tell how to feel about a situation by reading their mothers' facial expressions. By 2 years of age, children know that some things make people feel good and other things make them feel bad. Further development takes place during the preschool period; by 5 or 6 years of age, children studied by Richard Fabes and his colleagues were in agreement with adults 80% of the time in their assessment of other children's emotional states. Linda Michalson and Michael Lewis, studying 2- to 5-year-olds, found that the older children were better than the younger ones at assessing the emotions another person might feel, at least in more complicated situations.

B. Young children use various strategies to keep their emotions under control. For example, they may turn away from something frightening or use language to encourage themselves in the face of difficulty. They also become better able to resist temptation. Between 2 1/2 and 5 years of age, there is an increase in the use of *active engagement*—a strategy in which the child deliberately stops attending to a tempting but forbidden object and instead plays with an alternative object.

C. Babies are not born with the ability to regulate expression of their emotions in socially-acceptable ways, but parents begin shaping this quite early. By 3 years of age, North American children are able to express an emotion they do not feel.

D. Work in the area of emotional develop has shown us that each aspect of emotional development appears to go through a series of stages; we have also seen that emotional development, social development, and cognitive development are closely related.

Children who have high levels of social and emotional development and are able to use their skills in real-life situations are said to have *socioemotional competence*. Such children are better liked both by peers and by teachers, because they are easier for other children to get along with. Research on socioemotional competence has led to programs to improve children's ability to interact with others in acceptable ways.

V. TAKING ONE'S PLACE IN THE SOCIAL GROUP AS A DISTINCT INDIVIDUAL

By the end of early childhood, children have accepted that conformity to social rules is inevitable. While they are by no means completely socialized, they have developed their own distinct ways of thinking and feeling and are able to demonstrate their sensitivity to the social world in a variety of contexts.

Key Terms I

Following are important terms introduced in Chapter 10. In the space to the right, write the definition of the term. In the space to the left, write the letter of the example that best illustrates the term.

_____ aggression _____

_____ autonomous morality _____

_____ dominance hierarchy _____

_____ empathy _____

_____ explicit modeling _____

_____ heteronomous morality _____

_____ hostile aggression _____

_____ induction _____

_____ instrumental aggression _____

_____ prosocial behaviors _____

_____ relational aggression _____

_____ self-control _____

_____ social development _____

_____ socialization _____

a. The process by which children acquire their society's values, knowledge, and standards.
b. A mother appeals to her children's pride and their desire to be grown-up in explaining how they should behave toward others.
c. This occurs when someone hurts another person intentionally.
d. When this develops in a preschool, it determines who will typically be dominant and who will be submissive in an argument between two children.
e. Janet hits another preschool child in order to gain possession of the doll she is playing with.
f. Children have achieved this when they understand that rules are based on the agreement of those they govern and can be changed if everyone agrees.
g. This is a process with two aspects: in one, children become differentiated as individuals; in the other, they become integrated into the society of which they are members.
h. John calls a fellow kindergartner "stupid" just to hurt his feelings.
i. A baby cries when she hears another child crying.
j. Altruism, cooperation, and sharing are examples of these.
k. This is characterized by attention to the letter, rather than the spirit, of the law.
l. Becky demonstrates this when she is able to hold still and sit quietly while the hairstylist trims her bangs.
m. Parents demonstrate for their children how to "take turns" with a toy.
n. Jan and Linda tell Jessica that they don't like her anymore and don't want to play with her.

Key Terms II

Following are important terms introduced in Chapter 10. In the space to the right, write the definition of the term. In the space to the left, write the letter of the example that best illustrates the term.

_____ catharsis _____

_____ conscience _____

_____ gender schema theory _____

_____ identification _____

_____ internalization _____

_____ latency _____

_____ Oedipus complex _____

_____ personality _____

_____ phallic stage _____

_____ primary identification _____

_____ secondary identification _____

_____ self-concept _____

_____ social roles _____

_____ socioemotional competence _____

a.   The Freudian stage during which children develop sexual jealousy toward the parent of the same sex.

b.   A father encourages his children to hit a punching bag to "blow off steam," hoping it will prevent them from punching one another.

c.   The idea that children's conceptions of sex roles guide their behavior and affect the way they select and remember information.

d   This happens during infancy when babies notice that there are other things in the world like them.

e.   Freud's term for modeling oneself after another person.

f.   This has occurred when children have accepted social rules and make an effort to follow them on their own.

g.   Children's distinctive sense of themselves, including distinctive ways of thinking, feeling, and behaving.

h.   During this Freudian stage, sexual energy is channeled into acquiring technical skills.

i.   Jason tells his mother that he wants to marry her someday, "after Daddy dies."

j.   The way children conceive of themselves in relation to other people.

k.   This has been explained by psychologists in four major ways: affiliation, differentiation, social learning, and cognitive schemas.

l.   Children need to have internalized adult standards in order for this aspect of personality to develop.

m   Examples are "daughter," "student," and "wife."

n.   Ability to discern other people's emotions is an important component of this.

Fill-in Questions

Cover the list of answers next to the statements below and fill in each blank with the word or phrase that correctly completes the sentence.

1. One aspect of social development is _____, the process by which children acquire the standards, values, and knowledge of their society. A second aspect is _____ formation, the way in which children come to have a sense of themselves and distinctive ways of thinking and feeling.

   socialization

   personality

2. Part of socialization involves _____, in which children seek to look, act, feel, and be like significant people in their social environment.

   identification

3. In Freud's view, there are two kinds of identification: _____ identification, which occurs during infancy when babies realize their similarity to other people; and _____ identification, which takes place during early childhood when children want to be like a specific person.

   primary

   secondary

4. Freud believed that around the age of 3, children enter the _____ stage of development, during which they develop sexual feelings toward the opposite-sex parent and jealousy or resentment toward the same-sex parent. He called these feelings the _____ Complex.

   phallic

   Oedipus

5. According to Freud's theory, the personality has three parts: the unconscious and pleasure-seeking _____, the _____, whose task is self-preservation, and the _____, which represents the authority of the social group.

   id, ego

   superego

6. Freud believed that in boys, identification occurs through _____ while in _____ it occurs through affiliation.

   differentiation, girls

7. In Nancy Chodorow's formulation of sex-role development, boys achieve identity through separation and are threatened by _____, while girls achieve identity through _____ and are threatened by separation.

   intimacy, attachment

8. According to _____ theory, identification occurs through observation and imitation.

   social-learning

label

schema

9. In Lawrence Kohlberg's view, an important factor in sex-role identification is children's ability to _____ themselves as boys or girls; other psychologists have emphasized the importance of a gender _____ in guiding interests and behavior.

active
separate

10. Male infants are more _____ than female infants, and, by 2 1/2 years of age, most boys and girls like to play with _____ kinds of toys.

white

negative

11. Psychologists researching ethnic identity have been concerned over the tendency of minority preschoolers to prefer _____ dolls over black ones; however, this does not seem to indicate that they have _____ feelings about their own group.

constraint

12. Piaget labeled preschoolers' reasoning about moral issues heteronomous morality or a "morality of _____."

autonomous

13. During middle childhood, Piaget thought, children develop a more _____ morality, based on an understanding that rules are agreements between people and can be changed if people agree to do so.

internalized

14. By the end of the preschool period, children have _____ many adult standards for behavior.

self-control

plan

15. As they develop _____, children become better able to behave in socially-acceptable ways even when no one is supervising them; this is related to their increasing ability to _____ ahead.

Aggression

16. _____ is behavior that is intended to hurt another person.

instrumental
hostile

17. Whereas _____ aggression is performed in order to obtain something desirable, _____ aggression is person-oriented.

evolution

18. According to some students of animal behavior, aggression is an important mechanism of _____.

rewarded
model

19. Learning theorists point out that aggression increases when it is _____; children may also learn aggression from adults who inadvertently _____ aggressive behavior.

dominance

20. Formation of a _____ hierarchy reduces aggression by reducing the number of others an individual will fight with.

21. The idea that _____, or "blowing off steam," will reduce   **catharsis**
    people's hostile impulses has not been supported by research.

22. Because children are sometimes aggressive in order to gain
    attention, one way of reducing aggression is to _____ only   **reward**
    cooperative behavior.

23. Altruism, cooperation, helping, and empathy are _____   **prosocial**
    behaviors.

24. Two effective methods of promoting prosocial behavior are
    explicit modeling and _____.   **induction**

Multiple-Choice Questions

Circle the letter of the word or phrase that correctly completes each statement.

1. _____ is the process by which children learn the standards, values, and knowledge
   of their society.
   a.   Personality formation
   b.   Prosocial behavior
   c.   Affiliation
   d.   Socialization

2. According to Freud, identification in males
   a.   requires that they differentiate themselves from their mothers.
   b.   requires that they differentiate themselves from their fathers.
   c.   results in their remaining affiliated with their mothers.
   d.   occurs because they are rewarded for imitating appropriate behavior.

3. In thinking about moral issues, preschool children
   a.   have no sense of right or wrong.
   b.   believe in obeying the spirit of the law rather than the letter of the law.
   c.   judge the rightness or wrongness of actions by outcome, not intention.
   d.   are inclined to question the judgment of people in authority.

4. In Freud's theory, which part of the personality serves as a person's conscience?
   a.   The id
   b.   The ego
   c.   The superego
   d.   The unconscious

5. When children are able to pass up a small candy bar today to wait for a larger candy bar tomorrow, they are exhibiting
    a.   repression.
    b.   self-control.
    c.   internalization.
    d.   prosocial behavior.

6. The major developmental crisis of the preschool period, according to Erik Erikson, involves conflict between
    a.   trust and mistrust.
    b.   industry and inferiority.
    c.   autonomy and shame and doubt.
    d.   initiative and guilt.

7. When children exclude another child from a group or harm the other child's friendship with someone else, they are engaging in
    a.   a defense mechanism.
    b.   explicit modeling.
    c.   instrumental aggression.
    d.   relational aggression.

8. Children worry about "ownership rights" to toys and become serious about taking them from others
    a.   from early infancy.
    b.   only when they begin preschool.
    c.   beginning at about the time they can walk.
    d.   beginning at about 2 years of age.

9. Aggression among children is caused by
    a.   frustration.
    b.   adults who inadvertently reward aggressive behavior.
    c.   inborn tendencies to compete with others.
    d.   All of the above are causes

10. Physically punishing children for aggressive behavior
    a.   may make children even more aggressive.
    b.   is the most successful way to inhibit aggressive behavior.
    c.   has no effect on children's level of aggression.
    d.   provides catharsis for parents and helps them cope better with their children's behavior.

11. When newborns cry in response to another baby's crying, they are displaying the first signs of
    a. self-control.
    b. frustration.
    c. empathy.
    d. learning.

12. Ability to perceive the emotional states of others and to control the expression of one's own emotions are aspects of
    a. gender schema formation.
    b. socioemotional competence.
    c. the Oedipus complex.
    d. the process of differentiation.

Short-Answer Questions

1. Briefly describe the Freudian, social-learning, and cognitive approaches to explaining children's sex-role identification. What are the strengths and weaknesses of each?

2. Discuss what happens during each of Freud's stages of psychosexual development. How do Freud's stages differ from Erikson's stages of psychosocial development?

3. What factors are thought to be responsible for human aggression? What might help reduce aggression among children?

4. What is prosocial behavior and what is its course of development in children? How can prosocial behavior be increased?

Putting It All Together

In this section, material from Chapter 10 can be put together with information presented in Chapters 8 and 9.

I.   One of the major accomplishments of early childhood is the growth of children's ability to regulate their own behavior. Show how developments in language ability and the growth of scripted knowledge help children to exhibit self-control and to interact socially with others.

II.   Among preschoolers, the ability to reason about social categories such as sex is thought to influence the process of identification. Use examples to demonstrate the relationship between cognitive development and social development during early childhood.

Sources of More Information

Ames, Louise Bates, and Carol Chase Haber. *He Hit Me First: When Brothers and Sisters Fight*. New York: December, 1982.
This book discusses sibling rivalry from the biological-maturational perspective of the Gesell Institute.

Dunn, Judy. *The Beginnings of Social Understanding*. Cambridge, Mass.: Harvard University Press, 1988.
The author has studied children as they interact with their siblings in everyday family settings. The book is helpful in illustrating the relationship between cognitive and social development.

Eisenberg, Nancy (Ed.). *The Caring Child*. Cambridge, Mass.: Harvard University Press, 1992.
A discussion of topics related to theory and research on the development of prosocial behavior.

Freud, Anna. *Psycho-analysis for Teachers and Parents* (Trans. by Barbara Low). New York: Norton, 1979.
This book contains four lectures in which Sigmund Freud's daughter, a noted children's analyst, discusses the early stages of psychosexual development.

Galinsky, Ellen, and Judy David. *The Preschool Years*. New York: Times Books, 1988.
The authors present practical solutions to the problems faced by parents of preschool children.

Hall, C. S. *A Primer of Freudian Psychology*. New York: World, 1954.
This brief paperback account of Freud's thinking is one of the most accessible and comprehensive available.

Honig, Alice Sterling. "Compliance, Control, and Discipline, Part I." *Young Children*, January 1985, 50-58.

Honig, Alice Sterling. "Compliance, Control, and Discipline, Part II." *Young Children*, March 1985, 47-52.
These two articles discuss children's development of self-regulation and suggest techniques that can be used by adults to increase cooperation and compliance.

Answer Key

Answers to Key Terms I: c, f, d, i, m, k, h, b, e, j, n, l, g, a.

Answers to Key Terms II: b, l, c, k, f, h, i, g, a, d, e, j, m, n.

Answers to Multiple-Choice Questions: 1. d, 2. a, 3. c, 4. c, 5. b, 6. d, 7. d, 8. d, 9. d, 10. a, 11. c, 12. b.

The Contexts of Early Childhood Development

CHAPTER 11

Children's development is influenced by the many contexts of their lives; their families, for example, belong to communities that, in turn, are parts of larger societies. Child rearing varies from society to society: a family of nomadic herders in North Africa and a family living in a New York City high-rise apartment will not teach their children the same survival and social skills. There are also differences in child-rearing practices within societies and corresponding differences in children's behavior. Many factors influence a family's child rearing, including the personalities of parents and children, the parents' occupational status, and the life stresses that affect the family at any particular time.

Even within the family, children are influenced by the world outside. Media such as television, newspapers, and books help to shape the behavior and beliefs of family members in the United States. Research on the influence of television on children indicates that it can have both positive and negative effects, depending on how it is used. Print media, particularly books, provide children with an introduction to literacy.

During early childhood, many children are cared for by relatives besides their parents or by day-care providers, either in other families' homes or in day-care centers. While high-quality daycare does not harm children intellectually, it has both positive and negative social effects. Not all families are able to arrange the best possible care for their children, and the long-term effects of poor-quality day care have not been determined.

Children also have out-of-home experiences in preschools— sheltered environments oriented toward enhancing their development. Special preschool programs have been created for economically disadvantaged children in the hope of giving them an educational "head start," and there is some evidence that preschool experience has at least some long-lasting positive effects on such children's later school achievement.

By the end of the preschool period, children, while not completely socialized, will have a great deal of information about how their culture works and will be able to behave competently in the wide variety of situations with which they are familiar.

Chapter Outline

Chapter 11 highlights how the contexts in which preschool children develop influence the course of their development. These contexts—ranging from specific events within the family or preschool to global influences of mass media—may shape children's development directly or indirectly, through their effect on parents and other family members.

I.   THE FAMILY AS A CONTEXT FOR DEVELOPMENT

According to anthropoligist Robert LeVine, parents' childrearing practices share three goals: ensuring children's survival; ensuring that they acquire economically important skills; and ensuring that they acquire basic cultural values. North Americans tend to picture a family as a *nuclear family*, consisting of husband, wife, and two or three children (see Box 11.1 for a discussion of how siblings influence one another's development). However, a wide range of different family configurations can be found in the U.S. and Canada and throughout the world, and, in many societies, *polygyny* is the norm.

A.   When Beatrice and John Whiting organized observations of child rearing in six diverse locales around the world, they found differences, not only in the circumstances of children's lives, but in the overall patterns of their behavior. For example, children of the Gussi, an agricultural people in Western Kenya, displayed more "nurturant-responsible" as well as more "authoritarian-aggressive" social behaviors than the children of Orchard Town, U.S.A., who were rated more "dependent-dominant" and "sociable-intimate." Each cultural group socializes children in ways that will help them to fit in as adult members of that particular society.

B.   While child-rearing behaviors differ in many ways among U.S. families, psychologists conceive of parenting styles as varying along two dimensions: from control to autonomy and from affection to indifference.
•   Diana Baumrind and her colleagues found that, when they measured the parenting styles of the families they studied, 77 percent of the families they studied fall into one of the following categories: those following an *authoritarian parenting pattern*, in which parents try to control their children's behavior and stress obedience to authority; those following an *authoritative parenting pattern*, in which parents encourage individualism and independence, while setting high standards for behavior; and those who follow a *permissive parenting pattern*, in which parents provide less discipline and demand less achievement and maturity than do parents in the other categories. Baumrind found that the children of authoritarian parents tended to lack social competence and intellectual curiosity, that the children of authoritative parents were more self-reliant and self-controlled, and that the children of permissive parents were relatively immature and less responsible than those of the other groups. Later research has extended these findings to high school-age students.

There are limits to the generalizability of these findings: the studies were of white, middle-class, two-parent families. There is evidence that keeping close control over children's behavior—characteristic of authoritarian parenting—does not have the same effect in other ethnic groups, such as African Americans and Asian-Americans, as it did in the families Baumrind studied. In addition, children's own characteristics probably influence the child-rearing strategies adopted by their parents. Still, these findings have generated a great deal of interest and have inspired other researchers to investigate the effects of parenting strategies on children's behavior.

•   In 1993, 27% of U.S. children lived in single-parent households. What are the consequences of growing up in a single-parent family?
•   Many single mothers raising children are teenagers. Research has shown that children of unmarried teenage mothers are developmentally disadvantaged compared to children of older, married mothers.
•   Divorce leads to changes in children's lives that are often accompanied by academic and social difficulties. However, two longitudinal surveys that studied families who were not divorced at the time of the initial interviews found that many of the problem behaviors associated with divorce began well before the divorce, and were probably responses to parental conflict. The impact of divorce seems to be greatest on boys and temperamentally difficult children. An equilibrium is usually reached after several years, but may be disrupted when parents remarry.
•   Poverty has an influence on child-rearing patterns. Laboratory and observational studies have demonstrated that when mothers are under stress they are more likely to adopt an authoritarian parenting style. Stressful events occur more often in poor families; low-income parents are also more likely to use authoritarian or inconsistent styles of child rearing. As pointed out in Box 11.2, children living in poverty are more likely to be victims of child abuse, though the problem is found in other socioeconomic levels as well. Several researchers have found that parenting style also is

significantly related to parental occupation. Middle-class occupations tend to require independence and self-directed work, while working-class occupations often demand obedience and punctuality; parents tend to socialize their children in the direction demanded by their own occupations.

• In *extended families* , grandparents, cousins, nephews, and other relations often share a household. Extended families are common among some cultural groups and provide children with a buffer against the effects of economic hardship. The support provided by extended families is particularly important for children born to unmarried mothers.

II.   MEDIA LINKING COMMUNITY AND HOME

Children's behavior is shaped, not only by the members of their families and their communities, but by modern communications media such as books, television, newspapers, and radio. Chapter 11 examines the influence of television and books.

A.   There is no question that children learn from watching television. Even infants imitate language and actions they hear and see on T.V. However, young children's difficulties in distinguishing between appearance and reality can greatly affect their understanding of television. They may have difficulty separating the actors from the characters they portray or understanding that the events depicted are not really happening.

• Techniques of television production such as close-ups, flashbacks, and changes of camera angle have meaning for older viewers but are confusing to preschool children, who may be unable to keep track of much of what they see. The fast-paced nature of television also allows little time for reflection. Gabriel Salomon found that children socialized to learn from television had lower expectations of how much mental work was needed to learn from written texts. He also found that children who watched a great deal of television read less well and did fairly poorly in school.

• The content of television programs differs systematically from everyday reality. For example, prime-time programming tends to stereotype people by sex, age, ethnic group, and occupation.

• Television also contains many violent episodes, and psychologists have noted an association between viewing violent television programs and aggression in children's play.

• The family has some influence on how children are affected by television. Children whose playground behavior is less aggressive also tend to be those whose viewing is limited and restricted to educational and children's programs and whose parents also take them to parks, museums, and cultural events. Children can also benefit from having their parents watch television with them and discuss the content of the programs.

B.   Like television viewing, being read to requires children to construct meanings from words and pictures that represent elements of the everyday world.

• Virtually all preschool children are involved with print media in some form every day, if only for a few minutes. Many are read to by their parents or other adults.

Children who are often read to at home generally learn to read easily once they begin school. As was found in a study by Anat Ninio and Jerome Bruner, parents, in their interactions with children over books, often construct a *zone of proximal development*, asking questions suited to their children's level of knowledge. Grover Whitehurst and his colleagues have developed a parent-child activity called *dialogic reading*, which has been shown to have a positive effect on several measures of children's cognitive development.

• Adults have much greater control over the content of the books they read to children than over the content of television programs children watch. Some adults worry that certain literary forms such as fairy tales or nonsense verse are harmful to children's development; still others defend them as beneficial. Box 11.3 touches on this question. It is difficult to characterize the influences of media in general terms—their effects depend on the social setting for which a child is being prepared.

III. THE YOUNG CHILD IN THE COMMUNITY

Children are often left in the care of people other than their parents for several hours a day. This changes both the nature of their experiences and the nature of their parents' control over those experiences.

A. At the present time, more then 60 percent of U.S. mothers with preschool children were working and using some form of day care.
• In *home care*, children are cared for in their homes by relatives or babysitters.
• In *family care*, children are cared for in the day-care provider's home, along with children from outside their families. Family day-care providers may be licensed by state, county, or local government, but most are unlicensed.
• Licensed *day-care centers* generally place more emphasis on formal learning experiences. Those serving fewer than 60 children tend to be more flexible and more responsive to individual children than larger ones; within a center, children receive more individual attention when placed in a group of less than 15 to 18 children.

B. There is disagreement among psychologists about the effects of day-care experience on children's development.
• Since much early research on day care was conducted in high-quality, university-affiliated centers, the results may not be generalizable to other settings. The longterm effects of day care have not yet been studied. And families who use day care may vary in significant ways from those who do not, raising the possibility that some "effects of day care" could be only effects of family situations.
• The intellectual development of middle-class children in day care is at least as good as that of their stay-at-home peers; low-income children seem to actively benefit from day-care enrichment programs.
• Children who attend day-care centers in the U.S. are more self-sufficient and independent, more cooperative, and more comfortable in new situations, though also less polite, less compliant with adults, and more aggressive than children who do not

attend day care. Children in day-care centers and nursery schools engage in a great deal of group play and must therefore learn social skills such as how to enter groups of children who are already playing together and how to handle themselves when other children reject their overtures.

C. *Preschools* serve a primarily educational purpose; the children, who may range in age from 2 1/2 to 6, typically spend 2 1/2 to 3 hours per day engaged in a variety of activities designed to enhance various aspects of their development. The emphasis is usually on exploration rather than on performing correctly on preassigned tasks. Preschools in other cultures may provide different kinds of environments, socializing children to become members of those societies (see Box 11.4 for a discussion of differences between American and Japanese preschools).
    • Project Head Start was begun in 1964 in an attempt to narrow the educational gap between low-income and middle-class children by providing preschool-aged children with learning experiences they might miss at home. Soon, it was a year-round program serving 200,000 children.
    • Although initial reports were promising, the Head Start program lost favor after a 1969 study reported that the beneficial effects disappeared during the first years of elementary school. In 1989, however a review of follow-up studies showed that children who had attended a preschool program were less likely to be assigned to remedial classes than children with no preschool experience. The study also found, that special model Head Start programs had additional beneficial effects on rates of delinquency, teen pregnancy, and unemployment. However, the effects of preschool programs faded out unless they were followed up by special programs later in children's educational careers. Debates over longterm effectiveness and about the proper ways to spend government money make the future of compensatory preschool education uncertain. However, the Head Start program has become a symbol of a commitment to help children out of poverty through self-improvement.

IV. ON THE THRESHOLD

By the end of the preschool period, children have accumulated a great deal of knowledge about a wide variety of contexts; their ability to think about the world, to interact with other children, and to control their own behavior have all increased as well. In these ways they indicate their readiness to take on the roles and responsibilities they will face in middle childhood.

Key Terms

Following are important terms introduced in Chapter 11. In the space to the right, write the definition of the term. In the space to the left, write the letter of the example that best illustrates the term.

_____ authoritarian parenting pattern _____

_____ authoritative parenting pattern _____

_____ day-care centers _____

_____ dialogic reading _____

_____ extended family _____

_____ family care _____

_____ home care _____

_____ nuclear family _____

_____ permissive parenting pattern _____

a. Janet's parents expect a lot of her and are fairly strict, but they are willing to explain the reasons for their decisions and to listen to her point of view. Janet gets along well with other children and is generally happy with her home life.

b. John's behavior is relatively immature for his age, but his parents are not especially concerned. They believe that children should learn through their own experiences. When John is ready to accept more adult responsibilities, he will indicate it through more mature behavior, they feel.

c. Jack is a quiet and well-behaved child, though his behavior seems to lack spontaneity. His parents are insistent that he follow the rules they set, and Jack knows that if he questions these rules he will be punished. In general, Jack prefers playing alone to dealing with the problems that accompany social interactions among children.

d. In this type of care, children's daily routines ar least disrupted.

e. This provides support that is especially important to the children of young, unmarried mothers.

f. The smaller in size among these are more flexible and responsive to children's needs.

g. This parent-child activity has had a beneficial effect on children's cognitive development.

h. This arrangement is considered the norm among North Americans, but is not typical in many other cultures.

i. Providers of this type of care may have licenses; however, many are unlicensed.

Fill-In Questions

Cover the list of answers next to the statements below and fill in each blank with the word or phrase that correctly completes the sentence.

culture

1. Beatrice and John Whiting's study of child rearing in six different locales revealed how differences in _____ are associated with differences in children's behavior patterns.

authoritarian, permissive

2. Diana Baumrind characterized the U.S. parents in her study as _____ authoritative, or _____ with respect to child rearing.

authoritative

3. Children of _____ parents tend to achieve more and be better adjusted socially both as preschoolers and as adolescents.

conflict

4. Studies of families who subsequently divorced suggest that some of the academic and social problems that accompany divorce may actually be results of parental _____.

stress

authoritarian

5. Because lower-income families are subject to more _____ than well-to-do families, their parenting styles can be expected to be more _____.

obedience

6. While middle-class occupations stress self-direction, working-class occupations place greater emphasis on _____ and punctuality.

extended

7. In some cultural groups, _____ families help to buffer children from the stresses of low socioeconomic status.

reality

8. Three- and 4-year-old children may not understand some television programs because of problems distinguishing between appearance and _____.

stereotyped

9. Frequently, television programs depict ethnic groups, women, and certain occupations in _____ ways.

parents

10. Children learn more from watching television when their _____ watch with them.

literacy

11. Children acquire the beginnings of _____ at home, by being read to, looking at the writing on cereal boxes, or watching their parents read the newspaper.

12. The way parents interact with their children over picture books prepares them for the way they will be asked questions in _____. **school**

13. A major difference between preschoolers' experiences with books and television is the greater _____ adults have over the content to which they are exposed. **control**

14. The most popular day-care arrangement for preschool children is _____ care, in which children are cared for in their own homes; _____ care, in which children are cared for in the home of a nonrelative, is the next most frequently used arrangement. **home** **family**

15. In day-care centers, children receive more individual attention when cared for in groups of less than _____. **15 to 18**

16. Attendance at well-staffed day-care centers has no negative effects on children's _____ development. **intellectual**

17. In daycare centers, children's interactions with one another usually occur around a shared _____, such as playing with blocks. **activity**

18. _____ came into being to "promote experiences of mastery within a child-sized world." **Preschools**

19. Follow-up studies of Head Start programs have shown that the effect of preschool programs tends to _____ with time if not followed up with special programs later in children's school careers. **decrease or disappear**

20. Preschoolers display surprising competence and maturity of reasoning when operating in familiar _____ for which they know the appropriate scripts and the roles they are to play. **contexts**

Multiple-Choice Questions

Circle the letter of the word or phrase that correctly completes each statement.

1. Diana Baumrind and her colleagues found that the parenting styles of middle-class Americans vary along dimensions of
    a. aggression and love.
    b. control and affection.
    c. guilt and initiative.
    d. confidence and empathy.

2. Compared with working-class parents, middle-class parents are
    a. more concerned about their children's futures.
    b. less concerned about their children's futures.
    c. more likely to emphasize self-reliance.
    d. more likely to emphasize obedience.

3. All children are affected when their parents divorce, but _____ in particular seem to suffer the greatest effects.
    a. temperamentally "difficult" children
    b. boys
    c. girls
    d. both a and b

4. Which is a possible source of misunderstanding when preschoolers watch TV?
    a. They may not know how to interpret special techniques such as scene changes or flashbacks.
    b. They may not understand that the events on the screen are not really happening.
    c. They may not be able to distinguish the actors from the characters they play.
    d. All of the above

5. Which is true about the effects of TV violence on children's behavior?
    a. Unrestricted viewing of violent programs is associated with more aggressive behavior.
    b. Children who watch nonviolent children's programs like Mr. Rogers' Neighborhood are just as aggressive as those who watch violent programs.
    c. Only children who are predisposed to be violent are affected by violent programs.
    d. Children who "blow off steam" by watching violent programs are less aggressive in their play than children who watch nonviolent programs.

6. Which of the following serves as a "literacy experience" for young children?
   a. Listening to their parents read a letter aloud.
   b. Looking at the message on cereal boxes.
   c. Bringing home a note from their preschool teacher.
   d. All of the above

7. Kornei Chukovsky, a Soviet poet, argued that nonsense verse
   a. is harmful to children's cognitive development.
   b. helps strengthen children's sense of reality.
   c. is fun for children but doesn't teach them anything.
   d. is confusing to children because they think the nonsensical things really happen.

8. Differences in _____ have been found between children who attend day care and those cared for at home.
   a. social development
   b. intellectual development
   c. attachment to their parents
   d. sex-appropriate behavior

9. The most widely utilized form of day care for preschool children is
   a. care in organized childcare centers.
   b. care in the child's own home.
   c. family care.
   d. All are utilized equally

10. Preschool-aged children have less trouble joining a group of children already playing together if
    a. they are girls.
    b. the group they are joining is composed of unpopular children.
    c. they ask the other children to explain what they are doing.
    d. they act as though they are already part of the group.

11. The main purpose of preschools is to
    a. take care of young children while their parents work.
    b. give children a head start in learning academic skills such as reading and writing.
    c. provide children with opportunities to practice developmental skills in a scaled-down environment.
    d. get children ready for school by teaching them to perform correctly on assigned tasks.

12. The most recent follow-up studies of Project Head Start showed that
    a. the program had no effect on children's development.
    b. the program had a positive effect on children's achievement which lessened with time unless followed up with special school programs.
    c. the program had no long-lasting effects on school achievement or on occupational aspirations.
    d. the program left disadvantaged children even worse off than before.

Short-Answer Questions

1. What differences can be observed among children whose parents use authoritarian, authoritative, and permissive child-rearing strategies? Why is it hard to say whether the strategies actually cause the differences in children's behavior?

2. In what ways do parents' occupations and socioeconomic status influence the child-rearing strategies they use?

3. What problems may young children have in understanding what they see on TV? What similarities and differences are there between the way children learn from TV and the way they learn from books?

4. In what ways do day-care and preschool experiences affect children's intellectual and social development? What positive effects have been noted? Negative effects?

Sources of More Information

Clarke-Stewart, Alison. *Daycare*, 2nd ed. Cambridge, Mass.: Harvard University Press, 1992.
A discussion of scientific and practical issues surrounding day-care by a researcher with considerable experience in the area.

Fields, Marjorie V. *Literacy Begins at Birth*. Tucson, Ariz.: Fisher Books, 1989.
The author discusses how children learn to read and write and how parents and teachers support the process.

Greenfield, Patricia Marks. *Mind and Media: The Effects of Television, Video Games, and Computers*. Cambridge: Harvard University Press, 1984.
The author shows how various media can be used to enhance children's learning and to promote social development.

Singer, Dorothy G., Jerome L. Singer and Diana M. Zuckerman. *Teaching Television: How to Use TV to Your Child's Advantage*. New York: Dial Press, 1981.
This book reviews the problems and possibilities of television watching, discusses how TV shows are put together, and covers stereotyping, violence, and other timely issues.

Trelease, Jim. *The New Read-Aloud Handbook* (2nd Rev. ed.). New York: Penguin, 1989.
This book discusses how being read to affects children's development and includes a bibliography of suggested stories and books for reading aloud to children of various ages.

Trotter, Robert J. "Project Day-Care." *Psychology Today*, December 1987, 32-38.
The author interviews Ed Zigler, a psychologist who helped start Project Head Start, about possible solutions to the childcare crisis facing U.S. parents.

Wallerstein, Judith S., and Joan Berlin Kelly. *Surviving the Breakup: How Children and Parents Cope with Divorce*. New York: Basic Books, 1980.
A summary of findings from the Children of Divorce Project, written for general readers.

Wallis, Claudia. "The Child-Care Dilemma." *Time*, June 22, 1987, 54-60.
This article describes the crisis developing as day-care facilities fail to keep up with the demand created as greater numbers of mothers join the workforce.

Answer Key

Answers to Key Terms: c, a, f, g, e, i, d, h, b

Answers to Multiple-Choice Questions: 1. b, 2. c, 3. d, 4. d, 5. a, 6. d, 7. b, 8. a, 9. b, 10. d, 11. c, 12. b.

Cognitive and Biological Attainments of Middle Childhood

Between 5 and 7 years of age, children change in a number of ways. Their bodies and facial features become more streamlined and their smiles show gaps and permanent teeth coming in. Less visible changes in their brains support more graceful movements and more efficient thinking. They are entering the developmental period called middle childhood.

During middle childhood, children's height, weight, and strength increase steadily. These changes are matched by new cognitive abilities and increasing competence in the many social contexts to which they have been exposed since the end of infancy. Already skilled speakers of their language, these older children can follow complex directions and, when assigned tasks, can perform them without constant adult supervision. They are better at remembering things and their thinking is more consistently logical than it was during their preschool years.

A reflection of children's new abilities is that adults now send them to be educated in schools or assign them economically important work to do. These new activities, in turn, stimulate further cognitive and social development. The behavioral changes of middle childhood can be understood more clearly when they are considered in terms of the many contexts in which development takes place.

Chapter Outline

In many cultures the first loss of baby teeth marks the beginning of middle childhood. The accompanying physical growth and brain development are the sources of children's new capacities.

It seems to be universal among cultures that when children are between 5 and 7 years old, adults begin to expect them to take on new responsibilities that involve formulating goals and working independently. Chapter 12 investigates the biological and psychological changes that underlie children's greater abilities and justify adults' expectations of children during middle childhood.

I. COPING WITH INCREASED FREEDOM AND RESPONSIBILITY

During middle childhood, there is an increase in the amount of time children spend unsupervised by adults, and the range of contexts they inhabit increases greatly. Are the biological and cognitive changes of middle childhood indicators of a new stage of development, or can we best understand them as continuations of steady changes begun several years earlier?

II. BIOLOGICAL DEVELOPMENTS

During middle childhood, children increase in size and strength, putting on about 1 1/2 feet in height and 50 pounds in weight. Growth is not steady, but goes through rapid and slow periods.

A. Both genetic factors and nutritional status contribute to size differences among children. Illness slows children's growth; the deficit is quickly made up as long as nutrition is adequate.

B. Motor skills, coordination, and agility increase during middle childhood. Boys are slightly more advanced in activities that require power and force; girls are better at fine motor skills or activities that combine movement with balance. Sex differences are due partly to physical differences and partly to cultural expectations.

C.   Children's brains undergo changes between the ages of 6 and 8: myelination of the cortex continues; there are increases in the number of synapses and the amount of neurotransmitters produced; children's electroencephalograms (EEGs) reveal a shift from a predominance of theta activity (characteristic of sleep in adults) to a predominance of alpha activity (characteristic of engaged attention); there is an increase in *EEG coherence*, indicating greater coordination between the activities of different areas of the brain. Robbie Case has argued that these changes allow the brain's frontal lobes to coordinate the work of other brain centers, resulting in children's increasing ability to make plans and maintain goals. There is some evidence that children's patterns of brain activity are related to their performance on problem-solving tasks. However, because the evidence is correlational, it is difficult to be certain whether changes in children's brains are the actual causes of the changes in their behavior.

III.   A NEW QUALITY OF MIND?

Psychologists are interested in how changes come about in children's thinking during middle childhood and whether these changes represent a distinctive stage of cognitive development.

A.   According to Piaget, the new behaviors that accompany middle childhood represent a new form of thought. *Concrete operations* are internalized mental actions that fit into a logical system and relate directly to physical objects. Children's thinking is now more flexible and, when solving problems, they can consider alternatives and retrace their steps. It was Piaget's belief that concrete operational thinking has a significant effect on their social relations, which now become broader and more complex.
   • *Conservation* of properties such as quantity or number refers to children's understanding that these properties remain constant even when physical appearance changes, for example, when the level of water rises as the water is poured into a taller, thinner glass. Most 3- and 4-year-olds are misled by changes in physical appearance because they focus their attention on only one aspect of a stimulus, such as the height of the water. When children become able to conserve liquid quantity, they understand that, logically, the quantity of water must remain the same even though it appears different. They justify their insistence that "there is still the same amount of water" with one of the following arguments: *identity*, "nothing was added so they are still equal"; *compensation*, "the new glass is taller but it is also thinner"; and negation or *reversibility* "if you pour the water back into the original glass, it will reach the same level as before." The conservation of number task tests children's understanding that, when a one-to-one correspondence has been set up between two rows of objects, rearrangement of one of the rows does not change the number—the rows are still equal.
   • Piaget's observations have been replicated by other researchers. However, some research has demonstrated more overlap in the conservation abilities of preschoolers and older children than was reported by Piaget. For example, Rochel Gelman devised

a simplified task that showed that 3- and 4-year-olds have partial knowledge about numbers that is not tapped by the ordinary conservation of number task. There is also controversy over whether the repeated questioning typical of conservation tasks leads children to give illogical answers by making them think their original answers are incorrect.

• In logical classification, children show their ability to group objects according to more than one criterion. So, for example, a stamp collection might be organized by country, year, and denomination. Unlike preschoolers, 7- to 8-year-olds are able to answer questions requiring knowledge of the relationship between a category and its parts (for example, "Are there more roses or more flowers?").

B.   According to the information-processing view, children's improved performance on problem-solving and logical classification tasks results from increases in knowledge, skills, and processing capacity.

• Robert Siegler tested children of various ages on a version of Piaget's balance problem. He formulated a set of four different rules that could be used to solve balance problems and devised sets of problems that allowed him to determine which rule each child was using. Siegler's results showed that development of logical reasoning can be explained partly by changes in the rules children use. Another important influence is *encoding* of the important features of a task; for example, in the balance task, younger children tend to pay attention to the amount of weight on each side of the balance and ignore the distance of the weights from the fulcrum. Box 12.3 provides further information about children's difficulties in perceiving more than one aspect of a stmulus.

• In contrast with a stage theory approach, the information-processing view is that younger children can form complex categories just as older children and adults do, though only within a narrow range of contexts.

C.   Four factors seem to account for increased memory performance during middle childhood:

• Children are able to hold more information in memory. *Memory span* increases from early childhood into adolescence; older children are able to process information more rapidly and make more efficient use of their memory capacity. Cross-cultural work supports this view. For example, it takes young children more time to encode longer items in memory; therefore, the words for numbers being shorter in Chinese than in English, Chinese children can recall more digits than their American age-mates. However, when memory capacity is measured using lists of words that are equally long in Chinese and in English, no differences in memory capacity are found.

• Older children generally have a greater *knowledge base* and, therefore, better-elaborated concepts to draw on when they need to remember things relating to a particular topic. For example, Micheline Chi found that 10-year-old children who are expert chess players remembered positions on a chess board better than college students did, though they were not as good at remembering random numbers.

• While 1-1/2 to 2-year-old children have been observed using simple tactics to help them remember, during middle childhood children become better able to make use of memory *strategies*, deliberate actions that help them to remember. Studies by John Flavell and his colleagues have demonstrated that older children are more likely to use *rehearsal* in order to remember information. *Memory organization* also changes during middle childhood. For example, older children are more likely to link words to be remembered according to category (animal, color, etc.). Children who do not spontaneously use rehearsal or organizing strategies improve their performance when they are taught the techniques.

• Seven-and 8-year-olds know more about their own memory processes (*metamemory*) than younger children and are therefore more likely to correctly estimate how much effort will be required to remember particular items.

• These changes in different aspects of memory performance each appear quantitative and gradual. However, they add up to a sizable difference in memory performance between preschoolers and 7- to 8-year-olds.

D. Are the cognitive changes accompanying middle childhood universal or are they products of schooling and other characteristics of industrialized societies? Two of the most frequently studied cognitive abilities connected with middle childhood are concrete operations and free-recall memory.

• Most research has found that children in nonindustrial societies achieve concrete operations a year or more later than children in Western industrialized societies. However, Patricia Greenfield and other researchers found that many adults in certain cultures never showed an understanding of concepts like conservation. It has become evident that unfamiliarity with testing procedures is partly responsible for these results. For example, Pierre Dasen and his colleagues found that rural Australian aboriginal children showed greater understanding of conservation after being familiarized with a similar task in a brief training session. Children participating in cross-cultural studies also perform better on conservation tasks when tested in their native languages. In one study, Raphael Nyiti found that Micmac Indian children in Nova Scotia performed less well on a conservation task than children of European descent when tested in English, but equally well when tested in Micmac. There is also evidence that children in traditional societies may actually acquire some concepts—for example, understanding business transactions earlier as a result of their greater experience with activities such as helping their families market their products.

Apparently, concrete operations are an achievement of middle childhood for children in all cultures. However, cultural differences may influence children's performance on the specific tasks used to assess these skills.

• Cross-cultural studies show that the development of memory skills during middle childhood takes a somewhat different course in nonindustrial societies. For example, Michael Cole and his colleagues found that, unless they had attended schools, tribal children in rural Liberia did not demonstrate the regular increase in free recall performance characteristic of children in industrialized societies during middle childhood. Educated Liberian children, like their U.S. counterparts, learned the stimulus list quickly and made use of categories within the list (clothing, food, etc.) in recalling the items. The non-schooled Liberians, however, learned the list easily when the items were presented not randomly, but as part of a story. Items were clustered in recall according to their roles in the story. Barbara Rogoff and Kathryn Waddell found that Guatemalan children from a Mayan village also performed better on a memory task made meaningful in terms of their culture. Remembering, like concrete operational thought, is used by people in all societies, but specific forms of remembering—those most often studied by psychologists—are not universal, but associated with formal schooling.

E.   Although 5- to 7-year-olds are considered more competent and responsible than younger children, there are few visible physical changes that might explain the changes in their behavior. Improvements in technology show us that their brains are more mature; however, the exact relationship between brain maturation and improvement in cognitive skills remains unclear. To better understand the sources of changes in behavior during this period, it is also necessary to examine the social contexts in which children's development takes place.

Key Terms

Following are important terms introduced in Chapter 12. In the space to the write the definition of the term. In the space to the left, write with the letter of the example that best illustrates the term.

_____ compensation _____

_____ concrete operations _____

_____ conservation _____

_____ EEG coherence _____

_____ encoding _____

_____ identity _____

_____ knowledge base _____

_____ memory organization _____

_____ memory span _____

_____ metamemory _____

_____ rehearsal _____

_____ reversibility _____

_____ strategy _____

a. In answering a question about conservation, a child points out that two lumps of clay were the same weight to begin with and that nothing has been added or removed; therefore, they must still be equal although they now look different.

b. When asked if two lists of words are equally difficult to learn, a boy says that it will take longer for him to learn the longer list.

c. Understanding that objects' basic physical properties, such as weight, volume, and quantity, remain the same despite changes in appearance.

d. When applied to memory, this is a deliberate procedure that helps people remember things more effectively; for example, tying strings on their fingers or writing themselves notes.

e. A child realizes that the transformation performed in a conservation task can be undone; for example, by pouring the water back into the original container.

f. Ways of transforming information (combining, separating, etc.) that fit into a logical system.

g. A 10-year-old gets a phone number from "directory assistance" but has no pencil to write it down; she keeps it in memory by repeating it to herself over and over.

h. A boy notices that, when liquid is poured into another container, the greater height of the second glass is balanced by a decrease in width.

i. Children take advantage of internal structure in remembering a list of words, grouping the mammals together, the flowers together, and the fish together.

j. In a conservation task, this occurs when a child notices and makes mental representations of the height and width of a container.

k. This gets larger the more experience children have with particular topics or activities.

l. This is evidence that activity of the frontal lobes is coordinated with activity of other brain areas.

m. This increases from early childhood into adolescence.

Fill-In Questions

Cover the list of answers next to the statements below and fill in each blank with the word or phrase that correctly completes the sentence.

1. In many cultures, children are considered ready for new responsibilities when they begin to get their second set of _____.

                                                                                    teeth

alpha

2. Between 6 and 8 years of age, children's electroencephalograms begin to shift from a preponderance of theta activity to a preponderance of _____ activity.

coherence

3. Greater coordination between areas of the brain is reflected in greater EEG _____.

operations

4. When children mentally transform objects and information in a logical manner they are engaging in concrete _____.

Conservation

5. _____ is the Piagetian term for understanding that an object's underlying properties remain the same when its appearance is changed.

reversibility, compensation

6. Children explain their correct answers on conservation tasks in terms of negation or _____, identity, and _____.

classify

7. Middle childhood also sees an increase in children's abilities to logically _____ a collection of objects into groups and subgroups.

encoding

8. According to Robert Siegler, 5-year-olds perform poorly on Piaget's balance task because of difficulties _____ both of the relevant stimulus dimensions.

9. Information theorists point out that young children, like older children and adults, can make use of complex categories, though the _____ in which they can apply them are limited.

contexts

span

10. Memory _____ is a measure of children's short term memory capacity.

11. It is not known whether older children have greater memory capacity or whether they simply perform memory tasks more _____.

efficiently

12. We can say that a boy who has read many books about dinosaurs has a greater _____ base on this topic than one who has not.

knowledge

rehearsal organization

13. Two effective memory strategies are _____ and memory _____.

14. _____,—knowledge about their own memory processes—is more developed in older children than in preschoolers.   **Metamemory**

15. Many cross-cultural studies of cognitive development show that children from nonindustrial societies attain _____ a year or more later than children from industrialized societies.   **concrete operations**

16. _____ them on conservation tasks is one way to determine whether children from traditional cultures understand conservation but fail to show their knowledge because of unfamiliarity with the task.   **Training**

17. Children with a great deal of practice in a particular activity attain concrete operations related to that activity _____ than children without comparable experience.   **earlier**

18. Some cultural differences on conservation tasks are due to experimenters' lack of fluency in the subjects'_____.   **language**

19. Children who have not attended school typically perform poorly on _____ memory tasks, in which a large number of objects are presented to subjects in random order.   **free recall**

20. When items to be remembered are presented as part of a _____, unschooled villagers are quite skilled at recalling the items.   **story**

Multiple-Choice Questions

Circle the letter of the word or phrase that correctly completes each statement.

1. Between 6 years of age and the start of adolescence,
    a.   children grow at the same rate as they did during the preschool period.
    b.   children increase in height by 1 1/2 feet and in weight by 50 pounds, on the average.
    c.   children grow faster than at any time since early infancy.
    d.   do not grow appreciably.

2. When children are between the ages of 6 and 8, their brains
    a.   become more myelinated, especially in the frontal lobes.
    b.   achieve greater EEG coherence.
    c.   shift their electrical activity to a preponderance of theta waves.
    d.   All of the above

3. A child who, in correctly answering a question about conservation of liquid quantity, says, "They're still the same because, even though the level now looks higher, the second container is skinnier" is justifying her answer in terms of
    a. negation.
    b. reversibility.
    c. identity.
    d. compensation.

4. When shown a display of six daisies, three roses, and one daffodil, which child is likely to answer correctly when asked, "Are there more daisies or more flowers?"
    a. A 3-year-old
    b. A 5-year-old
    c. An 8-year-old
    d. All of the above

5. One reason for preschoolers' problems on conservation tasks is that they focus their attention on
    a. only one aspect of the stimulus situation.
    b. two aspects of the stimulus at the same time.
    c. other stimuli besides the ones presented.
    d. their own actions with respect to the stimuli.

6. Some of the increase in memory performance during middle childhood can be attributed to
    a. more efficient use of memory capacity.
    b. increased use of strategies such as rehearsal.
    c. an increasing knowledge base.
    d. All of the above

7. Metamemory refers to a person's
    a. memory capacity.
    b. knowledge relating to the information being recalled.
    c. knowledge about the process of remembering.
    d. use of organization to help remember a list of items.

8. People from traditional, nonindustrial societies perform better on conservation tasks when
    a. the experimenters are fluent speakers of their language.
    b. they are familiarized with the tasks through training sessions.
    c. Both a and b.
    d. None of the above—conservation performance is not greatly affected by task variables.

9. Schooled people have an advantage over unschooled people on which aspect of memory performance?
   a. rehearsal
   b. free recall tasks
   c. memory capacity
   d. remembering stories

10. What is the relationship between children's memory and their knowledge base?
   a. The greater the knowledge base children have about a topic, the better their performance on a topic-related memory task.
   b. If children have a large knowledge base on one topic, their performance is improved on tasks related to other topics as well.
   c. Knowledge base affects the memory performance of adults but not that of children.
   d. Knowledge base has no effect on children's memory performance.

Short-Answer Questions

1. Why is it difficult to determine the extent to which biological development during middle childhood causes the changes in behavior that characterize this period? Give examples.

2. How do changes in task presentation affect the ages at which children are able to perform tasks measuring concrete operations? Give examples.

3. What important changes take place in children's memory performance during middle childhood? How are these changes affected by cultural context?

4.   What cultural factors affect the age at which children attain concrete operational thought in a particular content area? What aspects of task presentation are important?

Putting It All Together

As children grow older, they learn more and more about the world. One thing they learn is that certain properties of people and objects remain the same despite changes in the way they look. Using examples, show how this knowledge develops in various ways during infancy, the preschool period, and middle childhood.

Sources of More Information

Cole, Michael, and Silvia Scribner. *Culture and Thought*. New York: Wiley, 1974.
This book describes studies of cognitive development carried out in Liberia.

Elkind, David. *Children and Adolescents: Interpretive Essays on Jean Piaget* (3rd ed.). New York: Oxford University Press, 1981.
This book of essays was inspired by Piaget's theory of cognitive development.

Inhelder, Barbel, and Jean Piaget. *The Early Growth of Logic in the Child*. New York: Norton, 1969.
The authors discuss the development of children's skills in logical classification.

Kail, Robert. *The Development of Memory in Children* (3rd ed.). New York: W.H. Freeman, 1990.
The author takes up important topics such as use of strategies, metamemory, and the role of knowledge base in memory.

Rogoff, Barbara, and Lave, Jean (eds.). *Everyday Cognition: Its Development in Social Context*. Cambridge, Mass.: Harvard University Press, 1984.
This is a collection of essays by psychologists and other social scientists on the effect of context on the process of cognitive development.

Serpell, Robert. "Measures of Perception, Skills and Intelligence: The Growth of a New Perspective on Children in a Third World Country." In Willard Hartup (Ed.), *Review of Child Development Research*. Chicago: University of Chicago Press, 1982.
The author reviews research on cross-cultural variations in perceptual and cognitive tasks and discusses ways that imposing Western cultural interpretations on behavior can be avoided.

Tanner, J. M. *Fetus into Man: Physical Growth From Conception to Maturity.* (Rev. Ed.) Cambridge: Harvard University Press, 1990.
This is a comprehensive review of normal growth and development.

Answer Key

Answers to Key Terms: h, f, c, l, j, a, k, i, m, b, g, e, d

Answers to Multiple-Choice Questions: 1. b, 2. d, 3. d, 4. c, 5. a, 6. d, 7. c;,8. c, 9. b, 10. a.

Schooling and Development in Middle Childhood

Throughout the world, middle childhood is a time when children are expected to begin to learn the skills they will need in order to be productive adult members of their societies. In modern, industrialized countries, children of this age spend much of their time in school, learning literacy, mathematics, and other culturally valued knowledge.

When children begin school, they already know a great deal about language and may know the names of the letters of the alphabet, a system that represents each significant sound with a different symbol. They can usually count numbers and objects, using their fingers or other body parts to help keep track of quantity. They are also experienced at making inferences on the basis of partial signs; for example, they know that, if the car is not in the driveway, their friend next door may not be at home. In school, children will build on these skills, working within a specialized environment with its own rules and even its own ways of using language.

Most of the cognitive changes associated with middle childhood are not direct results of schooling; however, children who have been to school perform better on tasks that resemble school activities. Schooling has its greatest effect on opportunity: children who are not educated have little chance for later economic success.

Because of the importance of schooling for later success, there has been great interest in tests that will predict school performance, and intelligence tests are now routinely used for that purpose. In fact, psychologists do not agree on what intelligence is, but since tests of intelligence seem primarily to measure aptitude for schooling, they are moderately successful in predicting who will do well and who is likely to have problems. In addition to aptitude, students need environments conducive to learning in order to succeed academically. For many students, school atmosphere and teacher expectations can make a difference between success and failure.

Chapter Outline

Education is important in shaping children's later lives. As described in Box 13.1, many children have difficulty in some particular area of learning. Therefore, the study of learning and development in school contexts is an active area of research for developmental psychologists.

I.   THE CONTEXTS IN WHICH SKILLS ARE TAUGHT

Although all children are raised to learn the basic knowledge, beliefs, and skills important in their culture, *education*—the deliberate teaching of specialized knowledge and skills—is not an important activity in all cultures. In hunter-gatherer societies, skills are taught as a part of everyday activity. Once societies become more complex, *apprenticeships*, which combine instruction with productive work, provide training for specialized occupations. In contrast to children taught in schools, apprentices learn through observation and practice, put their skills to work from the beginning, and are taught through oral rather than written language. The workshop is likely to contain people of all ages, and the master is a parental figure to the young apprentices.

II.   THE HISTORICAL DEVELOPMENT OF LITERACY AND SCHOOLING

Chapter 13 presents schooling in a historical context and describes the many factors that affect children's school performance.

A.   Written notation systems serve as a form of memory, extending language in space and time. The earliest writing system, traced back to abut 4000 years ago, was *cuneiform writing*, in which wedge-shaped symbols, representing the sounds of language, were inscribed on clay tablets. Since cuneiform writing was difficult to master, schools were established to train young people to be scribes.

B. It is only in more recent times, since the industrial revolution, that mandatory schooling and mass literacy have become widespread. At first, only children of the elite received a high level of education; today, many societies expect all children to attain such a level. This can, however, be a challenge to modern educational systems, which use teaching methods—based on drill and practice and oral imitation of the teacher—developed for large groups, and which are faced with an ever greater volume of information considered part of "the basics."

C. The modern alphabet was developed by the ancient Greeks and is a descendant of cuneiform writing. Each letter corresponds to a different basic sound or phoneme. In other kinds of writing systems, each symbol corresponds to a basic concept or to a unit of sound. For English and many other languages, a phonetic system is the most efficient, allowing all words to be represented using only 26 symbols.

III. DEVELOPMENT AND ACADEMIC SKILLS

A. Reading is a complex cognitive skill, and the process of learning to read is still not well understood.

An important aspect of reading is *decoding*, the process of learning letter-sound combinations. A difficulty in learning to read English is that there is often not a one-to-oone correspondence between letters and sounds. Written letters are pronounced differently in different contexts and it is difficult to isolate individual phonemes, which normally do not occur alone.
• Reading requires coordination of "top down" processes (integrating materials with previous knowledge) and "bottom up" processes (sounding out letters to make words, adding these together, etc.).
• There is disagreement over how much emphasis should be given to each type of process in early reading instruction.

Jean Chall, an advocate of the "code emphasis first" approach, has classified children's mastery of reading into stages. In Stages 1 and 2, children learn mainly how to relate print and sound. In Stage 3, children make the transition from "learning to read" to "reading to learn."

The current view is that teachers should include both decoding and comprehension training in early reading instruction by integrating the use of interesting and motivating literature with specialized training in work attack skills.

• *Reciprocal teaching*, a method created by Annmarie Palincsar and Ann Brown, integrates decoding and comprehension training through group discussion, including asking questions about content, summarizing, clarifying, and predicting what will happen next. This approach is an application of Vygotsky's idea of a "zone of proximal development." Studies have shown the procedure to be effective in improving children's reading skills.

B.   Learning arithmetic requires the coordination of: *conceptual knowledge* (the ability to understand the principles that underpin a problem); *procedural knowledge* (the ability to carry out a sequence of actions to solve a problem); and *utilization knowledge* (the ability to know when to apply particular procedures). Most children have some of each kind of knowledge when they arrive at school; even societies with no traditions of literacy or schooling have developed ways of counting and solving arithmetic problems. Children's rudimentary knowledge of numbers expands with age and instruction.

Disagreement about the best way to teach mathematics centers on the importance of drill and practice, supported by the work of E. L. Thorndike, versus emphasizing the importance of understanding, advocated by William Brownell. Today, it is agreed that drill in computation and practice in generalizing computations to meaningful problems are both important and necessary parts of mathematics instruction. These methods are increasingly supplemented by the use of computers, as discussed in Box 13.2.

C.   In school, language is used in ways that are different from its typical use in other contexts.
• *Instructional discourse* provides students with information about the curriculum and with feedback about the correctness of their answers while providing the teacher with information about their progress. A feature of instructional discourse is the *initiation-reply-evaluation sequence*; frequently, this takes the form of questions to which the teacher already knows the answer. In the specialized language of school, context does not always help children interpret the teacher's questions and they have to focus on language itself in order to master the information presented. As discussed in Box 13.3, this can cause special problems when children come to school speaking a foreign language.
• Children also need to learn how to write numbers. First, the first ten digits are mastered; then, it becomes necessary to learn the concept of place value and the conventions for representing larger numbers. For most children, this takes several years.

IV. THE COGNITIVE CONSEQUENCES OF SCHOOLING

Schooling provides children with instruction in remembering and in problem-solving and greatly expands their knowledge base. In order to specify the contributions of schooling to changes in cognitive function that occur during middle childhood, psychologists compare the performance of children who have attended school with that of those who have not.

A.   In places where there is a minimum age for beginning school, it is possible to compare children whose birthdays are just before the cut-off date with those who have just missed the cut-off. Studies using the *school cutoff strategy* have shown that attending first grade apparently increases children's recall ability, their use of rehearsal, and their ability to analyze the sound components of words. In contrast, a study by Jeffrey Bisanz and his colleagues showed that, while conservation of number improved as a consequence of age, mental arithmetic improved as a consequence of schooling.

B.   Another method of assessing the cognitive consequences of schooling is to study societies in which schooling is available to only a portion of the population.

The evidence suggests that schooling does not affect children's attainment of concrete operations. However, school experience may increase children's familiarity with testing procedures, making their performance appear advanced compared with that of unschooled children.

• In the opinion of some psychologists, the organization of children's *lexicons*—the total store of words in their vocabularies—is affected by schooling. For example, children who have attended school are sensitized to the abstract, categorical meanings of words. They show this by responding with words from the same category when asked for associations to a particular word (a child might respond "salmon" to the word "trout").
• Schooling appears to be the factor underlying cultural differences on standard memory tests. These differences are most pronounced in cases in which the materials to be remembered are not connected by an everyday script; they disappear when the materials are part of a meaningful setting. No evidence suggests that schooling increases actual memory capacity.
• Schooling seems to influence the degree to which children can reflect on and talk about their own cognitive processes and explain how they reach solutions to problems. This ability is called *metacognition*. Schooling also affects *metalinguistic awareness*, children's ability to think about their own language-using skills.
• Schooling does not appear to change the basic cognitive processes associated with middle childhood in a general way. Schooled children have learned information-processing strategies that make them more effective in performing specific school-related tasks: reading, writing, calculating, and problem-solving. One of the most important effects of schooling on children's lives is the opportunity it gives them to command more highly paid jobs which lead to greater economic power and increased social status.

V.   APTITUDE FOR SCHOOLING

For many years, the idea of "intelligence" has influenced discussion of the question of why some children learn more easily in school than others. While all languages have words referring to problem-solving ability, the exact meanings of the terms differ across cultures.

In the United States, children's scores on intelligence tests influence the kind of education they receive.

A.   Once mass education became widespread, educators became interested in finding out why some children had difficulty learning in school. In 1904, Alfred Binet and Theophile Simon were commissioned by the French Minister of Public Instruction to develop a screening exam to identify children who needed special instruction. Binet and Simon based their test on the premise that a child who performed at the level of the average 7-year-old on their tasks had a *mental age* (MA) of 7, regardless of his chronological age. An intelligent child would have a mental age greater than his chronological age, while the MA of a dull child would be less than his chronological age. While Binet and Simon felt that performance on their test was determined by both "nature" and "nurture," they specified no way in which the effects of these factors could be separated.

B.   Binet and Simon's test came into use in many countries. In the United States, it was modified by Lewis Terman of Stanford University. An updated version of the Stanford-Binet is in use today, as are intelligence scales developed by David Wechsler for use with adults and children.

• The concept of *IQ* (intelligence quotient), introduced by William Stern, refers to MA/CA X 100. So, for example, a 10-year-old with an MA of 11 would have an IQ of 110. A further refinement was the development of the *deviation IQ*, based on the fact that the raw IQ scores of a large population form an approximately normal distribution. This makes it possible to compare the scores of children of different ages. The procedure underlying today's IQ tests, like those of the test developed by Binet and Simon, are as follows: create a set of test items on which the performance of children of the same age will vary; order the items in terms of difficulty; and make certain that performance on the test corresponds to school performance.

• The essential properties of intelligence continue to be a matter of debate for psychologists. Intelligence is usually thought of as a general characteristic of people's behavior, and indeed, performance on separate tasks within IQ tests is highly correlated. However, some scholars feel that IQ tests measure only those aptitudes which relate to success in school, and in fact school tasks do differ in systematic ways from those encountered in other settings. Some investigators have proposed the existence of many different kinds of intelligence. Not all of these are measured by traditional IQ tests.

• Disagreements about the nature of intelligence are complicated by differences found between the average scores of members of different ethnic groups. According to the *innatist hypothesis of IQ*, embraced by many psychologists during the 1920s, these differences are due to inborn variations and cannot be eliminated through training or other environmental manipulations. During the 1930s and 1940s, this view was balanced by the *environmentalist hypothesis of IQ*, which viewed intelligence as greatly influenced by experience. The debate became more heated during the 1960s when it grew to encompass the question of whether federally funded projects such as Head Start were capable of improving children's school achievement.

• Currently, psychologists recognize that both genetic and environmental factors contribute to the intelligence test performance of individuals. It is difficult to specify the exact contribution of each for the same reasons—detailed in Chapter 2—that it is difficult to specify the genetic and environmental contributions to any human behavior. Because all intelligence tests draw on a background of learning that is culture-specific, comparisons of intelligence between cultural groups are extremely difficult to make. Studies indicate that within-group differences may have a substantial genetic component; however, because of noncomparability of environments, there is no evidence that average score differences between ethnic groups are due to genetic factors. In addition, because heritability is a population statistic—meaning that it applies to groups of people, rather than to individuals—measures of heritability do not tell the percentage of a person's IQ score that is attributable to heredity; instead, they estimate the percentage of variability within a group of people (raised under similar conditions) that is attributable to heredity. When environment is radically changed—for example, by a change in socioeconomic status—IQ will reflect this. For example, although African Americans as a group score below the national average on standard IQ measures, Sandra Scarr and Richard Weinberg found that children of black working-class parents who were adopted by white middle-class families scored, as a group, almost precisely at the national average.

VI. THE SCHOOL AND THE COMMUNITY

Family and peer influences and school atmosphere affect the likelihood of children's success in school; as discussed in Box 13.4, culture also has important effects.

A. Parental involvement has a positive effect on school achievement. For example, studies of native Hawaiian children support the importance of a culture-sensitive approach that builds on some features of family socialization practices—for example, cooperation and harmony—while ignoring or reversing others—for example, the tendency to avoid looking directly at adults. And studies of southeast Asian immigrants found that many parents read to their children, and that homework was very much a family activity. Many of the children were strikingly successful in school despite contending with many disadvantages. Parents' use of language is also important. For example, anthropologist Shirley Brice-Heath found that the language patterns used by Anglo, middle-class parents in the southeastern U.S. prepared their children for the special language of schooling; the language of the working class African American parents she studied did not serve this function as well.

B. Peer interactions can have negative or positive effects on children's school performance. William Labov and Clarence Robbins peer groups studied some of the negative effects. Their study was carried out in central Harlem in New York City; the school performance of boys in grades 4 to 10 who participated in ganglike groups was compared with that of boy's who did not. Labov and Robbins found that, while reading scores increased as nongroup members moved from grade to grade, group members made virtually no improvement over the course of the study. On the positive side, studies have found that working collaboratively with peers improves children's performance on problem-solving tasks.

C.   Research by Michael Rutter and his colleagues indicates that schools are not helpless in the face of community and peer group influence, and that school atmosphere can make a difference in achievement. Studying secondary schools in central London, they found that the most successful schools were characterized by: an emphasis on academics; teachers who were skillful at coordinating class activities; greater emphasis on praise than punishment; and the expectation that students should take on some of the responsibility for a clean and pleasant atmosphere.

As discussed in Box 13.5, other research has shown that children's performance is influenced by teachers' expectations. Robert Rosenthal and his colleagues found improvements in IQ scores among a group of children whose teachers had been led to believe that they were likely to "bloom" intellectually during the school year. Not all studies have found effects of teachers' expectations, but this may be due in part to differences in the ways teachers respond to such suggestions. Work by Carol Dweck and her colleagues has indicated that teachers have different expectations for boys and for girls, and that these are reflected in the kinds of feedback they give children affecting children's expectations about their own behavior.

D.   Although schooling is an important part of middle childhood in many societies, it does not represent all of children's lives. Chapter 14 examines the characteristics of children's peer groups and the effects of peer interaction on development.

Key Terms

Following are important terms introduced in Chapter 13. In the space to the right, write the definition of the term. In the space to the left, write the letter of the example that best illustrates the term.

_____ apprenticeship _____

_____ conceptual knowledge _____

_____ decoding _____

_____ deviation IQ _____

_____ education _____

_____ environmentalist hypothesis of IQ _____

_____ initiation-reply-evaluation sequence _____

_____ innatist hypothesis of IQ _____

_____ instructional discourse _____

_____ IQ _____

_____ lexicon _____

_____ mental age (MA) _____

_____ metacognition _____

_____ metalinguistic awareness _____

_____ procedural knowledge _____

_____ reciprocal teaching _____

_____ school cutoff strategy _____

_____ utilization knowledge _____

a. A kind of verbal exchange frequent in schools, in which a teacher asks a question, a student answers, and the teacher provides feedback.

b. This would be equal to 8 for a child who can answer questions on an intelligence test as well as the average 8-year-old.

c. This method of calculating IQ takes into consideration the fact that children's mental development occurs more rapidly among preschoolers than among adolescents.

d. In older children, this is more developed than it is in preschoolers, as reflected by their greater ability to explain their solutions to problems.

e. This is an application of Vygotsky's idea of a "zone of proximal development."

f. This form of deliberate teaching is not characteristic of hunter-gatherer societies.

g. A kind of language used in schools that varies in important ways from everyday language.

h. A child knows that, to determine how many more candies Amy has than he has, he should subtract his number of candies from hers.

i. According to this idea, one would expect people's intelligence scores to be more highly similar the more closely related they are.

j. In this kind of job training, the participant often lives in the master's house.

k. When applied to inversion, an example is knowing that, if you add three cards to your pile and put 3 cards back, you will have the same number you started with.

l. A number used to compare the intelligence of different people.

m. An example is being able to tell whether or not a particular sentence is grammatically correct.

n. This idea is supported by evidence that improving children's environments raises their scores on IQ tests.

o. Knowing, for example, how to add two numbers to get their sum.

p. This is one way to assess the effects of formal education on cognitive development.

q. Learning this is the major task of beginning readers.

r. The total set of words a child knows.

Fill-In Questions

Cover the list of answers next to the statements below and fill in each blank with the word or phrase that correctly completes the sentence.

Education apprenticeship

1. _____ is a form of socialization involving deliberate teaching of specialized knowledge and skills; _____ is a form of education in which instruction and productive labor are combined.

cuneiform

2. The first writing system was _____writing on clay tablets.

schools

3. The first _____ were places where young men were trained to be scribes.

tutors

4. Before mass education became widespread, children of the upper classes were educated privately by _____.

knowledge

5. The rapid accumulation of _____ poses problems for modern systems of education.

alphabet

syllable

6. The _____ is based on a system of representing each separate phoneme with a symbol; in some languages, symbols represent basic concepts or each possible _____.

sounds or phonemes

7. In the alphabetic system, there is often not a one-to-one correspondence between letters and the _____ they represent.

bottom-up

knowledge

8. Reading requires both _____ processing, in which words are recognized and combined into phrases, and top-down processing, in which information is integrated with previous _____.

decode

9. A basic task of early readers is learning to _____ the sets of letters that make up words.

10. Late in the elementary school years, children read to _____ rather than simply learning to read.

    learn

11. _____ teaching is a method for increasing reading comprehension through guided discussions of a segment of text.

    Reciprocal

12. According to Rochel Gelman and her colleagues, learning mathematics requires: conceptual knowledge, the ability to understand the principles underlying a problem; _____ knowledge, the ability to carry out a sequence of actions to solve a problem; and _____ knowledge, the ability to know when to apply particular procedures.

    procedural

    utilization

13. Even societies with no formal schooling have developed systems for _____ and doing arithmetic problems.

    counting

14. Modern mathematics instruction includes both _____ in computation and practice in _____ computation skills to new problems.

    drill
    generalizing

15. One kind of instructional _____ is the initiation-reply-_____ sequence.

    discourse
    evaluation

16. _____ does not have an appreciable effect on children's development of concrete operations.

    Schooling

17. When asked for their associations to a word, children who have been to school are likely to respond with another word from the same _____.

    category

18. Schooled children do better than unschooled children at _____ lists of unrelated materials; they are also better able to describe the logic underlying their solutions to problems, an ability called _____.

    remembering

    metacognition

19. A child's _____ is arrived at by dividing _____ by chronological age and multiplying by 100.

    IQ, mental age

20. According to the _____ hypothesis of IQ, differences between people's intelligence scores are due mainly to inborn factors; the environmentalist hypothesis, on the other hand, views intelligence as being highly dependent on _____.

    innatist

    experience or environment

school

21. Modern intelligence tests are moderately good at predicting children's performance in _____.

culture

22. It has not yet proved possible to develop an intelligence test that is truly _____-free.

between

23. While about half the variability in IQ scores within ethnic groups may be due to inherited factors, there is no evidence that differences _____ groups are genetically based.

peer

24. Research by William Labov and Clarence Robbins demonstrated that participation in some _____ groups may negatively affect children's school performance.

academic
praise
teachers

25. Michael Rutter and his colleagues found that the most successful schools were those which had a strong _____ emphasis, which relied on _____ rather than punishment, stressed student responsibility, and whose _____ were skilled in coordinating the class.

Multiple-Choice Questions

Circle the letter of the word or phrase that correctly completes each statement.

1. In which way is apprenticeship training different from formal schooling?
   a. In apprenticeship training, relatively little explicit instruction is given.
   b. In apprenticeship training, knowledge is immediately put to practical use.
   c. The shop in which an apprentice works is likely to contain people of diverse ages and skill levels.
   d. All of the above

2. The symbols in the alphabet represent
   a. phonemes.
   b. morphemes.
   c. basic concepts.
   d. syllables.

3. When children can recognize the logo of their favorite fast-food restaurant
   a. it means that they know how to read.
   b. they are taking a first step in learning to read.
   c. they are using "bottom up" processing.
   d. it means that they have reached the stage of concrete operations.

4. Today, a typical reading curriculum emphasizes
    a.   the look-say method.
    b.   learning letter-sound correspondences.
    c.   reading for meaning.
    d.   both b and c

5. The school cutoff strategy allows researchers to investigate
    a.   the problem-solving abilities of children who drop out of school.
    b.   the effect of schooling on children's cognitive abilities.
    c.   differences in IQ among ethnic groups.
    d.   the effect of teacher expectations on achievement.

6. Which is an example of instructional discourse?
    a.   On the first day of school, the teacher asks a child, "What is your name?"
    b.   The teacher asks the class, "Has anyone seen my red pencil?"
    c.   After writing a word on the blackboard, the teacher asks, "What does this say?"
    d.   All of the above are examples

7. Schooling affects children's performance on which of the following?
    a.   Memory for items connected by an everyday script.
    b.   Concrete operations in everyday contexts.
    c.   Ability to describe their mental activities.
    d.   All of the above

8. A 9-year-old child with a mental age of 10 has an IQ of
    a.   90.
    b.   100.
    c.   119.
    d.   111.

9. Intelligence tests are composed of questions that
    a.   can be answered equally well by children of the same age.
    b.   are culture-free.
    c.   are ordered from least to most difficult.
    d.   are selected to be unrelated to school performance.

10. Studies of heritability of intelligence have shown that
    a.   differences in IQ scores within cultural groups is attributable, to some extent, to genetic factors.
    b.   differences in IQ scores between cultural groups are largely attributable to genetic factors.
    c.   about 50 percent of each person's IQ score is caused by genetic factors.
    d.   All of the above

11. While studying secondary schools in central London, Michael Rutter and his colleagues found that the most successful schools were those that
    a.   served students with higher IQs.
    b.   punished students whenever they misbehaved.
    c.   had more modern buildings and better paid teachers.
    d.   expected a great deal of students and emphasized academic achievement.

12. Carol Dweck and her colleagues, studying teachers' expectations of boys and girls in the classroom, found that
    a.   boys are better behaved than girls during elementary school.
    b.   overall, teachers criticize girls more than boys.
    c.   girls are likely to be praised for cooperation rather than intellectual accomplishments.
    d.   boys are less likely than girls to blame others for their own poor performance.

Short-Answer Questions

1.   Discuss the differences between apprenticeship education and school learning.

2.   What differences have been found between the performance of schooled and unschooled children on cognitive tasks?

3.   Describe the basic elements of standardized intelligence testing.

4.   What evidence is there for the importance of genetic factors in determining children's IQs? What evidence is there for the importance of environmental factors?

5.   Discuss the contribution children's families make to their success in school.

Putting It All Together

Look back at the information on gene-environment interactions in Chapter 2. On the basis of what you have learned from Chapter 2 and from Chapter 13, discuss why it is difficult to assess the role of genetic factors in intelligence. In what ways does feedback in gene-environment interactions complicate the picture?

Sources of More Information

Baumeister, Alfred A. "Mental Retardation: Some Conceptions And Dilemmas." *American Psychologist*, 1987, *42* (8), 796-800.
This discussion of mental retardation touches on some of the issues involved in the use of standardized tests to measure intelligence.

Bissex, Glenda L. *Guys at Work: A Child Learns to Write and Read*. Cambridge. Mass.: Harvard University Press, 1980.
This case study follows one child from age 5 to age 11 as he learns to read and write.

Copeland, Richard. *How Children Learn Mathematics: Teaching Implications of Piaget's Research*, 4th ed. New York: Macmillan, 1984.
This is a Piagetian approach to the learning of mathematics in the elementary classroom. There are good descriptions of the many numerical concepts children acquire as they learn to manipulate numbers.

Eisenstein, Elizabeth L. On the Printing Press as an Agent of Change. In David Olson, Nancy Torrance, and Angela Hildyard (Eds.), *Literacy, Language and Learning: The Nature and Consequences of Reading and Writing*. Cambridge: Cambridge University Press, 1985.
This is a discussion of social change as related to the invention of literacy.

Gardner, Howard. *Frames of Mind: The Theory of Multiple Intelligences*. New York: Basic Books, 1983, 1985 (paperback).
This book presents Gardner's theory that every person has a unique set of competencies that together comprise his or her intelligence. Gardner describes seven intelligences, some of which are not included in commonly used IQ tests.

Nichols, Robert C. "Schools and the Disadvantaged" (A Summary of the Coleman Report). In Urie Bronfenbrenner and Maureen Mahony (Eds.), *Influences on Human Development*, 2nd ed. Hinsdale, Ill.: Dryden, 1975.
A discussion of how the environment of education affects children's academic achievement.

Saxe, Geoffrey B. *Culture and Cognitive Development: Studies in Mathematical Understanding*. Hillsdale, N.J.: Erlbaum, 1991.
This book describes a series of studies of the development of mathematical thinking among children who sell candy on the street in Recife, Brazil.

Trotter, Robert J. "Three Heads Are Better Than One." *Psychology Today*, August 1986, 56-62.
This article presents Robert Sternberg's triarchic theory, which hypothesizes componential, experiential, and contextual aspects of intelligence.

Answer Key

Answers to Key Terms: j, k, q, c, f, n, a, i, g, l, r, b, d, m,o, e, p, h.

Answers to Multiple-Choice Questions: 1. d, 2. a, 3. b, 4. d, 5. b, 6. c, 7. c, 8. d, 9. c, 10. a, 11. d, 12. c.

Social Development in Middle Childhood

Although the changes that usher in the period called middle childhood are biological, behavioral, and social, it is in the social domain that the greatest discontinuities in development arise as children move from the shelter of parental supervision to new contexts and challenges. Six- to 12-year-olds are more often left to the company of their peers than they were during the preschool period. They are expected to take responsibility for their activities during this time, get along with other children, and follow the social rules of their society even when no one is watching. They are also expected to take on personal responsibilities, such as completing homework, practicing musical instruments, feeding pets, and regulating their own behavior in numerous other ways. Their play begins to include more complex and competitive games, and the role-playing of early childhood gives way to Scrabble and Monopoly.

These changes in social behavior depend to some extent on the cognitive abilities that children are developing. At the same time, new opportunities for interaction with other children serve in turn as stimuli for further cognitive development. Parents and teachers recognize children's greater competencies and adjust their expectations accordingly. And cultural variations in behavior become more pronounced as the adults in children's environments push them toward the kinds of skills and social interactions that are valued and useful in their particular societies.

Chapter Outline

During middle childhood, children spend more time than before with *peers*, children of their own age and status, and less time with parents. When playing with peers, children engage in different activities than they do when adults are present; also, their behavior is regulated by different forms of social control. Children's sense of themselves changes as they come to inhabit new contexts, and parental socialization techniques shift from physically removing them from danger to explanation and discussion. Because children spend more time away from adult supervision, it is also more difficult for psychologists to study their behavior in contexts outside of school.

I.   GAMES AND GROUP REGULATION

It appears that game-playing is an important area in which children develop the ability to regulate their own social interactions.

A.   In middle childhood, children continue the fantasy play, based on *roles*, begun in the preschool period; now, however, games based on *rules* move into a position of prominence. Rule-based games require children to pursue goals while keeping a set of overall task conditions in mind, to engage in social perspective-taking, and to coordinate their own actions with those of other players. Rule-based games often involve larger groups and typically last longer than preschoolers' interactions.

B.   According to Piaget, rule-based games are a manifestation of concrete operations in children's social spheres, and they contribute to development by providing structured circumstances in which children can practice balancing the rules of society against their own desires. Rule-based games are similar to social institutions, and the give-and-take of game-playing helps children develop cooperation and an understanding of social rules. As discussed in Box 14.1, organized sports such as Little League are important for some children in this age group. Piaget studied children's ideas about rules by observing them playing the game of marbles. He concluded that preschoolers had no particular idea of the rules or any sense of competition. During middle childhood, children began to play to win. At first, children would not agree to any alterations in the rules, believing that they had been handed down by authority figures and could not be changed; between the ages of 9 and 11, they began to treat the rules as social conventions that could be changed if the other players agreed. Piaget found that boys engaged in more competitive play based on rules than girls did during middle childhood, a finding that has been confirmed by Janet Lever's observations, and is discussed in Box 14.2. Boys also tend to play in larger groups. However, rule-based games increase in importance during middle childhood for children of both sexes.

II. RULES OF BEHAVIOR

During middle childhood, children must learn to understand social rules in several different domains. From most general to most specific, these are *moral rules*, such as prohibitions against killing and stealing and ideas about fairness that are found in some form in all societies; *social conventions* regulating such things as sex-typed behavior, which are specific to particular societies; *group norms*, which apply to small groups such as peer groups; and *personal rules*, which are created by individuals to regulate their own behavior. Three- and 4-year-old North American children are able to recognize differences between moral principles and social conventions; by middle childhood, they can rank the various types of rules by importance. Larry Nucci found that, when asked to compare violations of rules, children ranked moral violations as most serious, then violations of social conventions; they ranked violations of personal rules as least serious.

A. Piaget found that during middle childhood, children's *morality of constraint* began to give way to *autonomous moral reasoning*. This, he thought, paralleled their developing understanding about the rules of games. Lawrence Kohlberg modified and elaborated on Piaget's ideas about moral thinking. Based on subjects' responses to a series of story-dilemmas, Kohlberg classified moral reasoning into six stages—two stages at each of three levels—representing people's thinking from 3 years of age through adulthood. Kohlberg found that children at Stage 1 (coinciding with the preschool period and the beginning of middle childhood) adopt an *egocentric* point of view and base their judgments on objective outcome. Stage 2 reasoning appears at around 7-8 years of age. Children's viewpoints are still egocentric, and their judgments are characterized by *instrumental morality* (the idea that it is okay to use others for one's own interest). At 10 or 11 years of age, children's moral judgments are made on the basis of a *social-relational perspective*, in which agreement with others is seen as important and reasoning is similar to the Golden Rule.

B. In a different approach to the study of moral development, William Damon studied 4-to 12-year-olds' ideas about *positive justice*, how resources should be divided or rewards distributed. The responses he obtained indicated that, as with reasoning about breaking rules, ideas of fairness develop through a sequence of levels: under 4 years of age, children simply state their desires, giving no reasons for their choice; 4- to 5-year-olds state their desires but justify their choices on the basis of external characteristics ("The girls should get more," for example); 5- to 7-year-olds tend to believe that strict equality is the only fair treatment when dividing resources. From about age 8 on, notions of deservingness and merit enter children's reasoning; as they become older, children are better able to coordinate the factors involved to ensure a fair outcome in a particular situation.

Theresa Thorkildsen studied children's ability to consider context in reasoning about fairness. In a study of 6- to 11-year-olds, she found that children's judgments of when it was fair to help another person differed depending on the activity involved (for example, it was fair to help another child during a class lesson but not during a test or a spelling bee). The 6-year-olds were as good as the 11-year-olds in taking context into account.

C.   How does children's reasoning about fairness correspond to their actual behavior? Damon performed a study in which children were asked to divide candy bars given to their group as "payment" for making bracelets. He found that in about 50 percent of the cases, children's behavior matched their reasoning level; in 10 percent of the cases, their behavior was at a higher level; and in 40 percent, it was lower. Similar results have been obtained by other investigators.

D.   Elliot Turiel and his colleagues used an interviewing technique to study the development of children's reasoning about social conventions, such as the one that certain occupations are more appropriate for men or for women. He found that children passed through three levels of reasoning about conventions: at the first level, they treated conventions as reflecting the natural order of things; at the second, they rejected the need for conventions; and at the third level, they recognized that, although they are arbitrary, social conventions do serve some purpose in regulating social life. However, while cross-cultural studies have found similar results in many societies, there are cultures in which breaches of social conventions are considered more like moral violations than they are in the U.S.

III.   RELATIONS WITH OTHER CHILDREN

During middle childhood, children need more than ever to be able to make places for themselves within the social group.

A.   According to Willard Hartup, friendships serve four main functions: they allow children to develop and practice social skills; they provide children with information about themselves, others and the world; they provide fun and relieve stress; and they provide models of intimate relationships.
• Proximity is an important factor in determining who children become friends with. Friends are also likely to be of the same age, race, and sex and to feel the same way about school, sports, and music. In a study by John Gottman, pairs of 3- to 9-year-olds were given several opportunities to play together. Those that became friendly tended to have interactions characterized by: common-ground activity; communication clarity; exchanging information; resolving conflict; and reciprocity.
• During middle childhood, children are sensitive to their status among their peers and become more concerned about being rejected or having their feelings hurt. Gossip becomes an important aspect of social interactions and serves as a means for children to exchange information and find out what their friends think, so that they will know how to behave.

- During middle childhood, children tend to segregate themselves by sex, as discussed in Box 14.3, although boys and girls do participate in joint activities on many occasions. Boys tend to have larger groups of friends and to play more boisterous, competitive games; girls have fewer, more intimate friends with whom they share feelings and exchange confidences. The sexes mix more often during large-group activities and when the supply of potential companions is limited.

- Making and keeping friends requires *social competence*—skills that depend on being able to understand how others think and feel. In a study of social perspective-taking, Robert Selman found that those children who were skilled at taking another's perspective also had more sophisticated ideas about friendship. These results fit in with Piaget's idea that egocentrism restricts young children to their own points of view, while older children can keep more than one aspect of a problem in mind.

- Observations have shown that children with higher levels of reasoning about friendship are better at getting along with others; better skills in reasoning give children *social repair mechanisms* that allow them to remain friends when differences arise, thus permitting greater freedom from adult supervision.

B. The relative popularity of children in a group can be studied using the *nomination procedure* to construct a *sociogram* of friendship choices. The children named as friends by the most people are assumed to be the most popular. Researchers can also use *rating scales* to assess popularity. Using such data, Steven Asher and John Coie's system categorizes children as popular, rejected, neglected, or controversial.

- Many studies have found that popularity is related to physical attractiveness; this effect is stronger for girls than for boys. Intelligence and social competence also contribute to popularity. Studies have shown that children who are aggressive, and have lower levels of cognitive ability and social competence are most likely to be rejected by peers. Neglected children are less sociable than others but are not aggressive, and are better able to improve their social status than are rejected children. Controversial children may be aggressive but have compensating cognitive and social skills; neglected and controversial children tend not to be distressed by their lack of social success and to have at least one friend.

- Some studies of popularity have involved bringing unacquainted children together and observing the development of their relationships. In one such study of unacquainted boys, Kenneth Dodge found that those who became popular were helpful, reminded others of the rules, and were not aggressive; the boys who were rejected were more physically and verbally aggressive than the others and were also more talkative and active. Boys neglected by group members were those who rarely interacted with the others. According to Dodge, the ability to enter an existing group is important in differentiating popular from unpopular children. Work by Dodge and his colleagues has shown that aggressive behavior and low social status may be rooted in lack of social understanding. Other investigators have also found that, once children's social reputations are established they may become self-perpetuating; for example, a child's behavior may be viewed as unfriendly when, by objective standards, it is not.

• Rejected children have difficulty reading the emotional states of others and controlling their own emotions. The reactions of others to their behavior only makes things worse. Programs designed to shape more appropriate social behavior have produced improvements in social competence and peer acceptance.

• Even when adults are not present, they influence peer interactions through social norms that shape patterns of behavior. For example, Thomas Dishion found that socially rejected boys were exposed to more coercive family experiences and were judged more aggressive than their peers. Poverty acted as an indirect cause by increasing family stress, making coercive discipline more likely.

C.   The socialization patterns of cultural groups also influence children's behavior. For example, studies by Millard Madsen and his colleagues have explored the way that groups choose cooperation or competition to solve problems. He found that Israeli kibbutz children, socialized to cooperate, performed significantly better on a task requiring cooperation than did urban Israeli children. Research in other countries supports the finding that culture influences group interaction. As discussed in Box 14.4, just as children must learn to get along within a group, groups must learn to get along with one another. Muzafer and Carolyn Sherif, in a summer camp experiment, found that intergroup competition can lead to conflict and hostility. Simply getting the members of two feuding groups together under pleasant circumstances did nothing to reduce hostility, the Sherifs found. Mutual respect replaced dislike only when members of both groups had to cooperate to solve problems affecting everyone's welfare.

• Does experience with peer interactions help children to develop social-cognitive skills? Marida Hollos found that while Norwegian and Hungarian children growing up on isolated farms scored just as well as village and town children on tasks measuring logical operations, they were less skilled at social perspective taking tasks. Psychiatrist Harry Stack Sullivan believed the experience of friendship during middle childhood to be a necessary precursor of interpersonal intimacy during adulthood. It appears that peer interaction plays an important role in social-cognitive development during middle childhood; however, relations with parents also remain crucial.

IV.   CHANGING RELATIONS WITH PARENTS

By the time children, are about 9 years old, their parents are less willing to shelter them than they were previously; parents expect more adult behavior from their children and adopt different strategies for correcting misbehavior when it occurs. Now, more of children's activities are carried out away from adult supervision. This is especially true for children of working mothers. Research on the effect of maternal employment, reported in Box 14.5, suggests that it depends on such factors as socioeconomic status, race, family structure, parental attitudes, and where the family lives. Girls seem to be positively affected by having mothers who work, while sons of working mothers are somewhat less well-adjusted than boys whose mothers are not employed outside the home.

Parental child-rearing strategies shift during middle childhood; when children break the rules, the consequences are more likely to involve removal of privileges than spankings. *Coregulation*, in which responsibility for controlling children's behavior is shared by parents and children, increases as children grow.

V.   A New Sense of Self

Changes in children's social lives during middle childhood are accompanied by changes in their sense of themselves.

A.   At the start of middle childhood, children think of themselves as defined by their bodies and deny that what people say may not be the same as what they think. They next develop a sense of separate inner and outer experience but, according to research by Robert Selman, believe that these must be consistent. By about 8 years of age, children realize that outward appearance and inner experience may differ and that people have private selves which cannot always be read from their behavior.

B.   Children now begin to define themselves in comparison with other children, a process called *social comparison*. Diane Ruble and her colleagues studied the development of social comparison in middle childhood by manipulating the feedback they gave children about their performance on a basketball task. Nine-year-olds who were told the hypothetical scores of previous participants rated their own performance as good or bad relative to these scores; however, 5- and 7-year-olds were equally pleased with their performance regardless of the supposed scores of other children.

C.   The new expectations faced by children during middle childhood are challenges to their self-esteem. Susan Harter and Robin Pike found that by the time they are 8 years old, children's evaluations of their cognitive, social, and physical competence began to agree with the judgments of their peers and teachers. Stanley Coopersmith discovered that 10- to 12-year-old boys with high self-esteem had parents whose style of child-rearing included acceptance, clearly defined limits, and respect for individuality—characteristics similar to those of Diana Baumrind's "authoritative" parents. The key to high self-esteem seems to be a feeling of control over oneself and one's environment. A positive self-image during childhood is linked to happiness and satisfaction in later life.

VI. Middle Childhood Reconsidered

When the biological, behavioral, and social components of middle childhood are considered separately, development appears relatively continuous with that of the preschool period. However, the consequence of changes in these domains is a distinctive combination of factors resulting in a bio-social-behavioral shift to a new period of development.

Key Terms

Following are important terms introduced in Chapter 14. In the space to the right, write the definition of the term. In the space to the left, write the letter of the example that best illustrates the term.

_____ coregulation _____

_____ group norms _____

_____ moral rules _____

_____ nomination procedure _____

_____ peers _____

_____ personal rules _____

_____ positive justice _____

_____ rating scale _____

_____ social comparison _____

_____ social competence _____

_____ social conventions _____

_____ social-relational moral perspective _____

_____ social repair mechanisms _____

_____ sociogram _____

a.   "Start on homework right after school" is an example.
b.   A collection of skills that help along children's relationships with their peers.
c.   For young children, these are provided by caretakers; for older children, their ability to reason about interpersonal relationships is a source of these.
d.   For a child in the third grade, these would be other third-graders.
e.   This involves asking each child in a group which children he likes to play with.
f.   This characterizes children's moral judgments beginning at about age 10 or 11.
g.   "It is wrong to kill other people" is an example.
h.   A child describes herself as "the best reader in the class."
i.   The Girl Scout Laws are examples

j. Children learn, for example, how to divide a dozen cookies among five children.

k. Wearing a bathing suit to school would violate one of these.

l. This involves sharing responsibility for children's behavior between children and parents.

m. These graphic representations of social relations are often used in research.

n. A child using this might assign a number to how much he or she likes a particular other child.

Fill-in Questions

Cover the list of answers next to the statements below and fill in each blank with the word or phrase that correctly completes the sentence.

1. It can be difficult to study children's social development during middle childhood because much of their behavior takes place outside _____ supervision.

   adult

2. While the play of preschoolers is based largely on roles, that of older children is characterized by games based on _____.

   rules

3. Piaget felt that rule-based games are a manifestation of _____ in the social sphere.

   concrete operations

4. During middle childhood, children learn to understand social rules at three different levels: _____ rules, such as prohibitions against killing; _____ conventions, such as what clothes people should wear in public; and _____ rules, such as completing homework before watching TV.

   moral
   social
   personal

5. Boys are more likely than girls to engage in games based on explicit _____; girls tend to play less complex games in _____ groups.

   rules
   smaller

6. In the moral reasoning of Stage _____, characterized by "instrumental morality," justice is seen as an exchange system.

   2

7. In Stage 3 reasoning, achieved by 10 or 11 years of age, judgments are made on the basis of a _____ perspective.

   social-relational

8. William Damon studied children's ideas about _____ justice, the process of deciding how resources or rewards should be distributed.

   positive

fairness

9. Theresa Thorkildsen found that, for both adults and children, judgments about _____ depend on the activity being described.

behavior
lower

10. Damon found that about half of the time the level of children's reasoning matched their _____ in a real situation; those who did not match were likely to behave at a _____ level than their reasoning.

11. Elliot Turiel and his colleagues have demonstrated that reasoning about moral rules and reasoning about social conventions are _____.

independent

pretend

12. To 3- and 4-year-olds, the major focus of friendship is _____ play; belonging and acceptance are important themes in the friendships of _____ childhood.

middle

13. During middle childhood, children become aware of their relative social _____.

status

14. Girls tend to be socialized more for cooperation, while boys are socialized for _____.

competition

larger

15. During middle childhood, boys tend to have _____ groups of friends than girls, while girls' friendships tend to be more _____ than boys'.

intimate

16. According to Robert Selman, developmental changes in conceptions of friendship are a result of changes in children's ability to take another's _____; higher levels of reasoning provide older children with social _____ mechanisms that make relationships work more smoothly.

perspective
repair

sociogram

17. A _____ is a graphic representation of children's popularity within a group.

attractiveness
competence

18. Popularity is related to physical _____ and to having a high degree of social _____.

aggressive.

19. Kenneth Dodge and his colleagues found that social rejected boys were more active, talkative, and _____ than more popular children.

20. Unfortunately, children may be rejected by others if the group has already formed _____ opinions of them, even if the opinions no longer fit their behavior.

negative

21. Children from cultures that value group cohesion over individualism perform better on problem-solving tasks requiring _____.

cooperation

22. Muzafer and Carolyn Sherif found that by setting up situations requiring two groups of boys to cooperate with one another, they could reverse hostility caused by _____ between the groups.

competition

23. Marida Hollos found that children who had many opportunities for _____ interaction performed better on a perspective-taking task than those growing up in isolation from peers.

peer

24. According to psychiatrist Harry Stack Sullivan, if children fail to form _____ during middle childhood, their later interpersonal relationships will suffer.

friendships

25. Parents of older children expect their children to behave in a more _____ manner than they did when they were younger.

responsible

26. During middle childhood, parental control over children's behavior is gradually replaced by _____.

coregulation

27. Preschoolers have a physicalistic view of the _____, equating it with particular activities and physical characteristics; older children realize that a person's _____ appearance may differ from his or her _____ experience.

self

outer
inner

28. Social _____ becomes more important in children's self-definitions during middle childhood.

comparison

29. Parents who are accepting of their children, set clearly defined limits, and respect their children's individuality, have children with high _____.

self-esteem

30. Although the changes associated with middle childhood do not appear stagelike when viewed separately, taken together they form the pattern characteristic of a _____ shift.

bio-social-behavioral

Multiple-Choice Questions

Circle the letter of the word or phrase that correctly completes each statement.

1. Compared with parents of younger children, parents of children in middle childhood are more likely to
   a. restrict the time children spend with peers.
   b. use physical force to control their children.
   c. rely on coregulation in controlling their children's behavior.
   d. supervise their children closely.

2. During middle childhood, _____ become(s) more important in children's play.
   a. rule-based games
   b. role-playing
   c. props such as blocks and dolls
   d. fantasy

3. Compared to girls, boys' play during middle childhood
   a. is more complex.
   b. involves larger groups.
   c. is more competitive.
   d. All of the above

4. _____, such as prohibitions against killing and stealing, are found in all societies.
   a. Social conventions
   b. Personal rules
   c. Group norms
   d. Moral rules

5. During middle childhood, which type of social rule violations do children consider least serious?
   a. Violations of moral rules
   b. Violations of personal rules
   c. Violations of social conventions
   d. They consider all types of violations equally serious.

6. Lawrence Kohlberg studied children's moral reasoning by
   a. observing their behavior on the playground.
   b. asking them to react to moral dilemmas presented in stories.
   c. asking them about the morality of their own behavior.
   d. exposing them to real moral dilemmas and observing their responses.

7. William Damon found that children's reasoning about positive justice
   a. corresponds to their behavior in nearly all cases.
   b. corresponds to their behavior about half of the time.
   c. is usually at a lower level than their behavior.
   d. almost never corresponds to their behavior.

8. According to Robert Selman, children's increasing ability to _____ leads to changes in their conceptions of friendship.
   a. conserve
   b. remember lists of unrelated materials
   c. take another person's perspective
   d. engage in logical classification

9. Shapira and Madsen found that _____ children performed best on a task requiring cooperation.
   a. middle-class urban Israeli
   b. suburban U. S.
   c. U. S. farm
   d. Israeli kibbutz

10. Children whose self-esteem is high tend to have parents who
    a. are accepting of them.
    b. set clearly defined limits for them.
    c. have respect for their individuality.
    d. All of the above

Short-Answer Questions

1. Why did Piaget feel that rule-based games were an important part of development during middle childhood?

2. Give examples of the kinds of moral reasoning typical of children in Lawrence Kohlberg's Stages 1, 2, and 3.

3. What factors influence children's popularity within a group? What relationship exists between social status and level of social competence?

4. Discuss the effects of maternal employment on children's development, and the factors that influence these effects.

5. What major changes occur in children's sense of themselves during the years of middle childhood?

Putting It All Together

Look back at the material on play in Chapters 6 and 10 for help in completing this assignment.

I. Match each of the following examples of play to the developmental period of which it is most characteristic.

_____   1. Stirring a cup of sand "coffee" with a twig.
_____   2. Playing cops and robbers.
_____   3. Playing kickball.
_____   4. Banging a hammer on the table.
_____   5. Jumping rope.
_____   6. Cooking a meal on a play stove.
_____   7. Dressing up in extremely sex-stereotyped clothes.

a. Early infancy (less than 18 months)
b. Late infancy (18-30 months)
c. The preschool period
d. Middle childhood

II. Using an example from each period, show how children's play during infancy, the preschool period, and middle childhood reflects their increasing cognitive skills and how play, in turn, promotes further cognitive development.

Additional Resources

Chance, Paul. "Your Child's Self-esteem." *Parents Magazine*, January 1982.
This article discusses the advantages of strong parent-child relationships and early experiences of mastery for children's development.

Furth, Hans G. *The World of Grown-ups: Children's Conceptions of Society*. New York: Elsevier, 1980.
This book, based on interviews with British children, aged 5 to 11, applies Piaget's developmental model to children's understanding of society and its institutions.

Kohlberg, Lawrence. *Essays on Moral Development: Vol. II. The Psychology of Moral Development: Moral Stages, Their Nature and Validity*. San Francisco: Harper & Row, 1984.
This is a good source of material on Kohlberg's views of moral dilemmas and the theory behind them.

Piaget, Jean. *The Moral Judgment of the Child*. New York: Free Press, 1965.
A report of Piaget's original work on the development of moral reasoning.

Rubin, Zick. *Children's Friendships*. Cambridge, Mass.: Harvard University Press, 1980.
This book describes the evolution of children's friendships, with a special emphasis on middle childhood.

Sernaque, Vivienne. *Classic Children's Games*. New York: Dell, 1988.
This book contains descriptions of games appropriate for 2- to 4-year-olds, 4- to 6-year-olds, 6- to 8-year-olds, and 8- to 10-year-olds.

Soyinka, Wole. *Ake, the Years of Childhood*. New York: Random House, 1981.
An autobiographical account of growing up in an African village by a Nobel Prize-winning playwright, poet, and novelist.

Answer Key

Answers to Key Terms: l, i, g, e, d, a, j, n, h, b, k, f, c, m.

Answers to Multiple-Choice Questions: 1. c, 2. a, 3. d, 4. d, 5. b, 6. b, 7. b, 8. c, 9. d, 10. d.

Answers to Putting It All Together: 1. b, 2. c, 3. d, 4. a, 5. d, 6. c, 7. c.

Biological and Social Foundations of Adolescence

The end of middle childhood is announced by radical biological changes. During puberty, young people's bodies become adult, both in size and in their capacity for biological reproduction. In industrialized nations, the age at which puberty occurs has gradually fallen over the last 200 years; at the same time, technological developments have increased the amount of education young people need in order to become independent members of society. The result has been a shortening of middle childhood and a lengthening of adolescence—the transitional stage between biological maturity and the full independence of adulthood.

According to many theorists, adolescence is a time of emotional upheaval caused both by hormonal changes and by new social arrangements that characterize this stage. After a long period of relative segregation, boys and girls develop an interest in one another, and peer groups support them in establishing attachments with members of the opposite sex. Relations with parents are also in transition, as adolescents move from positions of dependence to more egalitarian relationships. Many adolescents hold paying jobs, contributing to their feeling of independence. Still, according to our society, adolescents are not ready for adult privileges and need to be protected from adult responsibilities. The resulting separation between biological, behavioral, and social aspects of development gives adolescence its unique character.

Chapter Outline

The bio-social-behavioral shift that marks the end of middle childhood includes major changes: the greatest biological transition since birth results in reproductive capability; boys and girls begin to interact in new social configurations; and children's relationships with their parents change as they become more independent.

I.   TRADITIONAL CONCEPTIONS OF ADOLESCENCE

Modern conceptions of adolescence still reflect the opinions of eighteenth- and nineteenth-century scholars who wrote of it as a distinct period of life. According to Jean-Jacques Rousseau, adolescents are characterized by heightened emotional instability as they *recapitulate* earlier stages of development; their cognitive processes undergo a change to self-conscious thought and logical reasoning ability. At the end of the nineteenth century, Rousseau's ideas were adopted by G. Stanley Hall and other psychologists, who attempted to construct a theory of individual development based on Darwin's ideas of evolution. In particular, Hall embraced *recapitulationism*, the idea that "ontogeny recapitulates phylogeny"—that is, the evolutionary history of the species is repeated in the development of the individual child. This idea is now discredited; however, it has influenced the ideas of many theorists.

II.   MODERN THEORIES OF ADOLESCENCE

Although no one theory of adolescence is widely accepted at this time, there are theories based on the four theoretical perspectives examined in the text.

A.   Two influential theorists have brought biological-maturation perspectives to the study of adolescence.
   • Arnold Gesell agreed with Hall and others that children's development recapitulates human evolutionary history; therefore, he thought, "higher" human traits such as abstract thought, imagination, and self-control appear late in development, during adolescence. Gesell believed that biological factors determine the basic pattern of adolescent psychological functioning.
   • In Sigmund Freud's theory, adolescence corresponds to the *genital stage* of development. Reawakening primitive instincts upset the adolescent's psychological

balance, producing conflict and erratic behavior, and young people must rework old conflicts associated with earlier stages.

• Some researchers have applied theories and methods from ethology to the study of adolescence. For example, Ritch Savin-Williams has studied social hierarchies and aggressive behavior among teenagers. Other studies have found that, in non-human primates, males go through a period between the juvenile and adult stages of life that resembles human adolescence.

B. Environmental-learning theorists have argued that biological-maturation approaches overestimate the degree of discontinuity between childhood and adolescence and overestimate the importance of biological factors in shaping behavior. For example, according to Albert Bandura and Richard Walter, aggressiveness in adolescent boys is not an innate predisposition but a product of reinforcement by others. According to the environmental-learning approach, the same principles that explain behavior in all other age groups can be applied to understanding the behavior of adolescents. Several strategies have been used to highlight the effects of environment on adolescent development: studying societies in which teenagers do not display some presumably universal characteristic of adolescence (for example, Margaret Mead's study in Samoa); looking at ways in which naturally-occurring variations within a cultural group affect behavior (for example, Diana Baumrind's work on parenting styles); and designing experimental programs to modify behavior (for example, Nancy Guerra and Ronald Slaby's training program for juvenile offenders).

C. The constructivist perspective is represented by the theories of Jean Piaget and Erik Erikson. Piaget and his colleague Barbel Inhelder emphasized the transition during adolescence from concrete to formal operational thought. This new mode of thinking, they felt, affected many aspects of adolescents' lives. According to Erikson, the main developmental task facing adolescents is to incorporate into a healthy personality their new sexual drives and the new social demands made upon them—to form an *identity*. Erikson views adolescence as an important time during which individual and social identity must be made compatible

D. Psychologists who view adolescence from the cultural-context perspective note that while in some societies adolescence appears to be a distinct stage of life, this is not universally true. For example, in some nonindustrial societies children reach biological maturity later than they do in industrialized nations; by the time young people in these societies are biologically mature, they are also competent to support themselves and raise a new generation. Children from industrialized nations, on the other hand, may require specialized education for many years after they reach biological maturity in order to be able to sustain themselves and their children.

III. PUBERTY

Puberty is a series of biological events that transform individuals from physical immaturity to physical and reproductive maturity. In the brain, the hypothalamus begins the process by signaling the pituitary gland to produce greater amounts of growth hormones and to produce hormones that will stimulate the *gonads*. The testes of boys will produce testosterone and the ovaries of girls will produce estrogen and progesterone; these, in turn, trigger the physical changes that accompany puberty.

A.   One of the first signs of puberty is a growth spurt during which boys and girls grow faster than at any time since infancy and reach 98 percent of their adult height. Different parts of the body develop at different rates: leg length typically reaches a peak first, followed by trunk length, and shoulder and chest width. The brain grows little, although the head increases in size as the skull bones thicken. Girls' hips widen and their breasts develop, while boys develop broader shoulders and thicker necks. Puberty also leads to differences in strength. Boys develop greater strength and greater capacity for exercise; girls, however, will on average live longer and be better able to tolerate long-term stress.

B.   The *primary sexual organs*, those involved in reproduction, become mature during puberty. In males, this means the production of sperm cells and semen; in females, it means that mature ova are released and menstruation occurs. During this time, *secondary sexual characteristics*—outward signs that distinguish males from females-appear.

Girls experience *menarche*, the first menstrual period, about 18 months after the growth spurt reaches its peak. Ovulation typically begins 12 to 18 months after menarche.

C.   There is wide variation between children in the age at which puberty begins. Both genetics and environment play a part in this. Identical twin girls reach menarche much closer in time than do fraternal twins, illustrating the role of genetics. The role of the environment can be seen in the effect of exercise on age of menarche. Dancers and other girls who participate in a high level of physical activity reach menarche later than average. Adolescents who experience a great deal of family conflict reach menarche earlier, according to several studies. In addition, a look at historical trends shows that in industrialized countries and some developing countries the age of menarche has been gradually declining during the last 150 years. Boys also seem to pass through puberty earlier than they did before. The events of puberty generally occur within a 4-year period, although this varies among individuals.

D.   The changes associated with puberty are perceived in varying ways by different individuals and by different cultural groups.
   • In many societies, *rites of passage* mark the transition into adolescence. These may take the form of formal initiation ceremonies.

- In societies in which there are no initiation ceremonies, individuals may not discuss publicly the events of puberty. Some researchers have studied adolescents' reactions to these events. For example, Jeanne Brooks-Gunn and her colleagues have studied girls' reactions to their first menstruation. They have found that girls' attitudes and beliefs about menstruation are strongly affected by expectations and previously-held assumptions as well as by their own direct experiences. Boys' responses to *semenarche* (their first ejaculations) depend on the context in which it occurs. Both boys and girls are secretive about the changes in their bodies. Girls may initially tell only their mothers, but eventually confide in their peers to a greater extent than boys do, thus receiving a greater amount of social support.

- Does the fact that an individual matures sexually earlier or later than his or her peers influence social adjustment, personality, or peer relations? In an early study, Mary Cover Jones and Nancy Bayley found early-maturing boys to be more psychologically and socially mature and better socially accepted than late maturers, who often compensated by attention-seeking behavior or withdrawal from social interaction. Later studies, however, have uncovered disadvantages of early maturation; for example, early-maturing boys are more likely to smoke, drink, use drugs, and get in trouble with the law. Studies of girls have also shown a mixed picture, but early maturation has fewer benefits for girls than for boys and is associated with increased social pressures and greater dissatisfaction with their bodies (see the discussion of eating disorders in Box 15.1). Little is known about how being an early or late maturer affects later life; by the time the boys in Jones and Bayley's study were approaching 40, differences between the groups had largely disappeared.

IV. THE REORGANIZATION OF SOCIAL LIFE

The biological changes that mark the end of childhood affect young people's social development in various ways.

A. Relationships with peers also change during adolescence. Peer interaction occupies more time and is less under the guidance and control of adults than it was before. Peer groups become larger and increasingly heterosexual.

- U.S. teenagers spend more time with peers than they do with their families or by themselves. While they now have more opportunities to meet people from different backgrounds, their friends tend to be even more similar to them than they were in elementary school. For 6- to 12-year-olds, participating in common activities is an important criterion for friendship; this is supplemented, in early adolescence, by common interests, similarity of attitudes and values, loyalty, and intimacy. Loyalty and intimacy are especially important to girls, who engage in a great deal of self-disclosure with close friends. This leads to a certain amount of possessiveness, which eases later in adolescence when girls need their best friends less and are therefore more tolerant of their friends' differences and their relationships with others. Fourteen- to 16-year-old boys form somewhat less close friendships than do girls. Because they are more concerned with their relationship to authority than girls are, boys need the loyalty and support of male friends to help then remain independent from parents and other adults. Friends serve adolescents of both sexes as a "secure base" that supports them as they confront and deal with anxiety-provoking situations. As more situations are negotiated successfully, dependence on friends lessens. Studies show that close friendships are beneficial for adolescents' social and personal development.

• Two new kinds of peer groups—family-sized *cliques* and larger *crowds*—become important during adolescence, and being considered a member of a particular crowd reflects on adolescents' social status. James S. Coleman found that both boys and girls felt that "having a good personality" was the most important characteristic for being in a "leading crowd" at school. Boys also ranked a good reputation, participation in athletics, good looks, nice clothes, and good grades as important; for girls, the other important things were good looks, nice clothes, and a good reputation. One out of five boys and girls said they would like to change themselves so as to be accepted by the leading crowd. In high schools with diverse student bodies, some crowds may be defined by ethnic group membership.

• Peer pressure to conform is strongest during early adolescence and then declines; however, it depends on the type of activity involved. While increased pressure increases the probability of misconduct, teenagers are, on the whole, less likely to give in when the suggested behavior is antisocial than when it is neutral. Some behaviors considered antisocial in adolescence—smoking and drinking, for example—are considered acceptable for adults, raising the possibility that adolescents may simply be modeling adult behavior when they engage in these activities. Box 15.2 discusses the problems of risk-taking and social deviance during adolescence.

• The most popular boys and girls often lead their peers in making the transition from participation in same-sex groups to participation in heterosexual groups. Dexter Dunphy studied this transition among Australian adolescents in the late 1950s. He discovered that, during early adolescence, young people tended to gather in same-sex cliques. Cliques became part of a larger crowd—a group of adolescents of both sexes who gathered at football games, ice cream parlors, and other public places. Next, adolescents began to form heterosexual relationships across cliques, going to parties and movies, while still spending much of their time in same-sex groups. Eventually, heterosexual cliques were formed and the crowd finally dissolved into loosely associated groups of couples. Contemporary evidence supports Dunphy's basic findings with two exceptions: today, marriage is delayed longer than it was at the time of his study; and crowds are not necessarily mixed male-female groups—some are all male or all female.

B. Social learning is important not only in developing sex roles, but in learning the behaviors associated with sexual activity. Harry Harlow's studies with monkeys highlighted the importance of interaction with other monkeys for later sexual behavior, and studies by Dr. Alfred Kinsey and his associates point out the importance of learning in such human sexual practices as petting, a practice that has become much more widespread during the twentieth century.

• Sexual behavior can be thought of as a scripted activity progressing from kissing through intermediate stages to sexual intercourse, according to John Gagnon and

William Simon. Their scripted knowledge gives young people an idea of the roles they are supposed to play and gives sexual meaning to activities such as holding hands and kissing. Scripted activities are not organized in the same way in all cultures. For example, as described in Box 15.3, in Kenya at the turn of the century, the traditional Kikuyu script for adolescent sexual behavior included *ngweko*, a culturally sanctioned kind of lovemaking that did not involve direct genital contact.

• Males and females bring to sexual activity different expectations as a result of their different histories. Some of the differences are biological, resulting from the fact that sexual arousal in males is more straightforward and boys are more likely to have had experience with masturbation. Because of these differences, dating and courtship tend to be processes during which females become more committed to sexuality and males become more committed to romantic love than they were before.

• Boys and girls approach their first sexual intercourse differently. While nearly all boys and girls have their first experience with someone they know, girls more often describe their partner as a "boyfriend," while boys often describe their partner as a "friend." Boys are likely to report that their first intercourse was a positive experience; girls are likely to report feeling ambivalent.

• Adolescents engage in sexual intercourse in greater numbers and at earlier ages than they did several decades ago. An increase in the availability of contraception may have played some role in this trend, but most sexually active adolescents are inconsistent users of contraception. Recent worries about AIDS and other sexually transmitted diseases have resulted in greater condom use; however, more than half of sexually active high school students do not report protecting themselves. As discussed in Box 15.4, while surveys show U.S. teenagers to be no more sexually active than those in other countries, they are more likely to become pregnant. About one third of the pregnancies of 15- to 19-year-old girls end in abortion and another 14 percent end in miscarriages. Girls who give birth are more likely to keep their babies, even if they are unmarried, than to give them up for adoption. Race, social class, educational aspirations, and religious beliefs all affect the likelihood of a particular decision. Teenage motherhood is likely to interfere with a girl's educational plans and lead to economic hardship. In addition, babies of adolescents have higher rates of mortality and illness than do those born to older women.

C. During adolescence, young people's changing relations with their peers are accompanied by changes in their relationships with their parents. Studies conducted in the U.S. indicate that puberty plays a part in a reorganization of relationships between adolescents and their parents. A period of more frequent disagreements is typically followed by improved relations and greater autonomy for adolescent children. More noticeable changes take place in adolescent-mother relationships than in adolescent-father relationships.

• Although teenagers' appearance, dress, and behavior often suggest membership in a separate "youth culture," research shows that adolescents and their parents are in agreement about many important issues. A majority of the high school students surveyed by Denise Kandel and Gerald Lesser considered themselves "extremely" or "quite" close to their parents and wanted to be like their parents in many ways.

Adolescents are more likely to discuss personal matters with their mothers, seeking out fathers primarily when special advice is needed. Adolescents spend fair amounts of time with parents. However, time with parents is largely devoted to everyday activities such as shopping and eating, while relaxation and play are activities most often shared with peers.

• What are the subjects of adolescent-parent conflict? Mihaly Csikszentmihalyi and Reed Larson conducted a study in which adolescents carried beepers and filled out reports on their thoughts and feelings each time they were "beeped." They found that many parent-child conflicts center around matters of taste. These, however, may actually be expressions of conflict over independence and responsibility.

D. According to a study by Andrew Fuligni and Jacquelynne Eccles, there is an interaction between the influences of peers and parents on adolescents' behavior. When parents behave in ways that are authoritative but not authoritarian, adolescents retain a closer relationship with them and orient themselves less to peers. Children of authoritative parents are also more competent in school and less likely to get into trouble. Families and peer groups play complementary roles in reorganizing adolescents' social lives.

E. In the United States, children's first work experience comes from doing he household tasks, perhaps followed by neighborhood jobs such as babysitting and newspaper delivery. By age 15, many adolescents have regular part-time jobs. Each successive job that adolescents hold tends to be more responsible and substantial. By their mid-twenties, young people are generally working in adult careers. Studies indicate that as many as 60 percent of tenth graders and more than 75 percent of high school juniors and seniors are employed at some time during the school year. The number of hours worked per week increases with age. Teenagers from less advantaged families tend to work longer hours, and boys work more hours per week than girls. Minority and less-advantaged teenagers are less likely to have jobs; when they do, however, they tend to work longer hours than middle-class youths. Part-time employment has both positive and negative aspects. While it increases adolescents' self-confidence and provides practical knowledge of the business world, it does not typically provide on-the-job training that will be useful in adulthood, nor does it keep teenagers out of trouble. Employed teenagers also are less involved with school and their grades may decline, especially if they work many hours per week. Often, however, these teenagers were less committed to school even before they began working.

V.   THE BASIC BIO-SOCIAL DILEMA OF ADOLESCENCE

The basic bio-social dilemma of adolescence is that, in societies where adult rights and responsibilities are delayed relative to puberty, adolescents are biologically mature but socially immature and dependent. The gap between puberty and adulthood has widened over the years and the organization of work and schooling tends to segregate adolescents from adults and increase the influence of peers. The next chapter will examine changes in the quality of mind that accompany adolescence, and the ways in which the biological, social, and psychological domains interact, within a cultural context, to influence children's transition to adulthood.

Key Terms

Following are important terms introduced in Chapter 15. In the space to the right, write the definition of the term. In the space to the left, write the letter of the example that best illustrates the term.

_____ clique _____

_____ crowd _____

_____ genital stage _____

_____ gonads _____

_____ menarche _____

_____ puberty _____

_____ primary sexual organs _____

_____ recapitulationism _____

_____ secondary sexual characteristics _____

_____ semenarche _____

a.   These are directly involved in reproduction.
b.   The age at which girls reach this developmental milestone has declined by more than a year since the turn of the century.
c.   These outward signs of being male or female develop as a result of hormonal changes during adolescence.
d.   This series of biological changes constitutes the most radical change in p h y s i c a l development since birth.
e. · This idea grew out of enthusiasm for Darwin's theory of evolution.
f.   A boy's reaction to this event depends on the context in which it occurs.
g.   These produce testosterone or estrogen and progesterone.
h.   This has about the same number of members as a family, including grandparents.
i.   In Freud's theory, the period of mature sexuality.
j.   Examples of these are "jocks," "nerds," and "brains."

Fill-In Questions

Cover the list of answers next to the statements below and fill in each blank with the word or phrase that correctly completes the sentence.

social

1. During adolescence, biological changes are accompanied by changes in _____ life.

emotional
recapitulate

2. Jean-Jacques Rousseau felt that adolescence was a time of _____ conflict and instability; he also believed that adolescents _____ earlier stages of life, an idea that influenced later theorists such as G. Stanley Hall and Sigmund Freud.

maturation

3. Some modern-day theories, such as those of Arnold Gesell and Freud view adolescence as primarily the result of biological _____.

genital

4. For Freud, adolescence was the beginning of the _____ stage of development.

Ethologists

5. _____ have pointed out that male non-human primates go through a period of life similar to human adolescence.

reinforcement

6. Environmental-learning theorists point out that societal _____ plays an important role in shaping adolescent behavior.

formal

7. Piaget believed that during adolescence, young people progress from concrete to _____ operational thinking.

identity

8. According to Erik Erikson, adolescents' most important developmental task is to establish _____.

stage

9. Psychologists who take the cultural-context perspective point out that in some cultures adolescence appears as a distinct _____ of development and in others it does not.

Puberty

10. _____ is a series of biological developments that transforms individuals from being biologically immature to being capable of sexual reproduction.

growth
legs

11. A _____ spurt is one of the first signs of puberty; generally, the _____ are the first area of the body to reach their peak.

12. By the end of puberty, _____ are the stronger and more athletic sex, while females, on the average, live _____ and are healthier.

males
longer

13. During puberty, the primary sexual organs—those involved in _____— enlarge and mature. At the same time, _____ sexual characteristics, such as breast development and voice changes, appear.

reproduction, secondary

14. _____, girls' first menstrual period, occurs about 18 months after the growth spurt reaches peak velocity; in some societies, the events of puberty are marked by rites of _____.

Menarche

passage

15. There is some evidence that _____ -maturing boys are also more psychologically and socially mature; however, the picture for _____ is not so positive.

early

girls

16. For U.S. children, puberty may be accompanied by a temporary _____ in conflict with their mothers.

increase

17. Adolescent girls tend to want friends who are _____, while boys want friends who will support them in troubles with _____.

loyal

authority

18. Both boys and girls agree that having a good _____ is important for getting into the "leading crowd" in high school.

personality

19. Adolescents tend to date and form friendships with others with _____ attitudes and values.

similar

20. In early adolescence, young people gather primarily in same-sex _____ but increasingly spend time in heterosexual _____.

cliques
crowds

21. Psychologists such as John Gagnon and William Simon point out that the actions making up sexual activity—hand holding and kissing, for example—can be thought of as a kind of _____.

script

22. Biological and social factors result in adolescent girls being more committed to romantic love and adolescent boys being more committed to _____.

sexuality

23. Surveys have revealed that males and females report different responses to their first intercourse; in general, _____ have more positive feelings about this experience.

males

pregnant

24. Although U.S. teenagers are no more sexually active than their European counterparts, they become _____ in much greater numbers.

conform

antisocial

25. Adolescents are somewhat more subject than younger children to peer pressure to _____; however, they are less likely to follow their peers' lead in _____ than in neutral behavior.

Conflict

responsibility

26. _____ between adolescents and their parents often centers on matters of taste; the real issues, however, may be the ability to make decisions and take _____ for themselves.

work

27. Teenagers who _____ in addition to attending school benefit in many ways but their schoolwork may suffer.

increased

28. The earlier onset of puberty and the increase in the education needed for economic productivity today have _____ the length of adolescence.

Multiple-Choice Questions

Circle the letter of the word or phrase that correctly completes each statement.

1. Jean-Jacques Rousseau believed that adolescents
   a.   are, in a way, being born for the second time.
   b.   recapitulate earlier stages of development.
   c.   are subject to emotional ups and downs.
   d.   All of the above

2. In Freud's theory of development, the period of adolescence corresponds to the _____ stage.
   a.   latency
   b.   Oedipal
   c.   phallic
   d.   genital

3. Adolescents must establish _____, a pattern of beliefs that reconciles the ways in which they are like others with the ways in which they are different.
   a.   identity
   b.   formal operational thought
   c.   autonomy
   d.   self-esteem

4. The _____ produce(s) the hormone that is responsible for the adolescent growth spurt.
    a. hypothalamus
    b. adrenal cortex
    c. pituitary gland
    d. ovaries and testes

5. Which is correct about the physiological differences between males and females in adolescence and adulthood?
    a. Males are stronger, healthier, and better able to tolerate long-term stress.
    b. Males have greater capacity for physical exercise but females are healthier and longer lived.
    c. Females have larger hearts and lower resting heart rates and can exercise for longer periods.
    d. There are no appreciable differences between males' and females' capacities for exercise and athletic performance.

6. The timing of the events of puberty
    a. is the same, on the average, in all cultures.
    b. is earlier in children from poor families than children from affluent families.
    c. is earlier in many societies than it was 100 years ago.
    d. is equally similar for identical and fraternal twins.

7. Adolescents tend to choose friends
    a. who live close by.
    b. with similar values and attitudes.
    c. who are several years younger.
    d. from a different socioeconomic background.

8. Which describes an adolescent clique?
    a. A group of 15 to 30 boys and girls
    b. A loosely associated group of couples
    c. A group of 6 or 7 friends, usually of the same sex
    d. All of the above

9. Cross-cultural studies of sexual behavior indicate that
    a. adolescents in many cultures do not yet have sexual feelings.
    b. traditional societies are generally less restrictive about premarital intercourse than industrialized societies.
    c. the standards for adolescent sexual behavior is the same in all cultures.
    d. different cultures may have very different scripts for learning sexual behavior.

10. Under what circumstance are pregnant teenagers likely to choose abortion?
    a.   If they are over 15 years of age
    b.   If their mothers are poorly educated
    c.   If they are doing well in school
    d.   If their families are on welfare

11. Adolescents generally report that
    a.   they spend little time with their parents and a great deal of time with their peers.
    b.   they are closer to their fathers than to their mothers.
    c.   they disagree with their parents on most important issues.
    d.   despite disagreements, they feel close to their parents.

12. Most of the time, adolescents' jobs
    a.   pay the minimum wage.
    b.   prepare them for future careers.
    c.   result in contact with many adults.
    d.   offer good opportunities for advancement.

Short-Answer Questions

1.   Discuss the interpretations different theorists have given Rousseau's idea that earlier stages of development are recapitulated during adolescence.

2.   What evidence is there that early maturation may be socially and psychologically beneficial to adolescents? What exceptions to this picture have been noted?

3.   In what ways do parents and peers develop different "spheres of influence" in their relations with adolescents?

4. Discuss the advantages and disadvantages of adolescents holding jobs outside school hours.

Sources of More Information

Berndt, Thomas J. "The Features and Effects of Friendship in Early Adolescence." *Child Development*, 1982, *53* (6), 1447-1460.
The author examines the literature on childhood and adolescent friendship and discusses the major findings in this area of study.

Cole, Sheila. *Working Kids on Working.* New York: Lothrop, Lee, and Shepard, 1980.
The author has interviewed more than two dozen working children about why they work. The book also deals with questions about working and the law.

Feldman, S. Shirley, and Elliott, Glen R. (Eds.) *At the Threshold: The Developing Adolescent.* Cambridge, Mass.: Harvard University Press, 1990.
A broad summary of research on adolescence written by outstanding scholars in the field.

Malinowski, Bronislaw. "The Social and Sexual Life of Trobriand Children." In Wayne Dennis (Ed.), *Historical Readings in Developmental Psychology.* New York: Appleton-Century-Crofts, 1972.
This observation, first published in 1929, describes the coming of age of children in a society very different from our own.

Rubin, Zick. *Liking and Loving: An Invitation to Social Psychology.* New York: Holt, Rinehart and Winston, 1973.
This book provides an entertainingly written account of how psychologists study friendship and love.

Ruble, Diane N., and Jeanne Brooks-Gunn. The Experience of Menarche. *Child Development*, 1982, *53* (6), 1557-1566.
This article reports the attitudes and emotional reactions of adolescents and preadolescents to menarche.

Savin-Williams, Ritch C. *Adolescence: An Ethological Perspective.* New York: Springer-Verlag, 1987.
This book describes a naturalistic study of adolescents at a summer camp. A good illustration of the way psychological processes are manifested in social interactions.

Youniss, James and Smollar, Jacqueline. *Adolescent Relations with Mothers, Fathers, and Friends*. Chicago: University of Chicago Press, 1985.
This book uses interviews to provide a picture of the social reorganization that occurs during adolescence.

Answer Key

Answers to Key Terms: j, h, i, g, b, d, a, e, c, f.

Answers to Multiple-Choice Questions: 1. d, 2. d, 3. a, 4. c, 5. b, 6. c, 7. b, 8. c, 9. d, 10. c, 11. d, 12. a.

The Psychological Achievements of Adolescence

Psychologists from various theoretical orientations agree that adolescents' thought processes are more sophisticated than those of younger children. Piaget felt that adolescence was characterized by the emergence of formal operations, a type of systematic, logical thinking, while other investigators feel that the characteristics of adolescent cognition can be accounted for by the development of more advanced problem-solving rules and strategies. Cross-cultural differences complicate the matter, but thinking skills that resemble formal operations appear in people of all cultures, applied in specific contexts in which they are appropriate.

Adolescents' improved thinking skills are applied to social, political, and moral as well as academic problems. Capable of seeing the faults in existing systems, they may feel frustrated by the seeming impossibility of social change. Young people face important personal tasks during adolescence. They must loosen their attachments to their parents and look outside their families for someone to love. At the same time, they must establish identities, developing and committing themselves to their own points of view in many domains, including sex role, occupational choice, and friendship as well as political and religious orientation.

Adolescence exists because of delays in some components of the bio-social-behavioral shift that mark the end of childhood. It is not surprising, therefore, that adolescence as a separate, unified stage of development is not universal across societies; in this sense it is more like a long transition period between middle childhood and adulthood than a separate stage of development.

Chapter Outline

Many theorists agree that the transition from middle childhood to adolescence is accompanied by the development of a new quality of mind.

I.   RESEARCH ON ADOLESCENT THOUGHT

Daniel Keating has suggested that adolescent thinking is characterized by the following: thinking about possibilities not present to the senses; thinking ahead, rather than considering only the present; thinking through hypotheses, considering "what if"; thinking about thought, including *second-order thinking*, which involves rules about rules; and thinking beyond conventional limits about such topics as politics, morality, and religion. While there is evidence for these characteristics of adolescent thought, psychologists now acknowledge the importance of problem content and context for adolescents' performance on tasks measuring thinking skills.

A.   Piaget felt that changes in the way adolescents think about themselves, their social relationships, and their society have their source in the development of *formal operations*, a new level of logical thought. In contrast to concrete operations, formal operations involve, he believed, the ability to think systematically about aspects of a problem.
• Analyzing the performance of children and adolescents on tasks such as the "combination of chemicals" problem, Piaget found that adolescents' reasoning could be described as a *structured whole*—a system of relationships—while younger children's reasoning was characterized by partial, unconnected links. Another Piagetian task—discovering the conditions under which a balance beam will balance—also requires formal operational thinking to arrive at a correct solution, since it is necessary to consider the roles of weight and distance at the same time. This task is discussed in Chapter 12.
• A consequence of second-order thinking is *deductive reasoning*, in which a general premise is followed by a specific premise and a conclusion. If the premises are true, the conclusion must be true. Formal deductive reasoning is rare before 11 to 12 years of age but becomes more likely with increasing age.

• Inhelder and Piaget's writings seem to suggest that formal operational thought is universal; however, the actual situation is complicated.

• Some studies have found formal operational thinking among only a minority of subjects. Robert Siegler and Robert Liebert found that 10- and 13-year-olds who were tutored in using a systematic approach on similar problems were able to solve a railroad-track switching problem analogous to Inhelder and Piaget's chemicals task; without tutoring, none of the 10-year-olds and only 20 percent of the 13-year-olds were successful, although all children who received tutoring were able to solve the problem. Failure to use a formal operational approach is not limited to young adolescents. Noel Capon and Deanna Kuhn found that only 20 percent of adult shoppers used formal operational thought when asked to judge which of two sizes of garlic powder was a better buy.

• There has been a great deal of interest in whether sex differences exist in formal operational reasoning. When Marcia Linn and Janet Hyde conducted a *meta-analysis* of studies involving formal operational tasks, she found that, while in many studies there were no sex differences in performance, when sex differences did occur they generally favored males. According to work by Joan Peskin, this may be caused by the content of formal operational tasks, which are often science-oriented and of greater interest to males. Peskin found that, among girls with little interest in science, performance was better on "female-oriented" versions of tasks. It appears that males and females have equal capacity for formal operational reasoning, but that the extent to which the capacity develops depends on experience.

• Are there cultural differences in the incidence of formal operational thought? Cross-cultural work indicates that people from small societies that are not technologically advanced rarely demonstrate formal operations when tested with Piagetian methods. Piaget considered two possible explanations. Perhaps a certain amount of environmental stimulation is necessary for formal operational thought to develop; life in small, traditional societies may not provide stimulation of the right kind. Alternatively, all normal people may attain formal operations, but may manifest this mode of thought "in different areas according to their aptitudes and their professional specializations." In the end Piaget found the second explanation a more likely one.

B. Alternative accounts of adolescent thought have been suggested by theorists who question Piaget's interpretation.

• Information-processing theorists disagree with Piaget's idea of a qualitatively different mode of thought emerging during adolescence. Instead, they argue, increasing information-processing capacity and more powerful problem-solving and memory strategies can account for the differences in performance between adolescents and younger children. When Robert Siegler applied the information-processing approach to Inhelder and Piaget's balance beam problem using 5- to 17-year-olds as subjects, he found that children of different ages used different rules for solving the problem. However, even the oldest subjects failed to solve all forms of the problem, indicating the absence of the generality one would expect in formal operational thought. Deanna Kuhn and her colleagues conducted a study in which 10-year-olds and adults participated over a 10-week period, reasoning about the causes of school achievement in a fictional school district. Neither the adults nor the children were logically consistent across problems; however, subjects in both age groups used more sophisticated reasoning strategies as they became more experienced.

• Theorists from a number of traditions view adolescent thought as strongly influenced by increasing ability to use abstract verbal concepts. Heinz Werner and Bernard Kaplan found that 11- and 12-year-olds were better able than younger children to integrate information over many examples when inferring the meaning of an unfamiliar word. And Philip Levinson and Robert Carpenter concluded that, while 9-year-olds found quasi-analogies ("A bird uses air, a fish uses ＿＿＿") easier to solve than true analogies ("Bird is to air as fish is to ＿＿＿"), 15-year-olds found both types equally easy showing a greater ability to coordinate the meanings of separate words into a logical system.

• While Piaget sought to describe adult thought with a single logic, cultural-context theorists attempt to understand adult thought by analyzing the different settings adults frequent and their associated scripts. This approach expects variability in thinking from one context to another, and cross-cultural studies have found evidence of such variability. For example, as discussed in Box 16.1, Edwin Hutchins showed that techniques used by Micronesian navigators to sail from one island to another were examples of formal operational thought. Yet, while they were sophisticated problem solvers during navigation, the same Micronesian subjects did not perform at high levels on a traditional Piagetian test of formal operations. Although high school-educated Micronesians did not know how to use the navigational system, some showed formal operations in the traditional Piagetian task, presumably because that task was more familiar from their school experiences.

People regularly demonstrate their ability to apply formal operations in everyday situations requiring organization and planning ahead; for example, arranging for a holiday meal. However, their reasoning in everyday contexts may vary (for example, by using short cuts) from their reasoning on formal tasks designed as logical puzzles. In fact, several studies of everyday reasoning have cast doubt on the hypothesis that once individuals become capable of formal reasoning, it becomes a general characteristic of their thinking. Judy Tschirgi found that even when the logic and materials of the problems are the same, subjects may respond differently depending on whether they view an outcome as positive (one they want to maintain) or negative (one they want to change). In Tschirgi's study, college students and second-graders were equally likely to follow this pattern.

It has also been observed that expert problem solvers such a s chess players and scientists often take shortcuts in reasoning, not looking at all possible combinations of factors, but only those that have proved important in the past. Taken together, these findings suggest that formal operations are, indeed, acquired in a context-specific manner. It is necessary to examine many different contexts to assess whether the cognitive changes from middle childhood to adolescence represent continuity or a stagelike change.

II.   ADOLESCENT THINKING ABOUT THE SOCIAL ORDER

Experimental tasks often measure adolescent thought in formal problem-solving contexts. How do adolescents reason about areas of personal concern to them?

A.   While children think seriously about social realities during middle childhood, their reasoning about politics changes in predictable ways during the course of adolescence.
  • Based on interviews with adolescents from several countries, Joseph Adelson and his colleagues concluded that, in contrast to 12- to 13-year-olds, 15- to 16-year-olds began to speak in terms of abstract principles when asked to respond to questions about society.
  • Older adolescents also viewed social control differently; while 12- to 13-year-olds tended to give authoritarian answers when asked about law-breaking and punishment, 15- to 16-year-olds thought in terms of reform and rehabilitation. This shift in reasoning corresponds to changes in mid-adolescence noted by Inhelder and Piaget in their studies of scientific problem solving.
  • Adolescents' more complex thinking is evident in their explanations for social problems such as homelessness.
  • Adolescents are especially interested in political and religious ideologies because of their new ability to think about ideal systems and to find inconsistencies in long-held beliefs. They may, however, find it difficult to work out alternatives to the existing social and political order.

B.   There is some evidence that, like thinking about politics or scientific problems, reasoning about moral issues undergoes development during adolescence. Stage 3, in Kohlberg's system, based on relations between individuals, remains the most commonly seen mode of reasoning, though Stage 4 reasoning makes an appearance during adolescence; Stage four reasoning is based on fulfilling duties to which one has agreed and focuses on relations between the individual and the group. Moral behavior is, therefore, behavior that maintains the existing social order. Stage 3 and stage 4 reasoning depend on partially attaining formal operational thought, according to Kohlberg. Stage 5 reasoning in Kohlberg's system generally does not appear until early in adulthood and is rarely seen even then. Rather than focusing on maintaining the existing social order, stage 5 thinkers seek possibilities for improving it. Stage 6 reasoning is even rarer and involves placing certain universal ethical principles above the rules of society.
  • Several controversies surround Kohlberg's theory of moral development. First, while most studies show subjects progressing through the stages in order, others have found regressions and skipping of stages. Responses to Kohlberg's moral dilemmas are also sometimes difficult to score reliably; the Sociomoral Reflection Measure (SRM) was developed by John Gibbs in response to this problem. It is a paper-and-pencil test that is simpler to score and correlates well with reasoning on the dilemmas. Problems have arisen as well with respect to the correspondence between moral and cognitive stages. Finally, there is uncertainty about the relation between moral reasoning and actual moral behavior. People who can reason morally may not always behave morally.

However, some evidence of correspondence is provided by a study carried out by Herbert Richards and his colleagues. They found that 9- to 14-year-old children who reasoned at Stage 2 on the dilemmas (based on immediate interest) had worse classroom behavior than those who reasoned at Stage 1 (oriented toward obedience and punishment) or Stage 3 (based on acceptance of shared social norms).

• In early tests of moral reasoning in adolescents, girls were found to score slightly lower than boys. Carol Gilligan has hypothesized that male-female differences may occur due to differences in "moral orientation," with males more oriented toward individual rights and females more oriented toward responsibility for others, which is not valued as highly in Kohlberg's scoring system. In fact, however, most studies show no significant differences between males and females on tests of moral reasoning, and both men and women are capable of reasoning from care-oriented and justice-oriented viewpoints.

• Cross-cultural studies reveal that people from small, technologically unsophisticated societies rarely reason beyond Kohlberg's stage 3, and often reason at stage 1 or 2. Kohlberg explained this as the result of differences in attainment of formal operational thought. Other investigators, such as anthropologist Richard Shweder, have pointed out that Kohlberg's stage sequence itself contains value judgments specific to Western traditions of liberal democracy. In any case, data from many societies indicates that, by the time they become adults, young people can reason at stage 3—on a level corresponding to the Golden Rule.

III. INTEGRATION OF THE SELF

It is widely believed that adolescence is the period during which an individual needs to form the basis of a stable adult personality.

A.   During adolescence, a new kind of self-description appears, in which personal identity is defined in terms of beliefs, values, and life plans. Adolescents' self-descriptions contain less concrete, more inclusive concepts and a greater variety of attributes than those of younger children. They also tailor their self-descriptions to the context they are asked about. Adolescents may find it disturbing that they behave like different people in different contexts; however, their different "selves" become more resolved and reconciled as time goes by.

B.   Adolescents frequently become preoccupied with themselves as their behavior differs from that which would be characteristic of their "real selves." Self-esteem becomes an important issue. During adolescence, attractiveness and peer acceptance are the attributes most strongly associated with high self-esteem. Attractiveness is especially important to girls, who have been found, on average, to have lower self-esteem than boys. Children's self-esteem seems to drop in early adolescence, (around the time of the transition to junior high school) but increases steadily thereafter.

C. Erik Erikson viewed *identity formation* as the fundamental task of adolescence. Erikson also believed that adolescent development involves reworking previous *developmental crises* involving trust, autonomy, initiative, and industry. Adolescents must resolve their identities in both the individual and the social spheres and establish "the identity of these two identities," according to Erikson. Erikson's descriptions about the thinking processes involved in adolescent identity formation correspond closely to Piaget's descriptions of formal operational thinking. Identity formation can be difficult, and is especially so for those who, as described in Box 16.2, are forming a homosexual identity. It is not easy to objectively evaluate Erikson's ideas about identity. Erikson himself carried out biographical case studies of famous men, but this method is not practical for use with large numbers of ordinary teenagers. Instead, James Marcia and his colleagues have used interviews to elicit information about the degree to which young people have adopted and committed themselves to well-thought-out views on politics, religion, occupation, friendship, dating, and sex roles. On the basis of the answers they obtained, the researchers identified four patterns of identity formation: *identity achievement*,,in which young people had experienced a decision-making period and decided on their own views; *foreclosure*, in which they had not gone through an identity crisis but had simply adopted their parents' identity patterns; *moratorium*, in which young people were experiencing an identity crisis at the time of the interview; and *identity diffusions*, in which they had tried on several identities but had not settled on one. Many studies have indicated that, as they grow older, more and more adolescents can be classified in the identity achievement category and fewer in the identity diffusion category, a trend that continues into adulthood. Harold Grotevant and Catherine Cooper examined the relation between identity achievement scores and family interaction; they found that family systems which offer support and security while allowing adolescents to create distinct identities are the most effective in promoting identity achievement.

D. In Freud's theory, adolescence is a time when young people must rework, in new forms, the conflicts of earlier stages. For example, reworking the Oedipus conflict results in seeking love outside the family, "one of the most painful psychical achievements of the pubertal period," according to Freud. Freud believed that the stresses of the new demands of adolescence made young people especially vulnerable to personality disorders.

E. Like Freud, Erikson believed that girls and boys tend to follow different paths to identity achievement; however, the evidence for sex differences is "weak and inconsistent," according to Waterman's review of the evidence. Some studies have found sex differences in the domain in which boys and girls most quickly achieve identity status.

F. According to Margaret Spencer and Carol Mardstrom-Adams, identity formation is especially complicated for minority group children in the United States. Jean Phinney has described three stages in the formation of ethnic identity: unexamined ethnic identity; ethnic identity search, which may involve forming an *oppositional identity* in rejection of the dominant group; and ethnic identity achievement. Because it is difficult to separate effects due to ethnicity from those due to socioeconomic class, there is much about identity formation in U.S. minority group children that is not well understood.

G. Identity formation can differ provoundly between cultures. For example, Hazel Marcus and Shinobu Kitayama describe differences between cultures with an *independent sense of self*—in which individuals are oriented to being unique, expressing their own thoughts and opinions, and pursuing their own goals—and those with an *interdependent sense of self*—in which individuals seek to fit into groups and to promote the goals of others. Adolescents in different types of societies need to resolve different sets of problems in developing a unified sense of identity. In addition, not all societies require the full range of decisions and choices—related to work, marriage, and ideology—that are faced by young people in North America.

IV. THE TRANSITION TO ADULTHOOD

The period between middle childhood and adulthood does not entirely fit the pattern of earlier stages. In some societies, puberty begins later than it does in industrialized countries and coincides closely with marriage and taking on adult responsibilities.

A. In societies such as our own with a long delay between puberty and adult status, biological, social, and behavioral changes are not coordinated in the same way as in earlier stages.

Adolescence in modern industrialized societies is closely associated with the existence of formal schooling or other specialized training. Schooling introduces a long delay in reaching economic self-sufficiency and prolongs the process of socialization. Therefore, while changes in certain social domains, for example, relations with the opposite sex, change in response to biological developments, in other social domains such as political participation and starting a family, full adult power and responsibility are delayed. This unevenness in the social sphere is most likely the reason for much of the unevenness in adolescents' thinking and behavior.

B. Current trends requiring higher levels of educational knowledge may, by delaying young people's working lives and prolonging their economic dependence, have the effect of prolonging adolescence or may even result in a new stage of development between adolescence and adulthood.

Key Terms

Following are important terms introduced in Chapter 16. In the space to the right, write the definition of the term. In the space to the left, write the letter of the example that best illustrates the term.

_____ deductive reasoning _____ _____

_____ developmental crisis _____

_____ formal operations _____

_____ identity formation _____

_____ independent sense of self _____

_____ interdependent sense of self _____

_____ meta-analysis _____

_____ oppositional identity _____

_____ second-order thinking _____

_____ structured whole _____

a. This is described by such labels as "collective," "connected," and "sociocentric."
b. Adolescents are doing this when, for example, they make mental comparisons between two possible systems of rules for electing class officers.
c. In Erik Erikson's system, one of a set of developmental tests that an individual must face before moving on to the next life task.
d. A kind of systematic logical thinking on which adolescent thought is structured, according to Piaget.
e. Piaget considered this system of relationships an important characteristic of adolescent thought.
f. According to Erikson, this requires the integration of the solutions to all the developmental crises of childhood.
g. This characteristic of identity is typical of American or Western European culture.
h. An example is "Dolphins are mammals; Flip is a dolphin; therefore, Flip is a mammal."
i. This may involve combining data collected by many different investigators.
j. When this applies to an African American adolescent, everything about "white" culture may seem wrong.

Fill-In Questions

Cover the list of answers next to the statements below and fill in each blank with the word or phrase that correctly completes the sentence.

ahead
second-order

1. Daniel Keating has suggested that adolescent thinking is characterized by thinking about possibilities; thinking _____; thinking through hypotheses; thinking about thought, or _____ thinking; and thinking beyond conventional limits.

formal

2. Piaget believed that the new forms of thought which characterize adolescence are based on a logical structure called _____ operations.

structured

3. Adolescents' performance on problems such as the combination of chemicals task demonstrates, in contrast to that of younger children, the presence of a _____ whole.

formal operational
tutoring

4. Studies have shown that many teenagers and adults fail to reason at a _____ level on Piagetian tasks; Siegler and Liebert found that providing children with _____ helped their performance on a combination of switches task.

males
science

5. While many studies of formal operations show no differences in performance between males and females, those differences that are found generally favor _____; females with little interest in _____ perform better on tasks with "female-oriented" content.

concrete
formal

6. While _____ operational abilities appear to be universal, it is possible that _____ operations develop in different areas of thought, according to an individual's aptitudes and interests.

rules

7. On the balance beam problem, adolescents' problem-solving skills can be described as a gradual acquisition of more powerful _____, according to Robert Siegler, an information-processing theorist.

language

8. Increasing ability to solve analogies is one sign of the changing relation of thought to _____ during adolescence.

9. The cultural-context perspective assumes that, while people in all cultures acquire the ability to think systematically, the settings in which this ability is used will _____.

vary

10. Diverse activities such as Micronesian-style navigation and planning a holiday meal require the use of _____ thought.

formal operational

11. In contrast to formal problem solving, when people reason about everyday situations, they may take _____ based on intuition.

shortcuts

12. Judy Tschirgi found that, when confronted with an everyday problem, people's expectations about the _____, not their cognitive competencies, may control their reasoning.

outcome

13. Joseph Adelson and his colleagues found that a major change occurs in adolescents' reasoning about politics at about _____ years of age.

14

14. While 12- to 13-year-olds suggest that severe _____ is the best way to deal with law-breaking, older adolescents think more in terms of reform and rehabilitation.

punishment

15. When separating themselves from the value systems of their parents, adolescents may seek out an _____ person or system to follow.

ideal

16. While adolescents' reasoning abilities make them skillful at identifying the faults of existing political and social systems, they find it difficult to work out _____.

alternatives

17. Stage 4—_____ reasoning—begins to appear during adolescence; however, most adolescents reason at stage _____.

moral

3

18. Stage 5 moral reasoning focuses on abstract principles of right and wrong, while stage 6, rarely encountered, is based on universal _____ principles.

ethical

19. Adolescents' _____ of themselves are complex, including attributes from many domains.

descriptions

20. Attractiveness and peer acceptance are associated with high _____ during adolescence.

self-esteem

identity   21. Erik Erikson believed that _____ formation is the most important developmental challenge of adolescence.

achievement   22. James Marcia and his colleagues found that adolescents' responses to questions about identity formation placed them in one of four categories: identity _____, foreclosure, moratorium, or _____ diffusion.
identity

family   23. A _____ that offers support and security can be helpful in promoting identity achievement in adolescence.

conflicts   24. According to Freud, a major task of adolescence is reworking the _____ of earlier periods of development.

identity   25. Adolescents from ethnic minority groups move through several phases while achieving an ethnic _____; along the way, an _____ identity may be adopted.
oppositional

self   26. Identity formation differs somewhat across cultures; some cultures encourage an independent sense of _____, while others encourage an _____ sense of self.
interdependent

stage   27. Only in societies in which there is a relatively long separation between biological maturation and the assumption of adult roles does adolescence seem to exist as a unified _____ of human development.

Multiple-Choice Questions

Circle the letter of the word or phrase that correctly completes each statement.

1. Which of the following are characteristics of adolescent thinking?
   a. planning ahead
   b. formulating hypotheses
   c. thinking about one's own thought processes
   d. All of the above

2. According to Piaget, which of the following first makes its appearance in formal operational thought?
   a. the ability to construct others' points of view
   b. a system of relationships that can be logically described and thought about
   c. conservation of liquid quantity
   d. the ability to generate a classification system

3. To which types of problems are adolescents and adults most likely to apply formal operations?
   a. Problems whose content is unfamiliar
   b. Problems that cannot be solved using concrete operations
   c. Problems of familiar and interesting content
   d. All of the above equally

4. According to the cultural-context perspective, formal operational thought
   a. is applied in the same contexts in all societies.
   b. occurs only among people whose culture stimulates them to develop it.
   c. does not occur in most normal people.
   d. is applied in different contexts in different cultures.

5. People from which age group tend to be authoritarian in their views on social control and to conceive of the law as a way to prevent antisocial behavior?
   a. 12- to 13-year-olds
   b. 15- to 16-year-olds
   c. College-age young people
   d. Adults

6. When adolescents reason about political processes
   a. they generally see no problems with current systems.
   b. they are able to suggest workable solutions to current political and legal problems.
   c. they can see problems in current systems, but find it difficult to work out alternatives.
   d. their approaches are not significantly different from those of younger children.

7. The most common mode of moral reasoning during adolescence is Kohlberg's
   a. stage 2.
   b. stage 3.
   c. stage 4.
   d. stage 5.

8. Which of Kohlberg's stages of moral reasoning is based on maintaining the existing social order?
   a. Stage 2
   b. Stage 3
   c. Stage 4
   d. Stage 5

9.   Which is an objection to Kohlberg's theory of moral development?
     a.   Some studies have found no correspondence between moral reasoning and cognitive development.
     b.   The method of scoring answers can be difficult to use.
     c.   The relationship between moral reasoning and moral behavior is unreliable.
     d.   All of the above

10. Freud believed that adolescents need to _____ earlier conflicts; for example, the Oedipus conflict.
     a.   rework
     b.   repress
     c.   succumb to
     d.   recognize

11. According to Erik Erikson, establishing _____ is the fundamental task of adolescence.
     a.   intimacy
     b.   identity
     c.   autonomy
     d.   foreclosure

12. Adolescence is a separate stage of development
     a.   in all societies.
     b.   only when there is a long gap between biological maturation and the granting of adult social status.
     c.   in males but not in females.
     d.   for the last 100 years.

Short-Answer Questions

1.   Discuss the differences between adolescents' thinking and the thinking of younger children. How are these differences explained by Piaget? By information-processing theorists?

2.   How does culture affect performance on measures of formal operational reasoning? How does it affect performance on moral reasoning tasks?

3. Discuss the important developmental tasks of adolescence according to Freud and Erikson.

4. What evidence is there that adolescence is a distinct stage of human development? What evidence is there that this is not the case?

Putting It All Together

Match each example with the stage at which it is most characteristic:

a. infancy
b. the preschool period
c. middle childhood
d. adolescence

_____ 1. Lisa is developing scripts that help her get through activities such as birthday parties, visits to the dentist, and meals in restaurants.

_____ 2. Anne views laws as beneficial, not just a means of preventing bad behavior.

_____ 3. When asked to figure out what combination of paints produces a particular color, Frank uses pencil and paper to keep track of the combinations he has tried.

_____ 4. Children of Janet's age are learning that other people have feelings that may not always show in their behavior.

_____ 5. Luke's major tasks in personality formation involve establishing first trust, then autonomy.

_____ 6. Games with rules are now important in Jonathan's play with his friends.

_____ 7. Michael no longer automatically accepts his parents' view of the world and is formulating his own opinions about politics, religion, and occupational choices.

_____ 8. To Susan, friends are playmates—other children in the neighborhood whom she sees frequently.

_____ 9. Richard's reasoning can be primitive or fairly logical, depending on his familiarity with the task and on whether he has scripted knowledge about the situation.

_____ 10. Sara needs a best friend to supply feedback about her behavior and her feelings about boys.

Additional Resources

Erikson, Erik. *Identity: Youth and Crisis*. New York: Norton, 1968.
The author discusses adolescent identity formation and some of the difficulties involved in this process.

Keating, Daniel P. Thinking Processes in Adolescence. In J. Adelson (Ed.), *Handbook of Adolescent Psychology*. New York: Wiley, 1980.
In this chapter, the author describes the characteristics of adolescent thought and takes up problems of stage versus continuity and competence versus performance.

Kohlberg, Lawrence. *The Psychology of Moral Development: The Nature and Validity of Moral Stages*. New York: Harper and Row, 1984.
This volume brings together many of Kohlberg's most influential papers on moral development.

Kroger, Jane. *Identity in Adolescence*. London: Routledge, 1989.
This book pays careful attention to each of the major theories of identity formation. The biographical accounts of the theorists place their work in a cultural-historical context.

Linn, Marcia, Cathy Clement, and Steven Pulos. "Is It Formal If It's Not Physics?" (The Influence of Content on Formal Reasoning). *Journal of Research in Science Teaching*, 1983, *20* (8), 755-770.
This article examine the effects of content and subjects' expectations on performance on tests of formal operational reasoning.

Marcia, James E. Identity in Adolescence. In J. Adelson (Ed.), *Handbook of Adolescent Psychology*. New York: Wiley, 1980.
In this chapter, the author discusses his findings on adolescents' identity statuses.

Piaget, Jean, and Barbel Inhelder. *The Origin of The Idea of Chance in Children*. New York: Norton, 1975.
Reasoning about chance and probability are examples of logical thought. Piaget and Inhelder report on their studies of the development of these concepts in children with reasoning levels from preoperational through formal operational.

Overton, Willis F., and Anita M. Meehan. "Individual Differences in Formal Operational Thought: Sex Role and Learned Helplessness." *Child Development*, 1982, *53* (6), 1536-1543.
The authors explore factors that can lead to sex differences in performance on tests of formal operations.

Siegler, Robert S. "Three Aspects of Cognitive Development." *Cognitive Psychology*, 1976, *8*, 481-520.
This article describes the author's information-processing approach to Inhelder and Piaget's balance beam problem.

Answer Key

Answers to Key Terms: h, c, d, f, g, a, i, j, b, e.

Answers to Multiple-Choice Questions: 1. d, 2. b, 3. c, 4. d, 5. a, 6. c, 7. b, 8. c, 9. d, 10. a, 11. b, 12. b.

Answers to Putting It All Together: b, d, d, c, a, c, d, b, b, d.